# Beachy head
# Shipwrecks
# of the
# 19<sup>th</sup> Century

# Beachy Head Shipwrecks of the 19th Century

## (Pevensey – Eastbourne – Newhaven)

David Renno

AMHERST

Copyright © David Renno 2004

David Renno has asserted his right under the Copyright,
Designs and Patents Act, 1988, to be identified
as the author of this work.

ISBN 1 903637 20 1

Printed in Great Britain

First published in 2004 by

Amherst Publishing Limited
Longmore House, High Street, Otford, Sevenoaks, Kent TN14 5PQ

**Distribution**
Copies of this book are available from:
David Renno, PO Box 212, Hastings TN35 5WT
www.shipwrecksofsussex.co.uk

In recognition of the brave coastguardsmen and
lifeboat crews who saved so many souls at sea

# Contents

# Introduction

The stories of the vessels mentioned in this book have, in the main, been researched from local news reports. However, it should be appreciated that such news reports are not generally available before the middle of the 19th century, and not all wrecks were reported in the newspapers. A consequence of this is that details of some shipwrecks are less full, and in some cases are almost non-existent, but these are included with whatever details are available. Similarly, not all the information is known about each feature of every vessel. However, what information is known is detailed for each shipwreck and where the master's name is not known, he is included in the number of crew. The Wreck Location shown is the actual site of the shipwreck or where the incident occurred to cause the vessel to become a wreck, if later recovered.

The very nature of reporting mishaps at sea during most of this period was only made possible when either the members of the crew were saved or when a vessel failed to arrive at its destination, bearing in mind that travelling by sea then, took considerably longer than it does today. The reporting of sea disasters was therefore often not made until days or weeks after the event, unless there were other vessels involved in any rescue attempt. In these cases the rescue was invariably within coastal waters such as those recorded within this book between the towns of Pevensey and Newhaven in East Sussex. A perfect example of how long it took for information to reach the wider world was shown on Wednesday 18th September 1889, when an Eastbourne fisherman, Philip Swain, picked up a bottle floating in the sea. Inside the bottle was this message, *"Firefly, private yacht, 9th February 1889, off Denmark – Dear friends who happen to read this – We were a party of friends, all told, when we were run into by a two-master; and I am now writing these lines which I hope will come into some person's hands who will send help to us as soon as possible. But I am afraid you will be too late to save us as now our boat is sinking fast. If by chance any of our remains be found, please let our friends know at Hastings, Sussex, England, and also the".* Here the letter written some seven months earlier ends.

The shipwrecks in this book are shown in chronological order of loss. Those seeking information on a particular named vessel should refer to the Alphabetical Index at the back of the book.

Details of 19th century wrecks between the towns of Pevensey and Rye can be found in the author's book *East Sussex Shipwrecks of the 19th Century (Pevensey-Hastings-Rye)*, published by The Book Guild, Lewes, East Sussex

# Types of Sail Rigging

Fore-and-aft
Where the vessel's sails are set parallel, or close to, the fore and aft centre line of the vessel.

Gaf
A type of fore-and-aft rigging where the largest sail on a mast is four sided, with its leading edge attached to the mast.

Lug
Also a type of fore-and-aft rigging where the largest sail on a mast is again four sided, with either the fore edge projecting forward of the mast, or the uppermost part of the sail projecting forward of the mast.

Sprit
A type of fore-and-aft rigging where a four sided sail is held in place on a long spar or sprit.

Square
The sails are attached to spars which are at right angles to the mast, and on the fore-and-aft centre line of the vessel.

# Vessel Sail Rigging

| | |
|---|---|
| Barge | Flat bottomed freight vessel with or without sails. |
| Barque/Barquentine | At least a three masted vessel with aftermost mast fore-and-aft rigged with other masts square-rigged. |
| Brig/Brigantine | Two masted vessel with fore one square-rigged and the other mast fore-and-aft rigged. |
| Sloop | Single masted vessel fore-and-aft rigged with mainsail and jib. |
| Cutter | Single masted vessel rigged like a sloop but with a running bowsprit. |
| Chasse-Maree | French 2/3 masted vessel lug rigged. |
| Galliot | Two masted vessel for North Sea and coastal work, with one gaff-rigged sail on the main mast and the mizzen mast with up to three square sails. |
| Ketch | Two masted vessel fore-and-aft rigged, with the mizzen mast stepped forward of the rudder. |
| Lugger | Lug-rigged vessel. |
| Schooner | Two or more masted vessel with fore-and-aft rigging, where masts are of either equal height, or where the foremost mast is lower than the aftermast. |
| Smack | Single masted gaff-rigged fishing or coastal vessel. |
| Snow | Two masted vessel square-rigged like the Brig. |

# South Coast Martello Towers

The Martello Tower is very much part of the local maritime history and it would be very remiss if a very short history of these towers was not given. By the year 1804, Napoleon Bonaparte had gathered together a vast army on the French coast near Calais, with the quite obvious intention of invading England. However, as can be appreciated, to convey such a large army across the English Channel without suffering great losses was a very difficult problem for him, especially as the English Navy at this time was in total control of the Channel.

On the English side of the Channel there were the inevitable discussions and meetings as to how best to defend this country against this threat if it eventually turned into a reality. One participant in these discussion was a Captain William Ford, who suggested the idea of Martello Towers. It is assumed, and is probably correct, that his idea was developed from his knowledge of the tower at Mortella Point, in the Bay of Fioprenzo, on the island of Corsica.

William Pitt, who was the Prime Minister of the day, agreed that a number of these towers should be built between Folkestone in Kent and Beachy Head, near Eastbourne, in East Sussex. To enhance the country's defence against an impending French invasion, Pitt also authorised the building of 30ft. wide canal (the Royal Military Canal) between Shorncliffe, Kent to Pett Level, East Sussex, at a cost of £200,000. It is clearly obvious to the present day observer (and also it must be said to some people at the time) that a 30ft/9m wide canal would probably have little or no effect whatsoever on the French army, when considered that to have reached this canal they had just crossed the English Channel. However, neither the Martello Towers or the Royal Military Canal were called upon to defend the country, as the French army never invaded, being defeated at Waterloo by the Duke of Wellington in 1815.

The Prime Minister having agreed to the building of the Martello Towers, seventy three were then built at a cost of £3,000 each, approximately 600 yards/550 metres apart, along the south coast between Folkestone and Beachy Head by 1808. The towers were numbered 1 to 73 from east to west, with two redoubt forts to act as a base for supplies and for overall control, at Dymchurch in Kent, and at Eastbourne in East Sussex. A further twenty nine towers were built along the east coast by 1812, between Brightlingsea in Essex and Aldeburgh in Norfolk being identified by letters, starting 'A' at Brightlingsea and ending with 'CC' in Aldeburgh.

Each 30ft high brick built tower was constructed in an inverted flower pot design using half a million bricks. The walls were smooth and tapered so as to deflect enemy cannon fire and to allow a wider downward firing range of the gun mounted on the roof of each tower. The towers were constructed such that the sea-facing part of the tower was approximately 13ft thick, whereas the land-facing part was only about 6ft thick.

Each tower had three levels. The ground floor was used for the storage of munitions and provisions and access was by ladder from the first floor. To prevent accidental explosions of the stored munitions, the lanterns used for light were separated from the munitions by glass. The entrance to the tower was on the first floor and access was gained to the tower entrance by either ladder or drawbridge from the ground. The flooring above the munitions store was secured by wooden pegs instead of metal nails so as to prevent any risk of explosion or fire. The first floor was divided into three parts in order to house one Officer and the twenty four men of the Royal Artillery, who manned these towers.

The upper floor of the tower or the roof area, was the tower's gun platform. Access to it from the floor below was by means of a staircase built into the outer wall of the tower. However, the door from these stairs to the gun platform always had to be kept closed when the cannon was being used, to prevent flashback. This required the door to have a hole in it so the ammunition could be passed through the door, but this hole itself had to have a cover over it. The cannon mounted on the roof, which was capable of being turned in any direction to be fired, was a two and a half ton gun capable of firing a 24lbs/11kg, shot over a mile. It will be appreciated therefore, that as these towers were on average only 600 yards/ 550 metres apart, any enemy vessel approaching the shore could be reached by the cannons of over a dozen different Martello Towers.

What is known of the fate of the towers between Pevensey and Newhaven is shown as follows:

| Tower No. | Note on Location | Fate |
|---|---|---|
| 56 | Towers 56-59 built at 600yd/550m intervals | No longer exists due to sea erosion |
| 57 | See Tower 56 | No longer exists due to sea erosion |
| 58 | See Tower 56 | No longer exists due to sea erosion |
| 59 | See Tower 56 | Demolished in 1903 |
| 60 | Pevensey Bay | Converted into a dwelling |
| 61 | Pevensey Bay built 1806 | Still stands within a housing estate |
| 62 | Pevensey Bay | Converted into a dwelling |
| 63 | | Blown up during WW II, rubble used at RAF Friston |
| 64 | Crumbles | Used as a store |
| 65 | | By 1935 was undermined by sea erosion and collapsed 3 years later. |
| 66 | Langney Point | Used by Coastguard Service |
| 67 | | No longer exists |
| 68 | Built a mile inland on a conical mound known as St Anthony's Hill | Demolished by using it as a military gunnery target - as were Tower Nos. 69-72 |
| 69 –72 | Between Langney Point and eastern edge of Eastbourne | Abandoned at various dates between 1850 and 1872 |
| 73 | Eastbourne, Wish Tower | Open for public viewing |
| 74 | Seaford built 1810, an isolated tower but considered necessary due to proximity of Newhaven harbour | Public Museum |

# Shipwreck Recovery

In 1859 it was becoming of great concern to the Board of Trade that the value of shipping and cargoes being lost at sea had reached £2,750,000. It was not only the value of the loss that was of concern but that a large proportion of the cargoes might well be salvaged if prompt and efficient action was taken. Thus far, there had been a great reluctance on behalf of owners and insurers alike to make any attempts to recover vessels and/or their cargoes. It was estimated at this time that about 150,000 tons of shipping were lost annually.

In an attempt to resolve this problem, the Patent Derrick Company was established at 27, Cornhill, London. This company had a number of floating derricks stationed at various points around the coast, which were designed to salvage shipwrecked vessels and their cargoes from the sea bed.

A similar company existed in America with such derricks and had been extremely successful in recovering shipwrecks. This company, the New York Derrick Company, had salvaged several hundred vessels and was so successful that it was paying a yearly dividend to its shareholders of forty per cent.

The Board of Trade's concern was not really surprising when considering that 1170 vessels were lost around the coast of the United Kingdom for the preceding year of 1858. This figure represented 199 vessels of under 50 tons, 352 vessels between 51 and 100 tons, 467 vessels between 101 and 300 tons, 96 vessels between 301 and 600 tons, 28 vessels between 601 and 900 tons, 23 vessels between 901 and 1200 tons, and 5 vessels of over 1200 tons.

*(Ref: HN 11.2.1859; 14.10.1859)*

# Coastguard and Lifeboat Stations

Due to the enormous amount of smuggling and the subsequent loss of revenue, the Preventive Waterguard was formed in 1809 to combat the smuggling problem. Their duties were also to include the assisting of saving life after a shipwreck. In 1817 the Preventive Waterguard was replaced along part of the Kent coast by Navy shore patrols known as the Royal Naval Coast Blockade Service. The Preventive Waterguard continued to serve around the rest of Britain's coast until 1822 when it was merged with a number of other preventive organisations under the command of the Customs Service to form the Coast Guard. By the time of this merger in 1822, the Coast Blockade Service had extended its line of operation westward from the Kent coast as far as Cuckmere Haven in Sussex having 16 stations between Pevensey and Newhaven. The Coast Blockade Service was to have a very significant effect on smuggling along this part of the country's coast. However, it became too expensive to maintain and in 1831 was disbanded with the Coast Guard taking over responsibility for that part of the Kent and Sussex coast previously patrolled by the Coast Blockade Service. In 1856, the Coast Guard was transferred from the Customs Service to Admiralty control to become the Coastguard.

In 1892, nine Coastguard Stations covered the coastline between Pevensey and Newhaven. They are listed below:

| Coast Guard Station | Rescue Equipment | Distance from Preceding Station |
| --- | --- | --- |
| Pevensey | Rocket Apparatus | 2 miles |
| 57 Tower | Belts | 2 miles |
| Langney | Belts and Lines | 2 miles |
| Eastbourne | Rocket Apparatus, Lifeboat | 3 miles |
| Birling Gap | Rocket Apparatus | 4 miles |
| Crow Link | Cliff Ladders | 1 miles |
| Cuckmere | Belts and Lines | 2 miles |
| Blatchington | Rocket Apparatus | 3 miles |
| Newhaven | Rocket Apparatus, Lifeboat | 2 miles |

The coast line of the UK is some 4000 miles and throughout that distance in 1851, there was a total of 90 Lifeboats, one for just under every 45 miles. Along the south coast there were 10 such Lifeboats to cover the 400 miles of coast line. It becomes apparent how inadequate this number was when in 1852 there were 1015 shipwrecks and collisions resulting in a total loss of 920 lives around the UK. However, some 40 years later the situation had improved considerably and in East Sussex between Camber and Newhaven in 1892 there were 5 Lifeboats. The others not shown in the table above were at Camber, Winchelsea and Marine Parade, Hastings.

The 'Rocket Apparatus' was based on 'Captain Manby's Life Saving Apparatus', designed by Captain George William Manby and first used in 1807. It was based on a brass 5½ inch/14cm mortar weighing 300lbs/136kg, and capable of firing a 30lb/13.6kg weight and line a distance of 275 yards/ 251m. A length of plaited ox hide was placed between the shot and line to prevent the line being burnt when the shot was discharged. However in 1821 this was modified to a 24lb/11kg weight and line, to give greater distance.

Captain Manby was born on 28th November 1765 near Downham Market, Norfolk and died 89 years later on 18th November 1854 at his home at Southtown, Yarmouth, Norfolk. At first glance he was perhaps an unlikely person to invent such an apparatus bearing in mind his background. He joined the Cambridge Militia achieving the rank of Captain but spent much of his life writing. However, it was 18th February 1807 that prompted Manby to design his Life Saving Apparatus as the result of the loss of the brig Snipe and all 67 soles on board, just 50 yards/46m from shore, during a storm off Yarmouth. From that day on he, *vowed, if Providence spared my life, I would apply myself to discover some means by which not only the sufferers might have been rescued, but similar occurrences prevented in future.'*

Manby was well regarded and on 12th May 1831 was elected a Fellow of The Royal Society. His sponsors were Sir Astley Cooper (a surgeon); John Caley (Secretary to the Commissioner on Public Records, with a great interest in Natural Philosophy); Sir David Pollock (whose interest was Science); and Thomas Joseph Pettigrew (a surgeon). Part of their citation for his election read, *'a gentleman well versed in various branches of Natural knowledge.'*

Captain Manby was no stranger to Sussex as on 23rd October, 5 months after his election to The Royal Society, he gave a lecture at Brighton entitled, *'The most efficacious means of preserving the lives of shipwrecked sailors, and the prevention of shipwreck.'* This lecture was a detailed description of his design with other life-saving inventions for those at sea.

*(Ref: The Royal Society; TCB; SE 10.5.1851; HN 14.10.1859)*

# Beachy Head

Beachy Head is probably the most well known point on the south coast if not the whole of the UK coastline, for a variety of reasons. Over many years vessels have become wrecks below these white chalk cliffs and many mariners have lost their lives as a consequence. Having been shipwrecked at the bottom of these cliffs the only access to dry land was by walking along the beach at low tide. It was this loss of live and shipping that prompted a 'light' to be built at this coastal promontory, but the first permanent and substantial light, the Belle Tout Light was not built until 1834.

However, long before this a number of caves appear to have been built in the cliffs to assist those unfortunate stranded mariners. Possibly the most well known set of caves is 'Darby's Hole' or 'Parson Darby's Cave' which was almost under the Belle Tout Light. Access was by a set of steps from the beach and a photograph of the entrance taken in 1899 is shown at page 23. Parson Jonathan Darby (1667-1726) constructed the caves because he was so concerned at the loss of life from vessels becoming wrecked at Beachy Head. Although constructed to assist mariners in distress there is little doubt that these caves were also used to assist the exploits of smugglers.

The steps from the beach led into a 10ft/3m wide long irregular chamber, at the end of which were more steps leading to an upper chamber 20ft/6m higher up and open to the sea. It seems it was here that Darby lit fires to warn mariners of the dangers of Beachy Head. It was believed that these caves had an access from the top of the cliffs but this has never been substantiated.

In 1875 the Rev. H.E. Maddock M.A. carried out a physical survey of the caves at Beachy Head. In the 'Darby's Hole' he found at the entrance a number of inscriptions, the oldest of which read '*S.R. 1743*' and elsewhere were a series of illegible names and the date '*1788*'. Also in his survey he found that two caves accessed from the same entrance, both 8ft/2.4m in from the cliff face and about 8ft/2.4m x 9ft/2.7m and 6ft/1.8m high, had been constructed about 15ft/4.6m above the high water mark. There was another cave again about the same height above the high water mark and of similar dimensions as the others further along the cliffs. The last one he found was about ¼ mile/402m from Birling Gap which had been hewn from the cliff about 25ft/7.6m above the high water mark and measured about 7ft/2.1m square and 6ft/1.8m high. Again there were a number of inscriptions but the oldest legible one was *'1805'*.

The Belle Tout Light was never as effective as had been hoped as it was often shrouded in mist. It was therefore decided to build a Light at the foot of the cliffs which would give a better light and therefore visibility would be increased for shipping. Hence the current Light now at the foot of the cliffs at Beachy Head came into service in 1902, with the Belle Tout Light ceasing to be operational in 1899.

The other Light in this vicinity is of course the Royal Sovereign Light, which marks the Royal Sovereign Shoal. From 1875 until 1971 there was a manned Lightship on station, and manning it was not without its dangers as was demonstrated on New Years Day 1891. One of the Lightship crew, Thomas Leeman, who lived at 9, Turners Street, Ramsgate, Kent, was attending to the lights when he fell from the lantern cage, 30ft/9m to the vessel's deck below. He suffered serious injuries to the left side of his body. The Lightship master was very concerned about Leeman's injuries and at about 1.30am fired a distress rocket signal which was seen by the coastguard at Eastbourne who assumed that there was a vessel in distress. The lifeboat coxswain, Jesse Huggett, was informed and the alarm bell was rung to summon the crew. With the crew mustered they wasted no time in getting the lifeboat *William & Mary* ready. Due to the state of the tide and with the lifeboat house being situated at the Wish Tower, which was not an ideal site for launching, it was decided to take the Lifeboat to the east of the town to launch. As there were no local horses immediately available the lifeboat was manually pushed on its carriage.Unfortunately when the lifeboat reached the end of Addingham Road the incline in the road was greater than the men could manage. It was here that at last three horses from Mr. Gausden's stables were used to haul the lifeboat carriage the last remaining distance to the beach, with the lifeboat finally being launched at about 3am. Eventually the *William & Mary* arrived at the Lightship and conveyed the injured Thomas Leeman to Eastbourne for medical attention. This event emphasised the poor siting of the lifeboat house, as the crew had always wanted it to be on the beach at the eastern end of the town near the fishing boats.

The Royal Sovereign Lightship remained on station until 1971 when the lighthouse that now stands there was completed. The current lighthouse navigation light is 91½ft/28m above sea level. The light was maintained by keepers until 1994 when the light was made totally automatic.

*(Ref: ST 1.2.1875; HI 3.12.1891)*

# Beaufort Wind Scale

| Force | Wind Speed (Knots) | Wind Description |
|-------|--------------------|-----------------| 
| 1 | 1 - 3 | Light |
| 2 | 4 - 6 | Light |
| 3 | 7 - 10 | Light |
| 4 | 11 - 16 | Moderate |
| 5 | 17 - 21 | Fresh |
| 6 | 22 - 27 | Strong |
| 7 | 28 - 33 | Strong |
| 8 | 34 - 40 | Gale |
| 9 | 41 - 47 | Severe Gale |
| 10 | 48 - 55 | Storm |
| 11 | 56 - 63 | Violent Storm |
| 12 | 64 + | Hurricane Force |

# Nautical Measurements

6 feet/1.85m = 1 fathom

100 fathoms = 1 Cable

10 Cables = 1 Nautical Mile

3 Nautical Miles = 1 Sea League

# Weights and Measures

*Liquor Measurements (Non spirits)*

1 Barrel = 36 gallons/164ltrs
1 Hogshead = 1½ Barrels (54 gallons/245ltrs)
1 Puncheon = 2 Barrels (72 gallons/327ltrs)
1 Butt of Ale = 3 Barrels (108 gallons/491ltrs)

*Liquor Measurements (Spirits)*

Hogshead of Brandy   = 60 gallons/272ltrs
    "     Claret   = 46 gallons/209ltrs
    "     Port     = 57 gallons/259ltrs
    "     Sherry   = 54 gallons/245ltrs
    "     Madeira = 46 gallons/209ltrs

*Weight Measurements*

Hogshead of sugar = 13 to 16 cwt./660kgs to 813kgs
Sack of coal = 224lbs/102kgs
Sack of flour = 280lbs/127kgs
Sack of potatoes = 168lbs/76kgs
Sack of wool = 364lbs/165kgs

Parson Darby's Cave, Beachy Head - 1899

By courtesy of Eastbourne Library

Eastbourne Lifeboat and crew - 1870

By courtesy of Eastbourne Library

***Thames*** - Ashore at Eastbourne, 3<sup>rd</sup> February 1822

By courtesy of Eastbourne Library

***Gannet*** - Ashore at Seaford, 14<sup>th</sup> February 1882

By courtesy of Seaford Museum and Heritage Society

***Tally Ho*** - Ashore at Eastbourne, 26th February 1886

By courtesy of Eastbourne Library

***Peruvian*** - Ashore at Seaford, 8th February 1899

By courtesy of Seaford Museum and Heritage Society

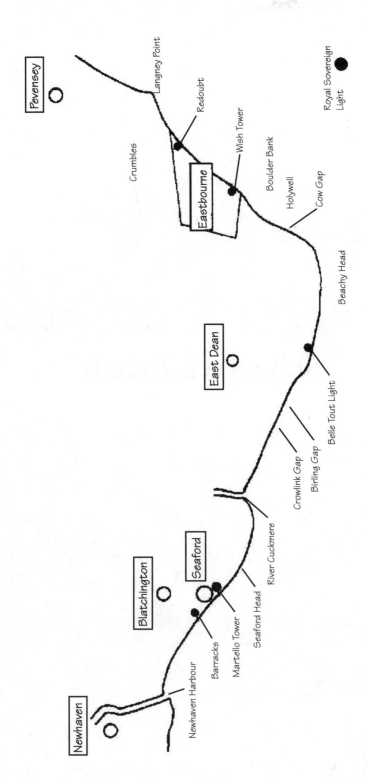

Newhaven

Blatchington

Seaford

Newhaven Harbour

Barracks

Martello Tower

Seaford Head

River Cuckmere

Crowlink Gap

Birling Gap

Belle Tout Light

East Dean

Beachy Head

Cow Gap

Holywell

Boulder Bank

Wish Tower

Redoubt

Eastbourne

Crumbles

Langney Point

Pevensey

Royal Sovereign
Light

# Shipwreck Details

# Key to Reference Sources

| | |
|---|---|
| BC | Bexhill Chronicle |
| BH | Beachy Head |
| BHB | Brett Historical Biographies |
| BPCP | Brett Premier Cinque Ports |
| BO | Bexhill Observer |
| CPC | Cinque Ports Chronicle |
| CNMM | Chronology at Newhaven Maritime Museum |
| DS | Dive Sussex |
| EC | Eastbourne Chronicle |
| EG | Eastbourne Gazette |
| ES | Eastbourne Standard |
| HC | Hastings & St. Leonards Chronicle |
| HI | Hastings & St. Leonards Independent |
| HN | Hastings & St. Leonards News |
| HO | Hastings & St. Leonards Observer |
| HT | Hastings & St. Leonards Times |
| LJ | London Jacket |
| LSRN | Lost Ships of the Royal Navy |
| MSSA | Memorable Shipwrecks & Seafaring Adventures |
| SAE | Sussex Agricultural Express |
| SE | Sussex Express |
| SEA | South Eastern Advertiser |
| SELB | The Story of Eastbourne Lifeboats |
| SES | South East Sail |
| SIBI | Shipwreck Index of the British isles |
| SMLH | Seaford Museum of Local History |
| SNLB | The Story of Newhaven Lifeboats |
| SOM | Sound of Maroons |
| SS | Seaford Shipwrecks |
| ST | Sussex Times |
| SUSH | Sussex Shipwrecks |
| SWA | Sussex Weekly Advertiser |
| TCB | The Coast Blockade |
| TMC | The Mariner Chronicle |
| TOTD | Toiler of the Deep |

# BRAZEN

| | |
|---|---|
| **Date:** | 26.1.1800 |
| **Wreck Location:** | Ave rocks west of Newhaven |
| **Description of Vessel:** | |
| **Gross Tonnage** | 425 |
| **Length** | 105ft/32m |
| **Beam** | 28ft/8.53m |
| **Vessel Type** | British sloop-of-war |
| **Date Built, Builder:** | c.1798 in France |
| **Owner:** | Royal Navy |
| **Ship's Master:** | Commander James Hanson RN |
| **Number of Crew:** | 115 |

This vessel was originally the French Privateer *L'Invincible General Bonaparte*, having been captured by the British vessel *Bodicea* in 1799.

During the night of 25th/26th January 1800 there was a terrible south-westerly storm and driving rain which increased throughout the night. Off the Sussex coast in these conditions was the vessel *Brazen*, a Royal Naval sloop armed with 18 cannons, on a routine patrol up the Channel. The *Brazen* had sailed from Portsmouth having the previous day taken into that port a French vessel captured off the Isle of Wight. Part of *Brazen's* crew were put on this captured vessel and consequently did not sail on the *Brazen* when she left Portsmouth on her last and fateful voyage.

The *Brazen* was no match for the horrendous weather and mountainous seas. It was soon after 5am on Sunday 26th January 1800 that the storm drove her onto the Ave Rocks, to the west of Newhaven. As soon as the vessel struck the rocks it went broadside to the sea, and to ease the situation caused by the constant battering of the huge waves on a rising tide, the crew cut down the main and mizzen masts. Despite their efforts, within a few minutes the *Brazen* rolled over on its side and very quickly started to go to pieces. By the afternoon it was to be a total wreck.

The crew, now realising their situation was desperate, started to jump into the raging sea and swim towards the shore. Others were using rafts or debris from the vessel as floats, to try and get ashore. The entire vessel's complement drowned in these attempts to get ashore except one, seaman Jeremiah Hill, who had joined the *Brazen* at Carysfort ten days earlier. He, like many other crew members, had been thrown into the sea but had sought refuge in the lea of the vessel's hull.

Captain Andrew Sproule of the Royal Navy at Brighton was in command of this part of the Sussex coast, and it was one of his men on watch that first saw the lights of the *Brazen* at about 5am. This watchman then heard crashing sounds and cannon fire over the winds of the storm. He originally thought that it was an attack but then heard the sound of men calling for help. He made his way to the scene along the beach together with a number of others, but all they could see was debris in the sea. As the tide was rising they had to retreat and wait till daylight.

About two hours later Captain Andrew Sproule was made aware of the situation and set out for Newhaven. When he and a number of his men arrived at the scene, it was still dark but by now the tide was at its height. The state of the tide and the condition of the sea made it impossible to answer the crew's cries of help from the beach.

A number of men then got two crane-machines kept nearby and dragged them to the top of the cliff above the stricken vessel. These crane-machines were in effect a mobile crane which raised and lowered a basket into which the casualty could be put. They were designed specifically for this type of rescue where the only approach to the casualty was from the cliff top.

When daylight finally broke the men with one of these crane-machines could see below them a seaman struggling in the cold sea. The sea was still crashing into the cliffs some 50ft/15.2m above the level of the beach. The basket was put out over the cliff edge above the seaman and two men went down in the basket to assist him. However, before they had got down the 300ft/91m to the sea below, part of the sail debris washed over the seaman and he was never seen again.

Daylight also made clear the full extent of this disaster. The *Brazen* could be seen firmly stuck on the rocks about ½ mile/800m from the shore, still with a number of the crew clinging to the wreck. One of the seaman still in the water was Jeremiah Hill, a non-swimmer, who was clinging to a drifting gunslide. He eventually drifted ashore where he was rescued.

At 3pm that afternoon the tide had receded sufficiently for Captain Sproule and his men to actually get on to the beach where they were met by the horrendous sight of 95 bodies strewn all along the water's edge from the wreck to Newhaven harbour. These bodies were recovered and taken away in carts to local churchyards and buried with 29 of them being interred at Newhaven's parish church of St. Michael's. The bodies of the remaining crew members of the *Brazen* were never found.

Commander Hanson's wife was only 20 years of age when he died in this shipwreck but she was to live to the age of 104 years.

An obelisk shaped stone monument designed by Henry Rhodes was erected in the graveyard at St. Michael's church to commemorate this tragic disaster. The inscription on the four faces of the monument read as follows:

Face one,

*Sacred*
*to the memory*
*of*
*Capt. James Hanson*
*The Officers and Company of His Majesty's Ship*
*Brazen;*
*Who were wrecked in a violent storm under the cliff*
*Bearing from this place S.W.*
*At 5 o'clock A.M. Jan 20ᵗʰ A.D. 1800.*
*One of the crew only survived to tell the melancholy tale,*
*By this fatal event, the country, Alas! was deprived*
*of 105 brave defenders at a time, when it,*
*most required their assistance;*
*The remains of many of them were interred near*
*to this spot,*
*By the direction*
*of the Lords Commissioners of the Admiralty.*
*"The waters saw thee O God!*

Face two,

*The Brazen, had been ordered to protect this part*
*of the coast, from the insolent attacks of the enemy;*
*and on the evening proceeding the sad catastrophy,*
*had detained a foreign vessel, which was put under*
*the care of the master's mate, a midshipman,*
*8 seaman and 2 marines; who were thereby saved from*
*the fate of their companions.'*

31

Face three,

*Names of the officers lost*
*James Hanson Esq. Commander*
*James Cook, John Denbry Lieuts.*
*Archibald Ingram Master*
*Patrick Venables, James Hanwell Midshipmen*
*John Braugh Purser Robert Hill Surgeon*
*Thomas Whitfield Boatswain*
*Robert Aalder Yawrte Gunner*
*John Teague Carpenter*

Face four,

*The Friends of*
*CAPT. HANSON*
*caused this monument to be erected*
*as a mark of their esteem for a deserving officer*
*and a valuable friend.*
*It was the will of Heaven to preserve him*
*during four years voyage of danger and difficulty*
*round the world, on discoveries, with Capt. Vancouver*
*in the years, 1791, 1792, 1793, 1794*
*but to take him from us*
*when most he felt himself*
*secure.*
*"The voice of the Lord is upon the waters."*

It was this disaster that prompted the setting up of a committee at Newhaven to investigate the possibility of having a lifeboat stationed at the harbour. In 1802 this committee approached Lloyds for assistance towards the cost and were awarded £50 with the balance being raised locally. The committee ordered the 22ft/6.7m long, believed six oared lifeboat, from Henry Greathead, which arrived on station in May 1803.

*Ref: SIBI; LSRN; CNMM; TMC; BPCP; SS; SNLB; LJ 31.12.1800-2.1.1801*

# JULIANA PROSPERA

| | |
|---|---|
| **Date:** | 17.5.1800 |
| **Wreck Location:** | Ashore near Crowlink Gap |
| **Description of Vessel:** | |
| **Vessel Type -** | Prussian sailing brigantine |
| **Cargo:** | 800 hogsheads* of Wine |
| **Voyage:** | Bordeaux to Emden (Stettin) |
| **Ship's Master:** | John Michael Bunger |

---

This vessel came ashore in terrible weather at Crowlink Gap and became a complete wreck. Fortunately all the crew were saved.

Half of the vessel's cargo of red wine from Embden was saved during the salvage operation, as was the hull and part of the rigging, all of which was subsequently sold to help towards the cost of the salvage.

* A hogshead is a liquid measure, the quantity of which varies upon the contents. If the contents are Claret or Madeira then the measure is 46 gallons/209 litres, Brandy 60 gallons/ 272 litres, Port 57 gallons/259 litres or Sherry 54 gallons/245 litres.

*Ref: SIBI; SWA 19.5.1800 & 26.5.1800*

# AID

| | |
|---|---|
| **Date:** | 31.12.1800 |
| **Wreck Location:** | Ashore near the east pier at Newhaven harbour |
| **Description of Vessel:** | |
| **Gross Tonnage -** | 106 |
| **Vessel Type -** | British sailing Brigantine |
| **Cargo:** | Coal |
| **Home Port:** | Sunderland |
| **Ship's Master:** | Thomas May |

On New Years Eve of 1800, this vessel was attempting to make for Newhaven harbour to seek refuge from the terrible weather and sea conditions. In making its attempt the vessel ran aground near the east pier and became a total wreck as a result of the pounding from the sea. However, the vessel's crew managed to save themselves by climbing onto the pier.

*Ref: CNMM; SWA 5.1.1801*

# FARMERS DELIGHT

**Date:**                                    1.1.1801

**Wreck Location:**                 Ashore near the east pier at
                                             Newhaven harbour

**Description of Vessel:**
**Vessel Type -**                    British sailing vessel

**Cargo:**                               Empty porter casks

**Home Port:**                       Hastings

**Voyage:**                            Cowes to London

**Ship's Master:**                  Fowler

---

On New Years Day of 1801, this vessel became a wreck, just eastward of the spot where the previous day the *Aid* became a wreck, as a result of the same fierce sea and weather conditions. Fortunately for the crew there were a number of persons ashore who saw the plight of the vessel and managed to get ropes to the crew and then drag them through the raging surf to the safety of the shore.

*Ref: SIBI; SWA 5.1.1801*

# VOLUNTEER

| | |
|---|---|
| **Date:** | 2.5.1801 |
| **Wreck Location:** | East off Beachy Head |
| **Description of Vessel:** | |
| **Gross Tonnage -** | 21 |
| **Vessel Type -** | British sailing sloop |
| **Home Port:** | Newhaven |
| **Voyage:** | Newhaven to London |
| **Ship's Master:** | Zacharia Stevens |

On the evening of 30th April 1801 this vessel left Newhaven harbour bound for London, but for reasons not clear the vessel foundered east of Beachy Head off Bexhill within 48 hours of setting sail. It was fortuitous that there was another vessel on the same course as the *Volunteer* that witnessed the event and put a boat off to rescue the stricken vessel's crew. By the time the rescue boat had reached the crew of the *Volunteer* it had almost sunk completely below the waves.

The *Volunteer* was subsequently raised and taken back to Newhaven

*Ref: LP 4.5.1801-6.5.1801 No. 4876; CNMM; SWA 4.5.1801*

# PRINCESS

| | |
|---|---|
| **Date:** | 23.4.1802 |
| **Wreck Location:** | Ashore at Beachy Head |
| **Description of Vessel:** | |
| **Gross Tonnage -** | 570 |
| **Vessel Type -** | British sailing merchantman |
| **Cargo:** | Cotton, drugs and general cargo |
| **Voyage:** | Smyrna to London |
| **Ship's Master:** | W. Lee |

This vessel's difficulties started at about 5am on Friday 23rd April 1802, when she was driven ashore at Beachy Head by the prevailing weather. However, the crew worked tirelessly and managed to re-float the *Princess* at about 3pm that afternoon. The vessel had not been afloat that long when the vessel unshipped its rudder. The inevitable result was that the *Princess* was driven back on the shore at Beachy Head. The cargo was of such great value, about £80,000, that the local Collector of Customs at Newhaven took over the supervision of cargo and crew who were kept in quarantine on the vessel. He sent a party of local dragoons to patrol the beach not only to keep an eye on the crew but also to prevent people plundering the cargo.

Over the following week a great part of the cargo was saved by removing it to smaller local boats which in turn ferried it to six brigs and four sloops that were at anchor off the wreck. This itself was not without dangers because on Thursday, 29th April 1802, two of the small ferrying boats foundered in a sudden squall, laden with part of the rescued cargo. The two crews were saved but the owners of these two smaller boats had to repay the value of the lost cargo which amounted to thousands of pounds. Shipbroker, Mr. St. Barb, is said to be the main owner of the cargo that was on board the *Princess*.

The *Princess* was a captured Spanish privateer which had been later sold as a merchantman.

*Ref: SIBI; SWA 26.4.1802 & 3.5.1802*

# DIANA

**Date:**                        31.5.1803

**Wreck Location:**        Ashore near East Dean

**Description of Vessel:**
**Vessel Type -**            British sailing vessel

**Voyage:**                  Porta Port to Hambro

**Ship's Master:**           Pirera

---

*Ref: SIBI*

# SOPHIA

| | |
|---|---|
| **Date:** | 15.11.1803 |
| **Wreck Location:** | West x south off Beachy Head |
| **Description of Vessel:** | |
| **Gross Tonnage -** | 95 |
| **Vessel Type -** | Sailing vessel |
| **Voyage:** | Guernsey to London |
| **Ship's Master:** | William Ingram |

---

This vessel had been recently purchased in Guernsey and was being taken to London to be surveyed and registered when it sank. Fortunately the crew managed to get off a jolly boat and came ashore in Seaford Bay.

*Ref: CNMM; SIBI*

# HOPE

**Date:**                            00.11.1804

**Wreck Location:**                  Off Beachy Head

**Description of Vessel:**
**Vessel Type -**                    Sailing vessel

**Cargo:**                           Pipe clay

**Home Port:**                       Liverpool

---

This vessel, on a date unknown in November 1804, was run down by a cutter while off Beachy Head but all the crew were saved.

*Ref: SIBI; EG 28.1.1885*

# BLANDFORD

| | |
|---|---|
| **Date:** | 8.2.1805 |
| **Wreck Location:** | Ashore near Bishopstone |
| **Description of Vessel:** | |
| **Gross Tonnage -** | 100 approx. |
| **Vessel Type -** | British sailing brig |
| **Cargo:** | Groceries, hops, tallow, iron, hemp |
| **Home Port:** | Poole |
| **Voyage:** | London to Poole |
| **Ship's Master:** | Jeffron |

Early on the morning of Friday 8th February 1805, the *Blandford* was driven ashore by the weather in Newhaven Bay near Bishopstone, with the loss of all hands. The vessel was smashed to pieces, so much so that only a few pieces of the hull could be seen. The cargo, also being at the mercy of the waves, was strewn along the coast. However, the Customs-house Officers and the Military tried to protect the cargo but with limited success. One of the items that was washed ashore was a case containing a marble tablet with an inscription of a nobleman engraved on it.

During that same afternoon a body was washed ashore near Newhaven and from the effects and clothing the body was assumed to be that of the owner. Two crew members were washed ashore at Newhaven on the following Monday, one of whom had an invoice in his pocket tending to suggest he may well have been the master. These two crew members were buried in the cemetery at Newhaven church.

*Ref: SIBI; SWA 11.2.1805 & 18.2.1805*

# CARL SOLOMON

| | |
|---|---|
| **Date:** | 27.12.1805 |
| **Wreck Location:** | Ashore near Beachy Head |
| **Description of Vessel:** | |
| **Vessel Type -** | British sailing vessel |
| **Cargo:** | Salt |
| **Voyage:** | Alicante (Spain) to Jacobstat (Sweden) |
| **Number of Crew:** | 14 approx. |

The *Carl Solomon* was driven ashore near Beachy Head in a terrific gale but fortunately all the crew were saved. The cargo was totally lost with only a few of the ship's items being salvaged. What was recovered was handed over to the Superintendent of the port of Newhaven, Mr. P. Simon, who retained the items under quarantine for 15 days, which the wreck-agents, Messrs. Burrows & Beckett of Eastbourne, fully agreed to.

*Ref: SIBI; SWA 30.12.1805 & 6.1.1806*

# ACTIVE

| | |
|---|---|
| **Date:** | 2.2.1807 |
| **Wreck Location:** | Ashore between Seaford and Cuckmere |
| **Description of Vessel:** | |
| **Vessel Type -** | British sailing brig |
| **Cargo:** | Timber |
| **Voyage:** | Swansea to Chatham |
| **Ship's Master:** | John Langford |

---

On the night of Monday 2nd February 1807 there was terrific gale which drove the *Active* on to rocks between Seaford and Cuckmere. Luckily none of the crew lost their lives although they lost all their belongings. Driven ashore in the same gale was the *Margaret* (see next page).

As five of the crew were Portuguese and therefore considered to be aliens, they were taken before a Magistrate at Newhaven the following Saturday to make application for the replacement of their lost passports. These were obviously granted and the men then made their way to the Portuguese Consul in London to assist their journey home.

*Ref: SWA 9.2.1807 & 16.2.1807*

# MARGARET

| | |
|---|---|
| **Date:** | 2.2.1807 |
| **Wreck Location:** | Ashore near Birling Gap |
| **Description of Vessel:** | |
| **Vessel Type -** | British sailing brig |
| **Cargo:** | Slate |
| **Voyage:** | Whitehaven to London |
| **Ship's Master:** | Gilderdale |

This vessel became a wreck when driven ashore near Birling Gap in the same gale as the *Active* (see previous page) on 2nd February 1807. All the crew and cargo were saved and the hull of the vessel was sold for scrap.

*Ref: SIBI; SWA 16.2.1807*

# SPECULATION

| | |
|---|---|
| **Date:** | 27.10.1807 |
| **Wreck Location:** | Ashore between the east pier Newhaven harbour and Bishopstone Mill |
| **Description of Vessel:** | |
| **Gross Tonnage -** | 101 |
| **Vessel Type -** | British sailing sloop |
| **Cargo:** | 228 quarters* of wheat, 200 sacks** of flour, 12 cases of glass bottles |
| **Home Port:** | Plymouth |
| **Voyage:** | Newhaven to Plymouth |
| **Ship's Master:** | Thomas Stile |

At 3pm the *Speculation* left Newhaven harbour bound for Plymouth and had only sailed down the English Channel for about 3 to 4 leagues (9 miles/14.5km to 12 miles/19km) when a sudden south westerly gale blew up causing damage to the bowsprit, jib and the mainsail. This left the vessel with only the foresail which considerably restricted manoeuvrability of the vessel to the effect that the vessel drifted eastward before the weather. The sea was in an increasingly bad state, such that eventually the waves broke over the stern of the *Speculation* and stove in the cabin skylight and washed the jolly boat off the deck.

The vessel continued to drift before the increasingly violent storm and raging seas until about 9pm when she was blown ashore between Newhaven east pier and Bishopstone Mill to the east of the harbour entrance. The sea and conditions were so terrible that those ashore could do nothing to assist either the vessel or its crew, who were left to their own devices to get ashore, which they did successfully and without loss. However, the same could not be said for the vessel or the cargo which were totally lost.

The wheat cargo was shipped by Rickman & Golley of Lewes, half of the flour was shipped by Edmund & William Catt of Bishopstone, with the remainder being shipped by Durrant & Co. of Lewes. The cargo of glass bottles was shipped by Stone of Newhaven.

The date this vessel became a wreck is also recorded as 22$^{nd}$ October 1807.

* A quarter is measurement of weight. A quarter of wheat weighs 480lbs/217kgs whereas a standard quarter weighs 8lbs/12.5kgs
** A sack of flour weighed 224lbs/102kgs

*Ref: SIBI; CNMM*

# FRIENDSHIP

| | |
|---|---|
| **Date:** | 22.11.1807 |
| **Wreck Location:** | Ashore near Seaford |
| **Description of Vessel:** | |
| **Gross Tonnage -** | 88 |
| **Vessel Type -** | British sailing brigantine |
| **Cargo:** | Ballast |
| **Home Port:** | Scarborough |
| **Voyage:** | Jersey to Scarborough |
| **Ship's Master:** | Matthew Crompton |

The brigantine *Friendship* left Jersey on 14th November 1807 bound for Scarborough and encountered severe weather conditions almost from the outset of the journey. However, by 4am on Sunday 22nd November the severe weather was showing signs of easing with a northerly wind and within two hours had lulled to a calm. The calm was not to last long, because by 8am the wind had freshened again to a southerly, and as a result the *Friendship* made good progress arriving off Newhaven about 10am the same morning, with an ever increasing wind.

The eastward progress was hindered at 11am with a further change in wind direction. With an increasing wind and rough sea conditions they tried to sit out the storm but by 9.30pm that evening the weather had won the struggle and the vessel was blown onto the beach at Seaford. To make the situation worse the vessel came ashore broadside which put the *Friendship* in a very precarious position. For the following 30 minutes the crew remained on board with the sea constantly breaking right over the vessel. It soon became apparent that the crew would have to abandon it, which they did safely with the help of those ashore, to watch their vessel be smashed to pieces within a further half an hour, by the action of the weather and the rough sea conditions.

*Ref: SIBI; CNMM*

# DOVE

| | |
|---|---|
| **Date:** | 23.11.1807 |
| **Wreck Location:** | Ashore west of Birling Gap |
| **Description of Vessel:** | |
| **Gross Tonnage -** | 97 |
| **Vessel Type -** | British sailing brigantine |
| **Cargo:** | 3790 bushels* of potatoes |
| **Home Port:** | Sunderland |
| **Voyage:** | Jersey to London |
| **Ship's Master:** | John Carr |

At about 9am on Thursday 19th November 1807, the *Dove* left St. Helier, Jersey under the escort of His Majesty's gun brig *Rebuff*. By 11pm that same day they had reached the Isle of Wight where the *Dove* left her escort. The *Dove* continued her journey up the Channel where at about midnight the following night, Saturday 21st November, as it was approaching Beachy Head the wind dropped and the vessel became becalmed. The master was aware that with an ebbing tide he had to get as far off land as was possible.

By 2am the next day, Sunday 22nd November, they were off Newhaven and by 4am they were off Cuckmere due to the flood tide. The weather then started to deteriorate with the wind increasing and sea getting ever rougher. The *Dove* spent the next 7 hours fighting the conditions and by 11.30am the crew found themselves about 6 miles/9.5km off Brighton with torn topsail. The master and his crew continued to fight the elements and slowly made their way up the Channel, when at about 8pm it was discovered that the vessel was starting to leak, so much so that both pumps had to be worked to keep the water level down.

At about midnight that same night the *Dove* ran aground just to the west of Birling Gap, in a very turbulent sea with still about 300ft/91m between the shore and the vessel. The vessel was now at the mercy of the sea as it washed right over the stricken vessel carrying away everything on deck.

As was the custom, the crew took to the main rigging as a safety measure. After they had been there for about 30 minutes it was noticed that the main mast was in real danger of breaking. The crew then moved from the main rigging into the fore rigging, just in time, as the main mast broke and fell over the side. The crew had been in the fore rigging for about a further 45 minutes when the action of the sea started to break the vessel up beneath them. It was becoming apparent that the crew would have to leave and take their chances in the surf. As the vessel broke up many of the crew took advantage of clinging to the floating debris and fortunately all managed to get safely ashore. Once ashore they then climbed up the cliff to a cave in the cliff face (see 'Beachy Head', page 19) and waited for the tide to drop sufficiently for them to walk along the beach and get to safety at Birling Gap. There they made for Birling Farm, the home of a Mr. Hodson, who gave them all the assistance he could.

* A bushel is a measure of capacity and weight, the quantity of which varies upon the contents. If the contents are potatoes then it weighs about 80lbs/36kgs, wheat weighs 60lbs/27kgs, barley weighs 47lbs/21kgs or oats weigh 40lbs/18kgs.

*Ref: SIBI; CNMM*

# INTEGRITY

| | |
|---|---|
| **Date:** | 20.12.1808 |
| **Wreck Location:** | Ashore east of Birling Gap |
| **Description of Vessel:** | |
| **Gross Tonnage -** | 229 |
| **Vessel Type -** | British sailing vessel |
| **Cargo:** | Coffee, sugar, rice, dyewood, hides, horns |
| **Home Port:** | London |
| **Voyage:** | Rio De Janeiro to London |
| **Owner:** | Mr. Atkinson of Seaford, Job Gardner and others |
| **Ship's Master:** | Job Gardner |

On the 15th September 1808 the *Integrity* set sail from Rio De Janeiro for London, and was to have quite an eventful journey up the Channel prior to becoming a wreck at Birling Gap nearly 3 months later. On 9th December 1808 the *Integrity* was finally in the Channel, having arrived the previous day. At 2pm that afternoon the crew saw a schooner to the westward which gave them some concern, believing that it may be an enemy vessel, especially when the schooner manoeuvred to the aft of the *Integrity*. Job Gardner, the master, was so concerned that they may be attacked during the coming night that he fired a gun and awaited a reply signal from the schooner, but none came. This more than convinced Gardner that the schooner was an enemy. Gardner then decided to fire four or five shots at the schooner, which appeared to have the desired effect as it sailed off westward and was not seen again.

The following morning with little wind, the *Integrity* was making little headway, when the crew saw a man-of-war brigantine bearing down on them at quite a pace. It transpired it was the *Sheldrake* with sails more suitable to these conditions. The *Sheldrake* sent a boat to the *Integrity* with three officers, all of whom stayed aboard the *Integrity* for about an hour before returning to their own vessel and sailing away.

On the night of 15th/16th December 1808 a strong north-easterly gale blew up which was to last for the next four days with extremely cold temperatures. At noon on 20th December 1808, the Isle of Wight was about 8 leagues (24 miles/13km) north east of the *Integrity*. By 6pm the same day the wind had increased and turned westerly accompanied by snow which was falling so heavily that the crew could see no further than half the length of the vessel. Three hours later the wind was coming from the southwest and was now hurricane force with so much snow it was not even possible to see as far as before.

At 11pm that evening Tuesday 20th December 1808, Gardner and his crew, much to their surprise, found themselves in surf and broken water, despite having two men stationed forward as lookouts. However, taking into account the conditions it is not really surprising that the lookouts did not see the surf beforehand. Once among the surf Gardner clapped the helm hard down to get out of it, but to no avail. The heavy sea and the strain of helm hard down caused the tiller wheel to sheer from its mountings. The vessel was now totally unmanageable with the result that the sea and weather drove it onto the rocks at Birling Gap. When the vessel came to rest, the position she lay in meant there was a real danger that the elements would cause the masts to tear the decks out. To prevent this, the crew cut away the main mast and let it float away.

The crew remained with the vessel until about 2.30am the following morning when the tide had ebbed sufficiently to leave the vessel high and dry. They then left the *Integrity* and walked eastward under the cliffs where they eventually met two men walking towards them who had heard of their plight and were coming to see if they could assist. The crew, although almost under Beachy Head, had no idea where in fact they were.

The master, Job Gardner having no boots, was suffering both from the cold and injuries to his feet, so he sent the mate back to the ship to recover all the vessel's papers and any other valuables that he could carry. This he did with the assistance of Customs staff and a Mr. Gabriel Burrows, who together with Mr. Hodson of Birling Farm, were appointed agents by Gardner to save what they could from the *Integrity*.

*Ref: SIBI; SWA 26.12.1808*

# ANNA

| | |
|---|---|
| **Date:** | 14.4.1809 |
| **Wreck Location:** | Ashore near Birling Gap |
| **Description of Vessel:** | |
| **Vessel Type -** | British sailing brig |
| **Cargo:** | 700 quarters* of oats |
| **Voyage:** | Waterford to London |
| **Ship's Master:** | Sly |

---

This vessel is also referred to as the *Aurora*.

This vessel and the *Susannah* (see next page), were to become wrecks within about 300yds/274m of each other on the same night, having been driven ashore. They were from the same port, Waterford, and were both bound for London.

The crew of the *Anna* all safely reached the shore and most of the cargo was saved.

\* A quarter of wheat weighs 480lbs/217kgs whereas a standard quarter weighs 28lbs/ 12.5kgs

*Ref: SIBI; SWA 17.4.1809*

# SUSANNAH

**Date:** 14.4.1809

**Wreck Location:** Ashore near Birling Gap

**Description of Vessel:**
**Vessel Type -** British sailing sloop

**Cargo:** 80 tons of bacon, marble blocks

**Voyage:** Waterford to London

**Ship's Master:** Thomas

---

This vessel and the *Anna* (see previous page), were to become wrecks within about 300yds/274m of each other on the same night, having been driven ashore. They were from the same port, Waterford, and were both bound for London.

Like the crew of the *Anna,* the crew safely reached shore and the bacon cargo was safely landed.

*Ref: SIBI; SWA 17.4.1809*

# SPEEDWELL

| | |
|---|---|
| **Date:** | 7.9.1809 |
| **Wreck Location:** | Ashore east of the Hope, Cuckmere |
| **Description of Vessel:** | |
| **Gross Tonnage -** | 74 |
| **Vessel Type -** | British sailing vessel |
| **Cargo:** | Timber |
| **Home Port:** | London |
| **Voyage:** | Littlehampton to London |
| **Ship's Master:** | Thomas Cluer |
| **Number of Crew:** | 2 |
| **Number of Passengers:** | 2 |

The *Speedwell* left Littlehampton at about 9am on Wednesday 6th September 1809 on its journey to London with a cargo of fir timber. The crew was Thomas Chapman, the mate, and an 18 year old youth. Also on board the vessel was the master's wife and young daughter.

At about midnight the *Speedwell* was off Beachy Head, when the impending weather looked very unsettled. As the deck was heavily loaded with the timber cargo, Thomas Cluer decided that they would seek protection off Seaford until the weather had passed. He also felt that if the weather turned really nasty he would be able to make a run for Newhaven harbour to seek shelter. However, the mate Chapman was very much against this idea.

It was about 2am the following morning that the *Speedwell* was finally at anchor and everybody turned in for the night leaving the mate on watch. The weather over the next couple of hours got steadily worse and by 4am the southerly wind had increased considerably accompanied by torrential rain. Thomas Chapman reported to the master both the state of the weather and how the vessel was coping in the conditions. He is reported to have said, "*Thank God she rides easy and we have a harbour to leeward, which we can run for should the vessel require it. She had better ride it out until daylight*".

As soon as daylight showed that morning, the mate went back to the master to report the fact. Meanwhile the other crew member, had gone on deck to find that there were in Seaford Bay and consequently nearer the shore than they believed to be the case. He informed the master and mate who returned to the deck. The master surveyed the situation and decided that the best thing to do was to ride out the weather at anchor and hope that the anchor cable would withstand the strain. The vessel remained in this position throughout the day until about 8pm, by which time the wind was blowing a hurricane from the north, still with torrential rain.

Thomas Cluer was becoming very concerned at their predicament and the likelihood of a very turbulent night in prospect. He decided for everybody's safety that they should all leave the *Speedwell* in the jolly boat, which was astern of the vessel. The jolly boat was brought to the side of the *Speedwell* and once everybody was aboard they started to row towards the shore and the turbulent surf that awaited them. They had managed to almost reach the shore with the waves breaking over them, when the jolly boat capsized throwing all the occupants into the sea with the loss of the lives of the master, his wife and young child. The mate and the 18 year old crew member managed to reach dry land safely with the help of a number of people who were on the shore.

It was not long after this that the *Speedwell* parted from her anchor cable and was driven ashore by the conditions at the Hope, Cuckmere where it was smashed to pieces.

*Ref: CNMM*

# HARLEQUIN

| | |
|---|---|
| **Date:** | 7.12.1809 |
| **Wreck Location:** | Ashore at Seaford Battery |
| **Description of Vessel:** | |
| **Gross Tonnage -** | 185 |
| **Vessel Type -** | British sailing man-of-war sloop |
| **Home Port:** | Plymouth |
| **Voyage:** | Plymouth to The Downs |
| **Date Built, Builder:** | c.1804 |
| **Owner:** | Royal Navy |
| **Ship's Master:** | Lieutenant Anstruther RN |
| **Number of Crew:** | 45 |
| **Number of Passengers:** | 4 |

The *Harlequin* was the escort for a fleet of 23 merchant vessels that left Plymouth for The Downs at about 3pm on Tuesday 5th December 1809. Among the merchantmen were the *Eunice (Unice); Albion; Weymouth; February; Traveller* and *Mitbedacht (Midbedach)*, see pages 60-65. The *Harlequin,* armed with 12 x 6 pounder cannons and 6 x 12 pounder cannons and with 45 crew under the command of Lieutenant Anstruther R.N., was there to protect this fleet against attack and in particular from French Privateers. Also on board when the *Harlequin* left Plymouth were four passengers, a man, his wife and their two children, one still a baby, the other 2 years old.

Although the fleet had met turbulent weather on its way up the Channel it was not to cause any great concern until the night of Wednesday 6th December, when the vessels were met by a hurricane, freezing temperatures and driving sleet. By the following morning, Thursday, there was a change in the weather in that the wind had subsided but the fleet was now surrounded by a thick fog with the sleet and freezing temperatures still present. It was in such conditions that the *Harlequin* constantly fired its cannons so as to alert the convoy astern, of her position. She was considered to be not only the fleet's protector but also the piloting vessel.

As the hours of Thursday 7th December passed, so the wind started to increase and by 4pm that afternoon it was gale force with poor visibility from fog and sleet. It was this lack of visibility that was to cause the *Harlequin* and six other vessels in the fleet, to become wrecks.

It was soon after this time that Lieutenant Anstruther, in the mistaken belief that the fleet had cleared Beachy Head, changed his course to further inshore. The fleet, observing this, all did likewise and the six foremost vessels, namely, *Eunice; Albion; Weymouth; February; Traveller* and *Mitbedacht,* were, like the *Harlequin,* all on course to run ashore in Seaford Bay. The first the crews were aware of their plight was when they found themselves among the extremely violent surf.

They now faced impending danger and in the darkness those on board could only hear the terrible sounds of the howling wind, breaking timbers, masts snapping and sails ripping, together with vicious seas constantly breaking right over the vessels. The breakers and the surf of the ebbing tide, were causing the vessels to crash against each other adding to the confusion and damage. However, despite all of this, the crew of the *Harlequin* continued to fire the cannons to warn the rest of the fleet of the danger they were in and the error of navigation that had been made. It is due to these efforts that the remaining sixteen merchantmen of the fleet successfully passed Beachy Head in safety.

The firing of the cannons to warn the fleet also roused the residents of Seaford who were unable to do much to assist due to the very thick fog and were unable to assess the true situation. In the meantime, those on board the stricken vessels were lashing themselves to the rigging to avoid being washed overboard, as many of the mariners were, and to await daylight. When daylight came the true horror of this disaster was realised. The most easterly of the wrecked vessels was *Mitbedacht* and to the west was the *February,* then the *Eunice, Harlequin, Weymouth, Traveller* and the most westerly vessel was the *Albion.*

Once daylight broke, a barrel was lowered from the *Harlequin* attached to a rope, and the action of the sea took the barrel ashore where the rope was then secured by people waiting to assist. This then allowed those still on board to get ashore including the male passenger. However, it was then found that his wife – albeit there are some reports that say this woman may have been Lieutenant Anstruther's wife – was still on board holding both the two children begging that they all be saved. Two of the *Harlequin's* crew that had just been rescued themselves got a small boat and went back through the breakers and surf at great risk to their own lives. They finally managed to get alongside the *Harlequin* but the woman would not leave the vessel until her children had been safely taken into the small boat. The two seamen climbed back onto the wrecked vessel and each lashed one of the children to their bodies and then lowered the woman into the small boat. Happily, they returned safely to shore, like the rest of the *Harlequin's* crew, with the exception of two of their number who were drowned.

Only a month earlier, The *Weymouth* and her master John Llewellyn, had been captured while in the Bristol Channel by a French privateer. The master, his wife and the ship's boy were cast adrift by their captors in a small boat when about 7 leagues/11km from land. They finally made shore at Land's End. Their captors' possession of the *Weymouth* was short lived because only a couple of days after seizing the vessel the British man-of-war sloop *Plover* recaptured the *Weymouth* under fire from the guns of the fort at St. Malo. The *Weymouth* was taken to the Scilly Isles where Llewellyn and the ship's boy rejoined the vessel. This subsequent disastrous voyage was the first since being recaptured and returning to Plymouth.

Of the *Weymouth's* total complement of 11, all but four safely reached the shore. These four mariners all drowned while trying to reach the shore in a small boat.

The American vessel *Eunice,* a few months prior to this fateful voyage, had a thousand pounds spent on her and was considered to be in excellent condition as a result. When the vessel ran aground a Mr. Close of Newhaven, together with a number of men from the 81st Regiment based at Seaford Barracks, rescued not only the master and his crew but also a large proportion of the cargo. These same men from Seaford Barracks also assisted in the protection of the cargoes that were washed ashore preventing them being stolen.

The crew of the *February* were, unhappily, not so fortunate as 14 of the total complement of 16 men were to lose their lives. The mate and ship's boy were the only survivors. Once the vessel ran aground the crew took to the rigging and as each part was washed away they all took refuge in the main mast. However, the weight of 16 men was too much and it finally gave way and all the crew were thrown into the boiling sea.

Of the total of 13 men on board the Prussian vessel *Mitbedacht* only one survived. Fortunately for this crew member, Lieutenant Derenzy of the 81st regiment based at Seaford Barracks saw him lose his grip on some wreckage and start to drift away. Lieut. Derenzy plunged into the sea and grabbed the mariner by the hair and managed to drag him to safety.

All those on board the *Traveller* were saved, as were those on board the *Albion*.

A total of 35 men lost their lives on 7th December 1809 as the result of Lieut. Anstruther believing that the vessels had passed Beachy Head.

*Ref: SIBI; MSSA; LSRN; SWA 11.12.1809*

# EUNICE

| | |
|---|---|
| **Date:** | 7.12.1809 |
| **Wreck Location:** | Ashore at Seaford Barracks |
| **Description of Vessel:** **Vessel Type -** | American sailing brig |
| **Cargo:** | Cotton, timber, ashes |
| **Home Port:** | New York |
| **Voyage:** | New York to Tonningen |
| **Ship's Master:** | William Bowers |
| **Number of Crew:** | 9 |

This vessel is also referred to as the *Unice*.

See *Harlequin* page 56.

# ALBION

| | |
|---|---|
| **Date:** | 7.12.1809 |
| **Wreck Location:** | Ashore at Seaford Barracks |
| **Description of Vessel:** | |
| **Vessel Type -** | British sailing schooner |
| **Cargo:** | Brandy, timber, saffron, cork, barilla (sodium carbonate) |
| **Home Port:** | Exeter |
| **Voyage:** | Gibraltar to London |
| **Ship's Master:** | John Tremond |
| **Number of Crew:** | 8 |

See *Harlequin* page 56.

# WEYMOUTH

**Date:**                        7.12.1809

**Wreck Location:**              Ashore at Seaford Cliff

**Description of Vessel:**
**Gross Tonnage -**              180
**Vessel Type -**               British full rigged sailing vessel

**Cargo:**                       Cork, tobacco, barilla (sodium carbonate)

**Home Port:**                   London

**Voyage:**                      Gibraltar to London

**Ship's Master:**               John Llewellyn

**Number of Crew:**              10

---

See *Harlequin* page 56.

# FEBRUARY

**Date:** 7.12.1809

**Wreck Location:** Ashore at Blatchington Battery, Seaford

**Description of Vessel:**
**Gross Tonnage -** 460
**Vessel Type -** Prussian full rigged sailing vessel

**Cargo:** Ballast

**Voyage:** Petersburg to unknown destination

**Ship's Master:** Martin Pramsschriber (from Danzig)

**Number of Crew:** 15

---

See *Harlequin* page 56.

# TRAVELLER

| | |
|---|---|
| **Date:** | 7.12.1809 |
| **Wreck Location:** | Ashore at Seaford |
| **Description of Vessel:** | |
| **Gross Tonnage -** | 109 |
| **Vessel Type -** | British sailing brigantine |
| **Cargo:** | Citrus fruits |
| **Home Port:** | London |
| **Voyage:** | Malaga to London |
| **Ship's Master:** | Coulson |
| **Number of Crew:** | 7 |

See *Harlequin* page 56.

# MIBEDACHT

**Date:** 7.12.1809

**Wreck Location:** Ashore at Seaford Battery

**Description of Vessel:**
**Gross Tonnage -** 350
**Vessel Type -** Prussian full rigged sailing vessel

**Cargo:** Wine, brandy, sugar

**Voyage:** Riga to Memel

**Ship's Master:** Johan G. Schults

**Number of Crew:** 12

---

This vessel is also referred to as the *Mitbedacht*

See *Harlequin* page 56.

# AURORA

| | |
|---|---|
| **Date:** | 15.12.1809 |
| **Wreck Location:** | Seaford/Newhaven area |
| **Description of Vessel:** | |
| **Gross Tonnage -** | 88 |
| **Vessel Type -** | British sailing brig |
| **Cargo:** | Timber |
| **Home Port:** | Sunderland |
| **Voyage:** | Southampton to Burlington, Yorkshire |
| **Ship's Master:** | George Hall |
| **Number of Crew:** | 4 |

At 10am on Thursday 14th December 1809 the *Aurora* left Southampton under its master George Hall, a mate, and three seamen. By the later part of the afternoon the weather looked quite threatening and by 5.30pm a strong south westerly gale was blowing. At this time the *Aurora* was 3 miles/4.8km south by east of the Owers Light with the sails much reduced. George Hall set a south easterly course so as to clear Beachy Head. However, by midnight the weather was deteriorating with heavy rain and stronger winds such that by 1am the following morning it was almost a hurricane and coming from the south. These terrible winds accompanied by ever increasing heavy seas washing over the vessel eventually caused the loss of part of the rigging which meant the crew had to stow the main sail. The vessel was now without sail and drifting towards the shore.

At 2am the crew could make out the cliff at Seaford above them, and although they were resigned to being washed ashore they did not want it to be among the rocks. The crew put the helm hard over, hoping the vessel would respond and then be able to drift ashore where the crew knew that their port side was free of rocks. Fortunately this manoeuvre was successful and it was not long before the vessel ran aground. No sooner had the vessel struck the shore than the topmast was torn away and the main mast snapped about half way up. The tide was on the flood and had been so for about two hours, and as a consequence each wave that struck the vessel pushed it further and further onto the shore.

The crew were now in a perilous state with the vessel breaking up beneath them. The master, George Hall, held onto the rigging so as not to be washed over board but unfortunately drowned. John Underdown, an 18 year old crew member, died while still on the deck and a further crew member drowned in attempting to reach the shore. Fortunately two of the crew, the mate Robert Jenes and another young crew member, survived this ordeal by hanging onto the main rigging until the high tide at 5am. They both then managed to jump from the vessel between the waves and with the assistance of those ashore were saved. They were both so exhausted, the younger man being unable to stand, that they were taken to a public house in Seaford, where the mate requested Mr. Goringe, a merchant and agent for stranded vessels, to take charge of the wreck of the *Aurora*.

*Ref: SIBI; CNMM;*

# REBECCA

| | |
|---|---|
| **Date:** | 6.2.1810 |
| **Wreck Location:** | Ashore under the cliffs at Seaford |
| **Description of Vessel:** | |
| **Vessel Type -** | American three masted sailing vessel |
| **Cargo:** | Tobacco, cotton, rice, flour, staves |
| **Ship's Master:** | Tayler |

During the night of Tuesday 6th February 1810 this American vessel ran aground in thick fog under the cliffs at Seaford. The vessel was stuck fast, so it was decided that the cargo should be got off, the majority of it being discharged over the following few days.

As each tide ebbed and flowed it was causing more and more damage to the *Rebecca*. However, with the cargo no longer in the vessel's holds, an attempt was made to re-float her the following Monday, 12th February. Unfortunately this attempt was not successful and it was clear that the *Rebecca* would eventually be smashed to pieces, so what remained of her was sold by auction on St. Valentines Day, Wednesday 14th 1810.

*Ref: SWA 12.2.1810 & 19.2.1810*

# PIPER

**Date:**                                    16.2.1810

**Wreck Location:**                          Ashore near Newhaven

**Description of Vessel:**
**Vessel Type -**                            British sailing vessel

**Voyage:**                                  Dartmouth to unknown destination

---

*Ref: SIBI*

# DRAPER

| | |
|---|---|
| **Date:** | 24.2.1810 |
| **Wreck Location:** | Ashore near Beachy Head |
| **Description of Vessel:** | |
| **Vessel Type -** | Irish sailing vessel |
| **Cargo:** | Linen, bacon, general provisions |
| **Home Port:** | Belfast |
| **Voyage:** | Belfast to London |
| **Ship's Master:** | William Gowan |

On the afternoon of Saturday 24th February 1810, in a fresh south westerly wind, five French Privateers were seen in pursuit of a number of vessels, including the *Draper*, *Graces* (see page 74), *Joseph* (see page72), and the *Danby* (see page 73). Some of them managed to gain the safety of Newhaven harbour but these four were not so lucky.

The *Graces, Joseph* and the *Danby* were all driven ashore by the pursuing Privateers, fortunately with no loss of life. However, some of the cargoes were damaged as a result of the vessels being wrecked.

As for the *Draper,* in trying to make good her escape with her cargo valued at £60,000, she was seized by two of the pursuing Privateers who put eleven men aboard her. However, the boarding party did not know how to sail the vessel and so they allowed the *Draper* to run ashore. Once aground, the boarding party took to a small boat, in ever freshening weather, presumably with the intention of rejoining their own vessels. They had not got far from the shore when their boat capsized in the rough sea resulting in three of them drowning. The other eight made for the shore where they were duly detained, the Collector and Comptroller of Newhaven putting the detainees in the custody of the Second Surrey Militia. The eight were then marched by the Militia to their Regimental Headquarters at Eastbourne for questioning.

At Eastbourne it was found that of the eight detainees three were Dutch, two were Spanish and the remainder were French. From interviewing them it was established that they were part of the crew of the French Privateer *Grand Duc de Berg* under the command of Captain De Rosse. Although the *Grand Duc de Berg* was not armed, apart from two small carronades,* it had seized a number of vessels in the Channel previously including the *Le Aliance,* a Spanish vessel of 300 tons off Dover, and the *Murray,* an English merchantman.

The detainees revealed that the *Grand Duc de Berg* together with fourteen other Privateers including the *Alexandrie, La Prevenir* and *La Caprice*, had left Dieppe earlier that day, but the *Draper* had not been the first vessel they had seized. It appeared that earlier in the day, the *La Caprice* had seized a brig with a full cargo.

One of the Dutch detainees, Gert Demuck, said that he could not get employment in Holland and so desperately needed money that he had joined the Privateer *Grand Duc de Berg,* as captains of such vessels paid large bounties. Captain De Rosse had paid Demuck twenty crowns/£5 for twenty days work.

The crew of the *Draper* all survived their ordeal and the cargo was later to be removed by the local Customs Officers intact.

*A short large-calibre gun

*Ref: SIBI; SWA 26.2.1810 & 5.3.1810*

# JOSEPH

| | |
|---|---|
| **Date:** | 24.2.1810 |
| **Wreck Location:** | Near Beachy Head |
| **Home Port:** | Sunderland |

See *Draper* page 70.

*Ref: SIBI*

# DANBY

**Date:**                           24.2.1810

**Wreck Location:**                 Ashore in Seaford Bay

**Description of Vessel:**
**Vessel Type -**                   British sailing vessel

**Home Port:**                      Sunderland

---

See *Draper* page 70.

*Ref: SIBI*

# GRACES

| | |
|---|---|
| **Date:** | 24.2.1810 |
| **Wreck Location:** | Ashore near Beachy Head |
| **Description of Vessel:** | |
| **Vessel Type -** | Irish sailing vessel |
| **Home Port:** | Belfast |
| **Voyage:** | Belfast to London |
| **Ship's Master:** | Caughey |

See *Draper* page 70.

*Ref: SIBI; SWA 26.2.1810 & 5.3.1810*

# HECTOR

**Date:**                              20.4.1810

**Wreck Location:**           Off Beachy Head

**Description of Vessel:**
**Vessel Type -**                British sailing vessel

**Cargo:**                          Coal

**Voyage:**                        Cardiff to London

**Ship's Master:**              Griffiths

---

During the night of Monday 20<sup>th</sup> April 1810 the *Hector* was run down by another vessel, the name of which was unknown. All the crew survived.

*Ref: SIBI*

# HAWKE

| | |
|---|---|
| **Date:** | 9.10.1810 |
| **Wreck Location:** | Off Beachy Head |
| **Description of Vessel:**<br>**Vessel Type -** | British three masted sailing schooner |
| **Voyage:** | London to Africa |
| **Ship's Master:** | Whitesides |

---

Many vessels sank during this era, with the circumstances or reasons as to why they sank not being known. The *Hawke* was just such a vessel, sinking on Tuesday 9th October 1810 with the loss of all hands.

*Ref: SIBI*

# UNKNOWN

**Date:**                                16.10.1810

**Wreck Location:**              Off Beachy Head

**Description of Vessel:**
**Vessel Type -**                  Three masted sailing schooner

---

The reason as to why this vessel, the name of which is unknown, sank on Tuesday 16th October 1810 is not known. However, it is known that she sank with the loss of the lives of all those on board.

*Ref: SIBI*

# HUNTER

| | |
|---|---|
| **Date:** | 25.9.1811 |
| **Wreck Location:** | Ashore at Birling Gap |
| **Description of Vessel:** **Vessel Type -** | British sailing vessel |
| **Cargo:** | Sugar, coffee, cotton |
| **Voyage:** | Martinique to London |
| **Ship's Master:** | Knight |
| **Number of Crew:** | 18 |

At 1am on Wednesday 25th September 1811, the severe gale that was blowing off the East Sussex coast was responsible for driving the *Hunter* and the *Hamilton* (see next page) ashore at Birling Gap. The crew of the *Hunter* were unable to get off the vessel until 7am that same day, during which time they were at great risk from the heavy seas and winds that constantly beat over the vessel. Fortunately there was no loss of life but the vessel did become a victim of the conditions and was wrecked.

The hull was auctioned on Thursday 3rd October in an attempt to recoup some of the underwriter's losses.

*Ref: SIBI; SWA 7.10.1811*

# HAMILTON

| | |
|---|---|
| **Date:** | 25.9.1811 |
| **Wreck Location:** | Ashore at Birling Gap |
| **Description of Vessel:** **Gross Tonnage -** | 400 |
| **Vessel Type -** | Sailing vessel |
| **Cargo:** | Rum, sugar, coffee, cocoa, cotton |
| **Voyage:** | Martinique to London |
| **Ship's Master:** | Martin |
| **Number of Crew:** | 25 |

This vessel like the *Hunter* (see previous page), was driven ashore by the fierce gale off the Sussex coast on the night of Wednesday 25th September 1811. Once the vessel was ashore the crew got safely off, to return later and recover all the cargo. However, the vessel was to become a wreck due to the combined effects of sea and weather, and like the *Hunter,* was auctioned on Thursday 3rd October in order to reduce the vessel's underwriting losses.

*Ref: SIBI; SWA 7.10.1811*

# NEW WALL

**Date:**                                10.12.1811

**Wreck Location:**              Near Newhaven

**Description of Vessel:**
**Vessel Type -**                    British sailing vessel

**Home Port:**                       Chichester

**Voyage:**                            Chichester to Shoreham

---

This vessel became a wreck on Tuesday 10th December 1811 near Newhaven, with all crew and cargo being safely rescued.

*Ref: SIBI*

# HENRY

| | |
|---|---|
| **Date:** | 15.2.1812 |
| **Wreck Location:** | Ashore near Beachy Head |
| **Description of Vessel:** | |
| **Vessel Type -** | British sailing vessel |
| **Cargo:** | Timber |
| **Voyage:** | Southampton to Shields |
| **Ship's Master:** | Abraham Reay |

---

On the evening of Saturday 15th February 1812 the *Henry* was being pursued by a French Privateer, which at about 10pm drove the vessel ashore near Beachy Head.

It was not until the following morning that John Hayter, an employee of Mr. Hudson, the owner of nearby Birling Farm, was made aware of the stricken vessel. Having got out of bed, Hayter instructed his informant to go and let the Customs Officers Messrs. West and Marsh know of the stranded vessel. Hayter himself took one of his employer's horses from the stables and rode down to the wreck where he found the crew still on board but all safe. However, the master was not on the vessel and Hayter was told by the crew that he had just walked off along the beach towards Eastbourne.

There was then much discussion between the crew and Hayter as to what was best to do in order to salvage as much as possible. They decided to take down all the sails, rigging and cables with the hope that these would be got off the vessel before the returning tide. To help with this work Hayter sent one Henry Miller back to Birling Farm to get a team of horses to help remove the salvaged items from the shore. Having arranged this he left the crew to get on with the work while he went off to Eastbourne to try and find the master.

Hayter finally found the master of the *Henry,* Abraham Reay, fast asleep on a bench in the tap-room of the New Inn at Eastbourne. When woken up, Hayter asked if he wanted more hands to help salvage items from his vessel. Reay said that he did not as there was no time because the vessel had run aground at low tide and the incoming tide would soon be covering the *Henry* and smash her to pieces. The New Inn landlady, Mrs. Comber, who was present during this conversation, was of the opinion that Reay was not well and could not have meant what he had just said. Reay finally sat up on the bench and Hayter told him what had been arranged with the crew regarding salvage and that a team of horses were on their way to assist. Hayter said that he believed that at least three wagon loads of salvaged items could be got off the vessel before the returning tide. Reay was indignant and insisted Hayter touch nothing from the vessel. Hayter pointed out that the horse teams would probably arrive at the wreck before he could return to the vessel.

Hayter left Reay in the New Inn, and returned to the *Henry* where he found the crew busy trying to salvage what they could. He told them of Reay's instructions, so they stopped work and the horse teams were sent away without removing anything. It was not long after this that the vessel was smashed to pieces by the advancing sea.

Abraham Reay subsequently made a protest about Hayter's actions before W.B. Langridge, a Public Notary, but the contents of it were not made public.

This wreck raised an additional problem in respect of access to the shore. The only road access was over land belonging to the owner of Birling Farm, Mr. Hudson, but he always kept the access gate locked. It was kept locked so as to maintain his right to the property and to keep trespassers out. Some people at the time tried to suggest that because the gate was locked it was hindering access to shipwrecked vessels, and that it had always been a right of way. Mr. Hudson said that he was quite happy for his locks to be removed from the gate provided those people removing the lock could justify their actions. Some of the local people who knew the previous Birling Farm owner, Mr. Dippery, said that he was also in the habit of keeping the gate locked but Mr. Dippery would never allow a wagon access when attending a wreck, until after his!

*Ref: SIBI; CNMM; SWA 24.2.1812 & 2.3.1812*

# NIMROD

**Date:**        17.2.1813

**Wreck Location:**    Near Beachy Head

**Description of Vessel:**

**Vessel Type -**     British sailing vessel

**Voyage:**       Honduras to unknown destination

**Ship's Master:**     Jack

---

The *Nimrod* became a total loss on Wednesday 17th February 1813 near Beachy Head. The master, two mates and nine crew were all drowned.

*Ref: SIBI*

# MOWBRAY

**Date:**                              00.4.1816

**Wreck Location:**          Seaford Bay

**Description of Vessel:**
**Vessel Type -**                British sailing vessel

**Cargo:**                          Coal

**Voyage:**                        Sunderland to Brighton

---

*Ref: SIBI*

# ALFRED

| | |
|---|---|
| **Date:** | 18.11.1816 |
| **Wreck Location:** | Near Newhaven |
| **Description of Vessel:** | |
| **Vessel Type -** | British sailing vessel |
| **Cargo:** | Coal |
| **Home Port:** | Sunderland |
| **Voyage:** | Sunderland to unknown destination |

---

On the morning of Monday 18th November 1813, the *Alfred* was driven ashore near Newhaven. All the crew were safely brought ashore.

*Ref: SIBI*

# NELSON

| | |
|---|---|
| **Date:** | 14.12.1816 |
| **Wreck Location:** | Near Birling Gap |
| **Description of Vessel:** | |
| **Vessel Type -** | British sailing sloop |
| **Cargo:** | Oats, nuts, furniture |
| **Voyage:** | Southampton to London |
| **Ship's Master:** | Atkins |

On the night of Saturday 14th December 1816 a very strong wind was blowing which led to the sloop *Nelson* being driven ashore near Birling Gap. Fortunately, she came ashore away from the rocks, which enabled the crew to get safely off the vessel. A proportion of the cargo was saved but the vessel was smashed to pieces by the combined effect of the sea and high winds.

The winds were so strong that numerous trees were blown over throughout East Sussex, including an old large yew tree in the cemetery at Ninfield. The minister had promised the tree to the sexton but before he could remove it, somebody had stolen it!.

*Ref: SIBI; SWA 23.12.1816*

# WILLIAM

**Date:** 1.7.1817

**Wreck Location:** Ashore east of Newhaven harbour

**Description of Vessel:**
**Vessel Type -** British sailing ketch

**Cargo:** Timber

**Home Port:** London

**Voyage:** Ross to London

**Ship's Master:** Bridges

**Number of Crew:** 3

---

At 10pm on the night of Tuesday 1st July 1817 the ketch *William* was at anchor off Newhaven trying to ride out the terrific gale that was blowing at the time. However, it was not long before the *William* broke free from its anchorage and was driven ashore by the turbulent seas and weather, where it was very quickly smashed to pieces. The master and the mate managed to save themselves, but unfortunately the other two crew members, aged about 20 years, drowned.

So vicious was the weather that night that not a single piece of the timber cargo could be seen the following morning.

*Ref: SIBI; SWA 7.7.1817*

# RUSSEL

**Date:**                                      17.3.1818

**Wreck Location:**                  Ashore near Newhaven harbour

**Description of Vessel:**
**Vessel Type -**                      British sailing brig

**Cargo:**                                   Coal

**Voyage:**                                Shields to Newhaven

---

On Saturday 14th March 1881, the *Russel* was attempting to enter Newhaven harbour, when it ran aground on the sand bar at the entrance. It was thought that the only way to save the vessel was to remove the cargo of coal, which would then make it possible to float the vessel off the sand bar. Over the next day or so the cargo was removed from the *Russel,* but unfortunately the vessel was not refloated and hence became a wreck.

*Ref: SIBI*

# WILLIAM & SARAH

**Date:**                              20.12.1818

**Wreck Location:**          Ashore near Newhaven harbour

**Description of Vessel:**
**Vessel Type -**              Thames sailing barge

**Home Port:**                  London

**Voyage:**                       Worthing to Shoreham

**Ship's Master:**            Swaine

---

The *William & Sarah* ran aground on the sand bar near Newhaven harbour on Sunday 20th December 1818 and sank. Luckily the crew were all saved.

*Ref: SIBI*

# JANE

| | |
|---|---|
| **Date:** | 20.10.1819 |
| **Wreck Location:** | Off Beachy Head |
| **Description of Vessel:** | |
| **Vessel Type -** | British sailing vessel |
| **Cargo:** | Coal |
| **Voyage:** | Sunderland to Weymouth |
| **Ship's Master:** | Pearce |

On Wednesday 20th October 1819 the *Jane* became a total wreck off Beachy Head, fortunately without the loss of any of the crew.

*Ref: SIBI*

# OCEAN

| | |
|---|---|
| **Date:** | 29.11.1819 |
| **Wreck Location:** | Ashore at Birling Gap |
| **Description of Vessel:** | |
| **Gross Tonnage -** | 200 approx. |
| **Vessel Type -** | Canadian sailing brig |
| **Cargo:** | 213 hogsheads* of sugar, 66 puncheons** of rum, 50 bales*** of cotton, 230 bags**** of coffee, 1 cask of arrow root. |
| **Home Port:** | Banff |
| **Voyage:** | Demerara to London |
| **Ship's Master:** | William Anton |
| **Number of Crew:** | 4 (possibly 5) |
| **Number of Passengers:** | 1 |

At 5am on Monday 29th November 1819, the *Ocean* was forced ashore near Birling Gap by the heavy seas and weather prevailing at the time. Such was the strength of the sea that within an hour it had been smashed to pieces, unhappily with the loss of the lives of the mate and one seaman. However, the master and remaining crew and the sole passenger on board survived the ordeal, having been rescued under extremely difficult circumstances by Midshipmen Kiltmeer and Jacobs of the Royal Navy, stationed at Birling Gap Coast Blockade Station.

The surviving crew lost everything they possessed as a result, but were suitably cared for by Kiltmeer and Jacobs. The majority of the cargo was lost with only 15 puncheons of rum, 12 bags of coffee, 50 bales of cotton and the cask of arrow root being salvaged.

As was often the case when a vessel became shipwrecked, it was not long before people ashore were removing any of the cargo left laying on the beach, and this case was no different. In his attempts to prevent this, Mr. H. Harrison, the Collector of Customs, was attacked by one of the thieves. However, the man was overpowered and detained and handed over to a Constable, but during the night, for reasons never explained, the detainee managed to escape custody.

The bodies of the two drowned crew members, Daniel Fell and Christian Goodwill, were soon found and an Inquest was held the following day. The Coroner, Mr. G. Gwynne, presided over the Inquest together with a jury, who returned a verdict of 'Accidentally drowned'.

* A hogshead of sugar weighed between 13 - 16 cwt./660kgs - 813kgs
** A puncheon of rum was 72 gallons/327ltrs.
*** A bale of cotton (USA) weighed between 400-500lbs/181 – 227kgs
**** A bag of coffee weighed between 140-168lbs/66 – 72kgs

*Ref: SWA 6.12.1819*

# PHOENIX

**Date:**                          00.12.1819

**Wreck Location:**               Ashore near Beachy Head

**Description of Vessel:**
**Vessel Type -**                 British sailing vessel

**Home Port:**                    Deal

---

When the *Phoenix* came ashore near Beachy Head in December 1819, the crew were saved by Midshipman Tom Caswell and two Coast Blockade men, at great risk to their own lives. Caswell was also involved in the rescue of another crew when the brig *Brothers* (see next page) became a wreck.

*Ref: TCB*

# BROTHERS

| | |
|---|---|
| **Date:** | 24.1.1820 |
| **Wreck Location:** | Ashore near Beachy Head |
| **Description of Vessel:** | |
| **Vessel Type -** | British sailing vessel |
| **Owner:** | Benjamin Lewes |
| **Ship's Master:** | Benjamin Lewes |

Monday 24th January 1820 saw the brig *Brothers* became a wreck near Beachy Head. Midshipman Tom Caswell, assisted by two others, offered much needed help to the master of the vessel.

*Ref: TCB*

# BROTHERS

**Date:**       14.3.1820

**Wreck Location:**   Off Newhaven

**Description of Vessel:**
**Vessel Type -**    British sailing vessel

**Home Port:**     Sunderland

**Ship's Master:**    Robert Whinney

---

This vessel became a loss off Newhaven on Tuesday 14th March 1820.

*Ref: CNMM*

# JEANE FANIE

| | |
|---|---|
| **Date:** | 18.12.1821 |
| **Wreck Location:** | Ashore near Beachy Head |
| **Description of Vessel:** | |
| **Vessel Type -** | French sailing vessel |
| **Cargo:** | Salt |
| **Home Port:** | Fannes |
| **Voyage:** | Marens to Dunkirk |
| **Ship's Master:** | Sylvester |
| **Number of Crew:** | 4 and 1 boy |

On Tuesday 18th December 1821 this small vessel was wrecked at Beachy Head having been forced ashore in a gale. It unhappily resulted in the loss of the master and his 12 year old son. The remaining four crew members survived and were tended to by men of the Coast Blockade Station at Birling Gap. The following day the survivors were taken to Newhaven to board a French vessel in the harbour, so they could return to France.

On arriving at the harbour their plight became known, and a number of local people went round raising money for the seamen. They collected £4 which was distributed among them. They were also given clothing and food to tide them over for the next few days until their vessel sailed for France.

As a result of this wreck, some Spanish Dollars and French Francs were washed up on the shore, together with a watch. Those who found this property were Joseph Thomas, William Pearson (both seamen of the Coast Blockade), Henry Miller, Henry Earle, Thomas Elliott and Thomas Shelley (all labourers from East Dean). The found items were subsequently handed to the Lloyds Agent, Mr. J.B. Stone, who was so taken by the honesty of the finders that he had their names mentioned in the local paper.

*Ref: SWA 24.12.1821, 31.12.1821 & 21.2.1822*

# THAMES

| | |
|---|---|
| **Date:** | 3.2.1822 |
| **Wreck Location:** | Ashore at Eastbourne |
| **Description of Vessel:** | |
| **Gross Tonnage -** | 1500 |
| **Vessel Type -** | East Indiaman* |
| **Cargo:** | Not known |
| **Voyage:** | From unknown port to China |
| **Date Built, Builder:** | c.1820, Barnett's Yard, Deptford, London |
| **Ship's Master:** | William Heaviside |
| **Number of Crew:** | 140 |

On the night of Sunday 3rd February 1822 the *Thames* (see photograph page 24), an East Indiaman* armed with 20 guns and built in 1820 at a cost of £52,000, was off Eastbourne in hurricane force winds and the accompanying very rough seas. It was this extreme weather that drove the vessel ashore at Eastbourne, despite the efforts of the master and crew. The distress guns and lights from the *Thames* were seen by, amongst others, those stationed at the Coast Blockade Station under the command of Lieutenant Edward Chappell. It was not long before there was a large crowd on the shore to watch the unfolding drama.

Lieutenant Chappell and two of his Midshipmen persuaded four local fishermen to launch one of their luggers to assist the stricken vessel. The surf through which the lugger was launched was described by Lieut. Chappell as *'the heaviest I have seen'*. Their efforts were successful as they managed to reach the *Thames* and put lines on her and bring those on board the East Indiaman ashore. However, between four and seven of the crew perished when they tried to effect their own rescue by making for the shore in a boat from the *Thames*.

A further local fishing lugger also attempted to put to sea to rescue those on the stricken *Thames*. The three fishermen on board this lugger together with, Midshipman Smith of the Coast Blockade, attempted to launch, but the surf at the shore was so rough that the lugger capsized. Midshipman Smith was washed away and drowned. His body was later found and returned to his home town of Margate in a hearse the following Thursday.

With the *Thames* ashore an inspection soon revealed that the hull had received serious damage from the horrendous beating it took from both wind and sea. To help repair the hull and make it watertight, two stagecoaches were engaged on two trips to London, to bring caulkers** to Eastbourne to repair the vessel's hull. While the repair work was carried out, the cargo, valued at £30,000, was got off the *Thames,* but not without a mishap. One of the men helping to unload the cargo was injured when a hogshead*** of beer which was being lowered to the shore between two slings, slipped and fell on him. He was a very lucky man considering the weight, as he only sustained minor bruising.

On Friday 22nd February 1822, nearly three weeks after the *Thames* first ran aground, the 100hp steam tug *Venus* and the 80hp steam tug *Swift* put lines on the vessel and slowly eased it into the sea in front of an excited crowd of thousands gathered at the scene. The *Thames* was then towed to Gravesend in Kent.

---

* The term 'Indiaman' was first coined in the 16th century when the Dutch East India Company (or VOC – Verenigde Oostindische Compagnie) built a number of ships for trade to the Dutch East Indies. However, the company ceased trading in 1799, but the term for such ships carried on. Hence the term seemed to refer to a defensively armed fully rigged three masted merchantman with one or two decks, that normally plied the trade routes, for a number of northern European countries between the Caribbean in the west (West Indiaman) and Asia in the east (East Indiaman).
 ** A Caulker made hulls watertight usually by pressing oakum (loose fibre obtained from picking old rope) into the seams of the hull.
*** A hogshead of beer was 54galls/245ltrs

*Ref: TCB; SWA 4.2.1822, 11.2.1822 & 18.2.1822*

# PHILLIPA

| | |
|---|---|
| **Date:** | 2.4.1823 |
| **Wreck Location:** | Ashore at Birling Gap |
| **Description of Vessel:** | |
| **Vessel Type -** | British sailing vessel |
| **Cargo:** | 13 casks of wine |
| **Voyage:** | Bristol to London |
| **Ship's Master:** | James Midge |

On the morning of Wednesday 2nd April 1823 the *Phillipa* found herself off Birling Gap in a very thick fog. As a result the vessel ran aground on rocks near Birling Gap and was immediately holed, with water pouring into the hull.

Two men from the local Coast Blockade, Darby and Bradley, assisted in getting the master James Midge and all his crew safely off the vessel. However, the fate of the cargo was not so fortunate as only 8 casks of the original 13 were saved.

During the following night the action of the sea smashed the stranded vessel to pieces.

*Ref: SIBI; TCB*

# BETSEY

| | |
|---|---|
| **Date:** | 30.11.1823 |
| **Wreck Location:** | Ashore at Seaford Bay |
| **Description of Vessel:** | |
| **Vessel Type -** | British sailing vessel |
| **Voyage:** | Richebucto to Hull |
| **Ship's Master:** | Hunter |

The *Betsey* became a total wreck on Sunday 30th November 1823 in Seaford Bay. It is not known how many passengers and crew were on the vessel at the time but only the second mate and one passenger survived.

*Ref: SIBI*

# THOMAS & HANNAH

**Date:**                         2.3.1824

**Wreck Location:**        Off Beachy Head

**Description of Vessel:**
**Vessel Type -**           British sailing vessel

**Home Port:**             Portsmouth

**Voyage:**                   Chichester to Rye

**Ship's Master:**          Trattle

---

This vessel became a total wreck on Tuesday 2nd March 1824, but none of the crew were lost.

*Ref: CNMM*

| | |
|---|---|
| **Date:** | 18.11.1824 |
| **Wreck Location:** | Ashore at Birling Gap |
| **Description of Vessel:** | |
| **Vessel Type -** | British sailing vessel |
| **Cargo:** | 1600 bushels* of Apples |
| **Voyage:** | Jersey to Leith (Glasgow) |
| **Ship's Master:** | Francis Le Fevre |
| **Number of Crew:** | 5 |

The name of this vessel is in some doubt as it is referred to as *Juno, June* and *Jemo.* What is not in doubt however, is that this vessel was driven ashore at Birling Gap on Thursday 18th November 1824 in a violent storm. Fortunately for the crew and the Pilot that were on board this ill-fated vessel, Lieutenant Joseph Clarke of the Coast Blockade was aware of their predicament. Although Clarke had only been on station a few weeks, he soon had eight of his men together and under his command they put off in a boat. This was at great risk to themselves in what were horrendous sea and weather conditions, but their endeavours were worthwhile as they managed to safely rescue the entire crew. Part of the cargo was also saved, i.e. 1200 bushels of apples, which were later sold at auction by the Customs at Newhaven

For his heroic efforts, Lieutenant Clarke was awarded a gold medal by the R.N.L.I. and each of his men were awarded two sovereigns/£2.

\* A bushel is a measure of capacity for dry goods and could be anything from 40lbs/ 18kgs for oats to 80lbs/36kgs for coal

*Ref: SIBI; TCB; SOM; SELB*

# ANTONIA ULRICA

**Date:** 11.3.1825

**Wreck Location:** Ashore 1 mile/1.6km east of Birling Gap

**Description of Vessel:**
**Vessel Type -** Dutch sailing brig

**Cargo:** Coffee, sugar

**Voyage:** From unknown port to Antwerp

---

On the night of Friday 11th March 1825, in thick fog, the *Antonia Ulrica* went ashore 1 mile/1.6km east of Birling Gap. Lieutenant Joseph Clarke of the Coast Blockade stationed at Birling Gap was soon launching one of their boats with a crew of his men. They navigated the rocks until they were able to rescue the crew and a young Portuguese boy who was a passenger on the vessel. The cargo was also saved and for the rescue of both crew and cargo Lieutenant Clarke was given a piece of plate valued at £5 by the Comptroller of Customs.

*Ref: TCB*

# SPEEDWELL

| | |
|---|---|
| **Date:** | 4.8.1825 |
| **Wreck Location:** | Ashore at Langney Point |
| **Description of Vessel:** | |
| **Vessel Type -** | British sailing vessel |
| **Cargo:** | Stone |
| **Voyage:** | Woolwich to unknown destination |
| **Ship's Master:** | Cosker |

The *Speedwell* was driven ashore on Thursday 4th August 1825 at Langney Point, and over the following days was to become a wreck as a result of the action of the sea and weather. The cargo of stone was recovered.

*Ref: SIBI*

# MAYFLOWER

**Date:**                              8.10.1825

**Wreck Location:**             Ashore at Seaford Bay

**Description of Vessel:**
**Vessel Type -**                  Sailing vessel

**Ship's Master:**               Robinson

---

On Saturday 8th October 1825, the *Mayflower* was leaving Newhaven harbour when it had a problem with it's rigging and ran ashore in Seaford Bay, becoming a compete wreck. The cargo was saved however.

*Ref: CNMM*

# ABEONA

| | |
|---|---|
| **Date:** | 8.11.1825 |
| **Wreck Location:** | Ashore near Birling Gap |
| **Description of Vessel:** | |
| **Vessel Type -** | British sailing vessel |
| **Cargo:** | 104 hogsheads* and 155 butts** of wine |
| **Home Port:** | Yarmouth |
| **Voyage:** | Cadiz to London |
| **Ship's Master:** | Thomas Cubitt |

---

At 5pm on Tuesday 8th November 1825, the *Abeona* was in a south-westerly hurricane accompanied by driving rain just off Beachy Head. The seas were mountainous and through this terrible weather the crew thought they could see chalk cliffs, however they were not sure as they thought it could also possibly be the sea. It was decided that the mate should go up into the rigging to ascertain whether it was land or sea that they were looking at. Unfortunately the visibility was so poor that he could not make his mind up. The master, who was at the helm, decided to err on the side of caution and set more sail in order for the vessel to haul away. However, with such horrendous winds and seas the vessel just did not respond.

For two and half hours the master and his crew fought these elements on board their vessel. During this period some of the sails were beginning to suffer from the considerable strain they were under and began to split. This now put the vessel in serious danger especially as the seas were now constantly breaking right over the vessel. As each sea washed over the deck, the crew were at risk of being washed over board.

At 7.30pm the *Abeona* was finally driven ashore among the raging surf. The master ordered that the sails be taken down which had the effect of turning the vessel broadside on to the sea. Once in this position and with the sea sweeping over her, the crew knew that they had to take to the rigging for their own safety. It was among the rigging that the crew remained for three and half hours being constantly beaten by sea, wind and rain. At 11pm the tide had turned and sufficiently ebbed to allow the crew to come down from the rigging, by which time 12 men of the Birling Gap Coast Blockade station under the command of Lieutenant Joseph Clarke had arrived on the scene. Lieutenant Clarke and his men went on board the *Abeona* and got all the passengers and crew safely off, who were then taken to the Watch-house to recover from their ordeal.

At 5am the following morning John Benjamin Stone, the local Lloyd's agent at Newhaven, together with James Hodson, took charge of the stores and cargo on board the *Abeona*. They then set about salvaging as much of it as possible over the following days and by Friday they had recovered 230 casks of the wine cargo before the vessel became a total wreck.

* A hogshead is a liquid measure, the quantity of which varies upon the contents. If the contents are Claret or Madeira then the measure is 46 gallons/209 litres, Brandy 60 gallons/ 272 litres, Port 57 gallons/259 litres or Sherry 54 gallons/245 litres.
** A butt is a liquid measure of wine or ale of 108galls/490ltrs.

*Ref: CNMM;*

# EMANUEL

| | |
|---|---|
| **Date:** | 7.4.1826 |
| **Wreck Location:** | Off Beachy Head |
| **Description of Vessel:** | |
| **Vessel Type -** | Dutch (possibly) sailing vessel |
| **Cargo:** | Cotton bales, sugar |
| **Voyage:** | Surinam to Amsterdam |
| **Ship's Master:** | Jisbrands Baarends |

---

The *Emanuel* was sailing up the Channel en route for Amsterdam with her 400 ton cargo when at 8pm on Thursday 6th April 1826 she came upon a very thick fog. At 3.30pm the following day the fog had still not lifted and the *Emanuel* was just off Beachy Head at low tide. The vessel had sailed too close to the shore and struck a rock reef. Luckily for those on board, a Dover Pilot boat was in the vicinity and took them safely off the stricken vessel.

Lieutenant Carter from the local Coast Blockade and his men, being aware of the wreck, reached the vessel later that day, by which time the crew had already been taken off by the Pilot boat. Lieut. Carter and his men, however, managed to salvage some of the cargo and convey it to the local Customs before the flood tide engulfed the vessel. The Coast Blockade was to later receive a letter of thanks from the Deputy Sergeant to the Lord Warden of the Cinque Ports for their efforts.

On the flooding tide the vessel drifted off the rocks and sank in 11 fathoms of water. However, on the following Monday 10th April, the *Emanuel* was seen floating off Eastbourne and a number of local boats put off and took the wreck in tow. They managed to tow it to ½ mile/800m off Cooden where the vessel was fixed to an anchor and moored, the intention being to later remove the remaining cargo. However, on the following Wednesday a very severe south westerly gale blew where upon the *Emanuel* broke from her moorings and became a complete wreck.

*Ref: SIBI; CNMM; TCB*

# LORD CRANSTOWN

**Date:** 7.12.1826

**Wreck Location:** Ashore ¾ mile/1.2km east of Birling Gap

*Ref: TCB*

# JOHANNA

| | |
|---|---|
| **Date:** | 1.3.1827 |
| **Wreck Location:** | Ashore Birling Gap |
| **Description of Vessel:** | |
| **Vessel Type -** | Dutch sailing galliot |
| **Cargo:** | Wine |
| **Ship's Master:** | Dows |
| **Voyage:** | Bordeaux to Amsterdam |

On Thursday 1st March 1827 this Dutch galliot was making for Amsterdam with its cargo of wine when it was driven ashore by the weather at Birling Gap. It was not long before the vessel became a complete wreck but only after Lieutenant Joseph Clarke of the Birling Gap Coast Blockade station and five of his men had safely rescued the crew.

In October of the same year the King of the Netherlands awarded Lieutenant Clarke a gold medal for his efforts in effecting this rescue. The five other men each received silver medals for the part they played.

*Ref: TCB; LL 6199 2.3.1827*

# JOLLY SAILOR

| | |
|---|---|
| **Date:** | 24.4.1829 |
| **Wreck Location:** | Ashore at Eastbourne |
| **Description of Vessel:** | |
| **Vessel Type -** | British sailing vessel |
| **Cargo:** | Coal |
| **Home Port:** | Whitby |
| **Ship's Master:** | Thompson |

On Friday 24th April 1829 this vessel and the *John & Mary*, also from Whitby with coal, were on the shore at Eastbourne. The *Jolly Sailor,* unlike the *John & Mary*, was not able to be got off the shore and so became a wreck.

*Ref: SIBI*

# BUFFALO

| | |
|---|---|
| **Date:** | 16.10.1829 |
| **Wreck Location:** | Off Beachy Head |
| **Description of Vessel:** | |
| **Vessel Type -** | British sailing vessel |
| **Cargo:** | Ballast |
| **Voyage:** | Chichester to Shields |
| **Ship's Master:** | Hall |

---

The report that the *Buffalo* had been in collision off Beachy Head with the *Hebden,* which was bound for Mauritius from London, was made on 16th October 1829 at Portsmouth by the crew of the *Hebden*. The date of the actual collision was therefore probably the previous day, when the *Buffalo* was holed to the water line causing the vessel to quickly fill with water and capsize.

*Ref: SIBI*

# UNKNOWN

**Date:**                              22.12.1829

**Wreck Location:**                    4 miles/6.4km off Eastbourne

**Description of Vessel:**
**Vessel Type -**                      Sailing brig

---

The circumstances of how this vessel became a wreck are not known. It was discovered on 22nd December 1829, when a passing vessel saw masts and rigging of what they believed to be a large brig, protruding above the surface of the sea. Due to the condition of the rigging it was assumed that the vessel must have gone down during the preceding week to ten days.

*Ref: SIBI*

# JOHN KERR

**Date:**                                    13.12.1830

**Wreck Location:**                 Off Beachy Head

**Description of Vessel:**
**Vessel Type -**                      British sailing vessel

**Voyage:**                                London to Bristol

**Ship's Master:**                    Allen

---

On Monday 13th December 1830, the *Joseph & Ann* put in at Dover to report that the vessel had been in collision with the *John Kerr* when off Beachy Head, and that the *John Kerr* had sunk as a result. Although the *Joseph & Ann,* bound for London, had received considerable damage in the collision, its crew managed to rescue all those on board the sunken vessel.

*Ref: SIBI*

# NEUTRALITEN

**Date:**                    8.4.1831

**Wreck Location:**          Off Beachy Head

**Description of Vessel:**
**Vessel Type -**           Sailing vessel

**Voyage:**                 Malaga to Stockholm

**Ship's Master:**          Bolin

**Number of Crew:**         11

On the morning of Friday 8th April 1831 the *Neutraliten* was off Beachy Head, when in collision with an unknown vessel (believed to be English). The impact was so severe that the *Neutraliten* sank with the loss of half the ship's complement, i.e. the master, mate and four of the crew. The remaining crew managed to get on board the jolly boat and came ashore near Pevensey that same morning.

*Ref: SIBI*

# AMBROOK

**Date:** 14.11.1831

**Wreck Location:** Ashore at Seaford Bay

**Description of Vessel:**
**Vessel Type -** British sailing vessel

**Cargo:** Coal

**Voyage:** Newcastle-upon-Tyne to Shoreham

**Ship's Master:** Eales

---

On the night of Monday 14th November 1831 the *Ambrook,* together with another vessel, the *Hope*, was making for Newhaven harbour. The *Ambrook* unfortunately got on the 'East Poles' which caused the vessel to drift into Seaford Bay and become a complete wreck. Luckily all the crew were saved after a difficult rescue, but only part of the vessel's stores were salvaged.

*Ref: SIBI*

# ADDER

| | |
|---|---|
| **Date:** | 00.12.1831 |
| **Wreck Location:** | Ashore near Newhaven |
| **Description of Vessel:** | |
| **Gross Tonnage -** | 182 |
| **Length -** | 85ft/25.9m |
| **Beam -** | 22ft/6.7m |
| **Vessel Type -** | British sailing man-of-war |
| **Date Built, Builder:** | c.1813, by Davy at Topsham, Devon |
| **Owner:** | H.M. Coastguard |

---

In 1826 this vessel, which had been moored at Rye, was converted from a 12 gun Royal Navy Gun Brig to a Watch Vessel (guard room and accommodation vessel) for the Coast Guard in the fight against smuggling around Beachy Head.

In December 1831 the *Adder* was at anchor off Newhaven riding out a terrific storm but as the storm intensified so the vessel started to drag its anchor. It soon became apparent that the *Adder* was going to become a risk to other shipping and so the decision was taken, by Lieutenant Belron of the *Confiance,* to cut the *Adder* free and allow it to drift ashore near Newhaven. The vessel soon became a total wreck although the hull was later salvaged and sold.

*Ref: SIBI; TCB; LSRN*

# DISPATCH

| | |
|---|---|
| **Date:** | 28.8.1832 |
| **Wreck Location:** | Ashore at Newhaven Bay |
| **Description of Vessel:** | |
| **Vessel Type -** | British sailing vessel |
| **Voyage:** | London to Bridport |

On the morning of Tuesday 28th August 1832 the *Dispatch* was driven ashore at Newhaven in a severe gale to become a complete wreck.

*Ref: SIBI*

# BACALHA

**Date:**                                    00.00.1833

**Wreck Location:**                 Near Beachy Head

**Description of Vessel:**
**Vessel Type -**                     British sailing vessel

**Home Port:**                         Newcastle

**Date Built, Builder:**          c.1799

---

*Ref: SIBI*

# JOHN

| | |
|---|---|
| **Date:** | 11.4.1833 |
| **Wreck Location:** | Ashore near Newhaven |
| **Description of Vessel:** | |
| **Vessel Type -** | British sailing vessel |
| **Home Port:** | Jersey |
| **Voyage:** | Jersey to Shoreham-by-sea |
| **Number of Crew:** | 4 |

---

The *John* was driven ashore by the weather on Thursday 11th April 1833 near Newhaven, while on its voyage from Jersey to Shoreham-by-sea. In order that the master and the four crew could be got off the stricken vessel the Coastguard had to use the rocket apparatus.

*Ref: SIBI; CNMM*

# BEN LOMOND

| | |
|---|---|
| **Date:** | 4.6.1833 |
| **Wreck Location:** | Near Newhaven |
| **Description of Vessel:** | |
| **Vessel Type -** | British steamship |
| **Voyage:** | Newhaven to Stirling |

*Ref: SIBI*

# INDUSTRY

| | |
|---|---|
| **Date:** | 27.6.1833 |
| **Wreck Location:** | Newhaven |
| **Description of Vessel:** | |
| **Vessel Type -** | British sailing vessel |
| **Voyage:** | Arundel to London |

*Ref: SIBI*

# DALHOUSIE

| | |
|---|---|
| **Date:** | 26.3.1833 |
| **Wreck Location:** | Off Beachy Head |
| **Description of Vessel:** | |
| **Vessel Type -** | British sailing vessel |
| **Voyage:** | London to Sydney |
| **Ship's Master:** | Butterworth |

Only one person was saved from this vessel, the remainder having drowned.

*Ref: SIBI*

# ZEPHYR

| | |
|---|---|
| **Date:** | 27.9.1835 |
| **Wreck Location:** | Ashore at the west pier Newhaven harbour |
| **Description of Vessel:** | |
| **Gross Tonnage -** | 106 |
| **Vessel Type -** | British sailing brig |
| **Cargo:** | Timber |
| **Home Port:** | Swansea |
| **Voyage:** | Newhaven to Swansea |
| **Ship's Master:** | Robert Day |

This vessel is also referred to as the *Zephur*.

On Sunday 27th September 1835, having discharged its cargo of timber, the *Zephyr* left Newhaven harbour under the command of a local pilot who disembarked once clear of the harbour. The vessel had not been long into the voyage to Swansea, when at about 10pm a strong south westerly gale blew up with heavy seas. The master, Robert Day the Younger, decided that it would be best to return to the safety of Newhaven harbour.

As the vessel approached the harbour entrance, a sudden and unexpected squall caused the *Zephyr* to collide with the head of the western pier. This collision was of such force that the starboard bow was stove in and before the crew were able to do anything it filled with water. The crew were in great jeopardy with the position of the vessel in such heavy seas and winds. It was only with the help of a number of men with ropes on the western pier that the crew managed to get safely off the *Zephyr*.

The weather continued to increase in violence and during the following day the vessel went entirely to pieces, however, not before the crew had worked relentlessly to save the vessel's stores.

*Ref: SIBI: CNMM*

# WILLIAM

| | |
|---|---|
| **Date:** | 18.11.1836 |
| **Wreck Location:** | Ashore 440yds/402m west of Birling Gap |
| **Description of Vessel:** | |
| **Gross Tonnage -** | 337 |
| **Vessel Type -** | British sailing barque |
| **Cargo:** | Coal, bricks, lime, grain, clothing, hardware |
| **Home Port:** | London to St. Vincent |
| **Ship's Master:** | James Hodnett |
| **Number of Crew:** | 15 and 3 boys |

On Sunday 6th November 1836, having taken on her cargo in London, the *William* set sail down the river Thames with a pilot on board. On the following Tuesday the vessel anchored in the Downs on both its port and starboard bow anchors, to allow the pilot off. The vessel remained at anchor for the next couple of days when, on the Thursday, it started to blow a really strong south-westerly gale. It was in these conditions that the starboard anchor cable broke leaving the vessel on one anchor. Although not known how, a message was got to Deal and another anchor was brought to the *William* at 4pm that same afternoon.

It was not until 6am on Tuesday 15th November, having been at anchor for a whole week, that the *William* actually got under way on her voyage down the Channel, in a moderate north westerly breeze. By 2pm on the Thursday, the *William* was about 15 miles/24km south east of Beachy Head and by 9.30pm that same day, about 4 miles/6km south of the same point. It was not long after this that the wind turned to the south-west and for the second time since leaving London, the *William* found herself in weather increasing to gale force with heavy rain and poor visibility. The vessel was now finding it hard to cope with these conditions and continually shipping water. The weather continued to worsen throughout the following hours when suddenly at 4am on Friday 18th November there was a break in the weather. It was then that the crew saw Beachy Head and the realisation that they were being driven ever closer inland by the wind. The master made all sail possible in an attempt to clear land, but with the wind dead on, the vessel was not responding. The master then decided to drop both anchors to stop the vessel's landward drift, but unfortunately she just dragged the anchors and finally at 5.45am struck the rocks about 440yds/402m to the west of Birling Gap. The force of the sea and the wind drove the vessel hard on to the rocks carrying away the vessel's rudder.

The Coastguard at nearby Birling Gap station were soon on the spot and assisted the crew in saving as much of the cargo as possible. On the receding tide it was possible for the master to make an inspection of the *William* and he found that she had been severely damaged. The vessel lay on these rocks being battered by each following tide until Thursday 24th November, when it finally went to pieces.

*Ref: CNMM; LL 7213 18.11.36*

# DIANA

| | |
|---|---|
| **Date:** | 5.4.1837 |
| **Wreck Location:** | Off Beachy Head |
| **Description of Vessel:** | |
| **Vessel Type -** | British sailing brig |
| **Cargo:** | Iron |
| **Home Port:** | Great Yarmouth |
| **Voyage:** | Newport to London |
| **Ship's Master:** | Robert Archbold |

The *Diana* left Newport on Sunday 26th March 1837 bound for London under her master Robert Archbold. However at 3am on Monday 3rd April the vessel sprang a leak when off Selsey Bill. The crew were set to work on both pumps but by midday the water level was rising despite their efforts. The master, realising their position, raised colours to indicate he needed assistance, which was answered by the *Reaper* of Scarborough which stayed with the *Diana* until 3pm. It was then decided that the master of the *Reaper* and five of his crew should go aboard the *Diana* to relieve at the vessel's pumps. However, an hour later they were joined by the Revenue Cutter *Victoria,* so the crew of the *Reaper* rejoined their own vessel and continued on their voyage to Quebec.

The mate, carpenter and eight crew from the Revenue Cutter went aboard the leaking vessel, again to relieve the crew, as it made towards Newhaven. At 8pm that evening both vessel's were off Newhaven harbour and the *Victoria* fired a signal gun for a pilot but unfortunately the signal was not answered. Both vessels were therefore compelled to start making for the port of Dover. During the following morning, Tuesday 4th April, the Revenue Cutter *Victoria* took the *Diana* in tow but by 10pm that same day the weather had become very stormy with strong winds, snow showers and poor visibility. It was in these conditions that the towing hawser broke. The *Diana* then started to drift, losing sight of the *Victoria* despite showing blue lights and firing pistols. The Revenue Cutter *Victoria* was not to be seen again.

The *Diana* was now at the mercy of the elements and with the leak still gaining on the work of vessel's pumps, it was hoped by those on board that the vessel would reach Newhaven. However, by 9am on Wednesday 5th April, with the waterlogged *Diana* now off Beachy Head and totally unmanageable, it was decided to take to the vessel's boat and leave the *Diana* to her fate. Within fifteen minutes of leaving the vessel she went down. The crew were finally picked up by a French fishing vessel and taken into Newhaven

*Ref: CNMM; SE 8.4.1837; LL 7253 7.4.37*

# HELEN

| | |
|---|---|
| **Date vessel sank:** | 21.1.1840 |
| **Wreck Location:** | Ashore near the Buckle Inn, Seaford |
| **Description of Vessel:** | |
| **Gross Tonnage -** | 58 |
| **Vessel Type -** | British sailing smack |
| **Cargo:** | Oranges |
| **Home Port:** | Maldon |
| **Voyage:** | St. Michael's to London |
| **Owner:** | Mr. Richmond |
| **Ship's Master:** | William Thom |
| **Number of Crew:** | 4 and 1 boy |

---

Although the *Helen's* master was William Thom, the sailing Captain was a man by the name of Mathews, and these two men, together with three other seamen and a boy, made up the full crew. The first time this vessel and its £400 worth of oranges encountered any problems, was on Monday 13th January 1840, when, at longitude 17 degrees 30 minutes west, it met a terrible storm. As a result the *Helen* lost its mast. Fortunately, at noon the following day, the *Elizabeth Walker* of Glasgow, came on the scene and was able to give them a spar for a jury-mast* which the crew managed to rig up. Their efforts were well rewarded because five days later they were off St Michael's Mount, Cornwall, having covered a distance of some 800 miles/1287km, and by the morning of Tuesday 21st January the *Helen* was off Worthing.

It was while off Worthing that the weather started to deteriorate from the south west, which caused the crew to reef part of the mainsail. It was while engaged in this that the mainsail tore into three pieces, but the crew were quick to react and soon had it replaced with a gib sheet. This unfortunately was insufficient sail and with the ever increasing gale the

*Helen* was drifting ever closer towards Newhaven. At 9am, to stop this drift, the anchor was dropped 880yds/804m off shore, east of Newhaven harbour entrance. With the anchor holding, the crew were satisfied that the vessel would be able to ride out the storm. Although close to land they had no means of communicating with those ashore, albeit the crew noticed some lights which they assumed was a signal not to run the vessel ashore.

At 7pm with the vessel close to shore and what was now an ebbing tide, the depth of water under the *Helen* was decreasing all the time. Suddenly the vessel struck the seabed as the sea rose and fell in the storm. In no time the vessel's cabin was full of water and Captain Mathews decided to cut the anchor cable allowing the vessel to drift ashore near the Buckle Inn, Seaford. Once ashore, a thousand spectators watched the crew tie a rope to a buoy which floated in land to those waiting on the beach, who in turn made the end fast. The crew then used this to come ashore. No sooner had the crew reached safety than the sea smashed the vessel to pieces.

The vessel's mate once ashore told his rescuers, *"I have been 14 times to St. Michaels and wrecked three times in two years and this time I have lost everything but what I have on."*

Unbeknown to the crew of the *Helen* there was much activity on shore while she was drifting towards Newhaven. At 7am on the morning of Tuesday 21st January, the *Helen* had been seen off Rottingdean with its broken mast and damaged rigging. The concern for the vessel by Captain Marsh of the Coastguards caused him to give orders that a boat, ropes and a small gun be taken to the beach in case the vessel came aground. The boat was on a small carriage and together with their equipment, Captain Marsh and his men pulled it along the beach at the same speed as the *Helen*, so as to remain opposite her. Eventually they arrived at the Newhaven harbour piers, and it was here that the Coastguard put the boat in the river and crossed to the other side. They took the boat and equipment out of the river and then carried it on their shoulders across land belonging to Mr. Catt, arriving at 10am at the point on the beach where all the spectators had gathered. There they waited until the *Helen* ran aground.

The following morning, with the vessel rapidly going to pieces, saw large numbers of people walking along the shore as far east as Cuckmere, collecting the oranges. It would appear that by the afternoon 100 oranges were being sold in Alfriston for 2s./10p. Several people were observed with sack loads of oranges on carts taking the fruit towards Brighton.

* A jury-mast is a temporary mast rigged to replace a broken one.

*Ref: SAE 25.1.1840; LL 8073 22.1.40; LL 8074 23.1.40*

# TWO FRIENDS OF DUNKIRK

| | |
|---|---|
| **Date vessel sank:** | 24.1.1840 |
| **Wreck Location:** | Off Beachy Head |
| **Description of Vessel:** | |
| **Gross Tonnage -** | 170 |
| **Vessel Type -** | French sailing schooner |
| **Cargo:** | Wine, brandy |

---

What caused this vessel to become a wreck and where, is not really known. However, what is known is that the upturned hull of the *Two Friends of Dunkirk* was first seen off Beachy Head on Saturday 25th January 1840 drifting east. The previous night there had been some very squally bad weather off Beachy Head and this is assumed to have been the cause of the loss of this vessel.

The vessel was next seen the following morning floating in a turbulent sea just off shore near the Galley Hill Coastguard Station, Bexhill. A number of small casks of wine had also been washed ashore nearby. However, the upturned hull continued to drift eastward until eventually being washed ashore near the Conqueror Hotel, on St Leonards seafront.

Mr. Harman of the Hastings Arms Inn was quick to get a number of men together and with ropes and anchors made the vessel fast. They then set about salvaging most of the cargo which was not without its risks as the sea was still very violent. The next morning, Monday, a hole was cut in the side of the *Two Friends of Dunkirk* and the remainder of the casks removed, most of which were marked '*Courtors and Von Reynschoote Cette.*'

*Ref: SAE 1.2.1840*

# UNNAMED

**Date vessel sank:** 00.6.1840

**Wreck Location:** Off shore between Blatchington and Crowlink

**Description of Vessel:**
**Vessel Type -** Small open boat

**Voyage:** Blatchington to Crowlink

---

Two Coastguardsmen, Messrs. Caddy and Malone were in this small boat travelling from the Coastguard Station at Blatchington to the one at Crowlink, because Caddy was being posted from one to the other. The boat was over laden with Caddy's possessions which is believed to have caused the boat to capsize throwing both men into the sea. Caddy unfortunately drowned but Malone stayed with the upturned boat and was eventually rescued.

Caddy was a married man with three young children and his death left them destitute as they now only had the clothes they were wearing. A collection made locally for Caddy's widow and children was put together with the small '*pittance*' the government paid in such cases.

*Ref: SAE 13.6.1840*

# UNKNOWN

| | |
|---|---|
| **Date:** | 3.7.1840 |
| **Wreck Location:** | Ashore near Birling Gap |
| **Description of Vessel:** | |
| **Gross Tonnage -** | 100 approx. |
| **Vessel Type -** | French sailing *chasse maree* |
| **Cargo:** | Salt |
| **Voyage:** | Unknown port to Boulogne |
| **Number of Crew:** | 4 and 1 boy |

On the night of Friday 3rd July 1840 a severe gale was blowing and this vessel, the name of which is not known, was driven ashore at Birling Gap in very thick fog. The crew had not seen the Beachy Head light due to the fog and as a result ran aground. The vessel immediately started to go to pieces and it was not long before it became a total wreck. However, throughout this ordeal the ship's boy had been kept in the cabin for his own safety, while the crew struggled with both the vessel and the conditions.

Fortunately it did not take long for the Birling Gap Coastguard, under the command of Lieutenant Horatio Blair, to arrive on the scene with their rocket apparatus. The first shot from this apparatus went straight through the rigging so they able to quickly get the four crew on deck off the vessel. In the crew's excitement and relief at being rescued they had totally forgotten about the ship's boy who was still in the cabin. Unfortunately by the time they realised, it was too late, and he was to become the only loss of life.

Lieutenant Blair was awarded a Silver Medal by the Royal National Lifeboat Institution for his gallantry in the rescue of these men.

*Ref: SELB; SAE 11.7.1840; CPC 15.7.1840; LL 8213 4.7.40*

# JOSEPH

**Date:** 13.11.1840

**Wreck Location:** Ashore between Martello Tower 72 and the Redoubt, Eastbourne

**Description of Vessel:**
**Gross Tonnage -** 178
**Vessel Type -** British sailing brig

**Cargo:** Coal

**Home Port:** Sunderland

**Ship's Master:** Timothy Ashford

**Number of Crew:** 7

---

On the evening of Friday 13th November 1840, a severe south-westerly gale was blowing off Eastbourne accompanied by heavy seas. The *Joseph* was off Shoreham when she sprung a serious leak in these terrible conditions. The master soon realised that he would not be able to make any local harbour with safety and so decided to run the vessel ashore in Eastbourne Bay.

At 7.30pm the Coastguard lookout at the Eastbourne Station saw the *Joseph* running before the gale with two topsails and heading towards the shore. Lieutenant Conduit the officer in charge of this station, soon had his men mustered with the rocket apparatus in readiness to assist in the rescue of the crew. In the meantime, the *Joseph* was slowly making for the shore on the rising tide. The situation was getting more critical as not only was she filling with water from a leaky hull, the violent sea was breaking over her with nearly every wave. As a result the crew had to take to the rigging and tie themselves to it to prevent being washed overboard.

Eventually at midnight the *Joseph* ran aground, falling on her port side, broadside to the shore and the masts towards the sea. Lieutenant Conduit got the rocket apparatus ready for firing, intending to get a line on the vessel. Unfortunately when it was fired, the rocket exploded and destroyed the launching ramp. Now, without the rocket apparatus, Cornelius Jones a boatman with the Coastguard, put his own life at great risk by diving into the raging surf, taking with him a small lead line. He got as near the vessel as he could and made numerous attempts to get the line on to the *Joseph* but none with any success. A local fisherman, George Hide, took over from Jones and dived into the surf with the lead line. The boiling waves threw him back towards the beach several times as he made his attempt to get near the stricken vessel. Eventually he was successful and managed to get the lead line on the *Joseph* which the crew secured having come down from the rigging. The crew then took it turns to tie a rope around their bodies as they were pulled safely to the shore.

The storm was to rage on for a further two hours during which time the *Joseph* was smashed to pieces by the ferocity of the waves on the rising tide. The cargo of coal was totally lost having been washed away by the actions of the sea. The crew were taken to Martello Tower 72 where the Coastguard tended to them as best as they were able. The majority of the crew's belongings were also lost but some items were returned to them having later been found ashore by Coastguardsmen, to the east of the wreck.

On Sunday 15th November the crew attended morning service at Trinity Chapel where the Rev A. Scrivener gave thanks for their safe rescue. During the evening service a collection was made among the congregation for the wrecked crew and given to the men to assist them in returning to their homes. The Shipwrecked Fishermen and Mariner's Benevolent Society, of which Lieutenant Conduit was the honorary agent, also contributed towards their costs to return home. For one of the married crew members this was the fifth time he had been rescued in such circumstances.

The *Joseph* was not the only vessel to succumb to the storm on this night, the *Friends* (see next page) was another casualty.

*Ref: SAE 21.11.1840 & 28.11.1840*

# FRIENDS

| | |
|---|---|
| **Date vessel sank:** | 13.11.1840 |
| **Wreck Location:** | Ashore near Wish Tower, Eastbourne |
| **Description of Vessel:** | |
| **Gross Tonnage -** | 160 |
| **Vessel Type -** | British sailing brig |
| **Cargo:** | 200 bushels* potatoes |
| **Home Port:** | Sunderland |
| **Voyage:** | Jersey to London |
| **Ship's Master:** | John Wright |
| **Number of Crew:** | 6 and 3 boys |

The *Friends* was the second casualty on the night of Friday 13th November 1840, the other being the *Joseph* (see previous page), but unfortunately with the loss of all hands.

The gale had driven the vessel ashore during the night near the Wish Tower at Eastbourne. But, nobody ashore knew of its fate until early next morning when discovered by a Coastguard. None of the crew was present and it had been so badly smashed to pieces by the sea that it was not possible to identify the vessel. It was not until Sunday 15th November that the identity was established, when a tin containing the vessel's papers was found.

All the bodies of the crew, except one, were later recovered along the shore line between the Wish Tower and Langney Point, including one believed to be the master. This assumption was made from the clothes on the body i.e. dark blue trousers, blue shirt, highloes**, and a black silk handkerchief round the neck. He was a man aged about 26 years.

\* A bushel of potatoes weighs about 80lbs/36kgs.
\*\* Highloes or Highlows were boots that reached above the ankle

*Ref: SAE 21.11.1840*

# ALERT

| | |
|---|---|
| **Date:** | 3.1.1841 |
| **Wreck Location:** | Near Beachy Head |
| **Description of Vessel:** | |
| **Length -** | 67ft/20.54m |
| **Beam -** | 18ft/5.46m |
| **Vessel Type -** | British sailing brig |
| **Home Port:** | Chichester |
| **Date Built, Builder:** | c.1803 at Great Yarmouth |
| **Owner:** | S. Facredell, Fishbourne |
| **Ship's Master:** | John Beale |

The *Alert* became a loss on Sunday 3rd January 1841 near Beachy Head.

*Ref: SIBI*

# MARY

| | |
|---|---|
| **Date:** | 5.3.1841 |
| **Wreck Location:** | Near Newhaven |
| **Description of Vessel:** | |
| **Vessel Type -** | British sailing brig |
| **Home Port:** | Newcastle |
| **Voyage:** | Alderney to London |
| **Date Built, Builder:** | c.1806 |
| **Ship's Master:** | Winter |

The *Mary* became a loss on Friday 5th March 1841 near Newhaven harbour.

*Ref: SIBI*

# MATRIMONY

**Date:** 11.10.1841

**Wreck Location:** Ashore at Seaside, Eastbourne

**Description of Vessel:**
**Vessel Type -** British sailing schooner

**Cargo:** Coal

---

On Monday 11th October 1841 the *Matrimony* was on the beach at Seaside, Eastbourne, discharging her cargo of coal when a severe south-westerly gale sprung up together with a very heavy sea. To safeguard the vessel it was decided that the vessel should be got off, but in the process her anchors dragged and the sea threw the vessel broadside to the beach. With each wave that struck the vessel on the rising tide, it pushed her further onto the beach and eventually over the groyne.

When the tide had receded it was found that *Matrimony's* bulwarks had been knocked away and that the hull had sustained serious damage. The damage was so severe as to be beyond repair and it was intended to break the vessel up.

*Ref: SIBI; SAE 16.10.1841*

# JANE

| | |
|---|---|
| **Date:** | 15.12.1841 |
| **Wreck Location:** | Ashore near East Pier, Newhaven |
| **Description of Vessel:** | |
| **Vessel Type -** | British sailing brig |
| **Cargo:** | 340 tons of coal |
| **Home Port:** | Sunderland |
| **Voyage:** | Sunderland to Newhaven |

---

On the morning of Wednesday 15<sup>th</sup> December 1841 there were very strong winds and heavy seas, and a number of vessels had sought refuge in Newhaven harbour. Two such vessels were the *Jane* and the *Friends* (see next page).

The *Jane* and its cargo of coal for T. Berry of Lewes, was running for the harbour but would not respond to the helm, which resulted in the vessel running ashore to the east of the eastern harbour pier. Great efforts were made by the crew and others, under the supervision of Mr. Cole, the Lloyds agent, not only to save the cargo, but to reduce the vessel's weight in order that it could be re-floated. However, with each tide the *Jane* filled with water dashing any hope that it would ever be re-floated.

There was no loss of life.

*Ref: SE 18.12.1841; LL 8666 17.12.41*

# FRIENDS

| | |
|---|---|
| **Date:** | 15.12.1841 |
| **Wreck Location:** | Ashore east of Newhaven harbour |
| **Description of Vessel:** | |
| **Vessel Type -** | British sailing vessel |
| **Cargo:** | 300 tons of coal |
| **Home Port:** | Sunderland |
| **Voyage:** | Sunderland to Newhaven |
| **Ship's Master:** | Simms |

On the morning of Wednesday 15th December 1841 there were very strong winds and heavy seas and a number of vessels had sought refuge in Newhaven harbour. Two such vessels were the *Friends* and the *Jane* (see previous page). The *Friends,* in running to seek the safety of the harbour, struck the eastern pier smashing her bowsprit, and stoving the bows as well as other serious structural damage. The seas and weather then carried the vessel ashore to the east of the eastern pier close to where the *Jane* had earlier run ashore. Fortunately there was no loss of life.

As in the case of the *Jane,* Mr. Cole, the Lloyds Agent, took over the supervision of the salvage operations in respect of the cargo. It was again hoped that with the removal of the cargo it would be possible to re-float the *Friends*. However, it too filled with every tide, making it highly unlikely that she would ever be floated again.

*Ref: SE 18.12.1841; LL 8666 17.12.41*

# HEBBLE

**Date:**                                 16.12.1841

**Wreck Location:**          Off Beachy Head

**Description of Vessel:**
**Vessel Type -**             British sailing vessel

**Cargo:**                          Coal

**Home Port:**               Whitby

**Voyage:**                      Newcastle-upon-Tyne to Le Havre

**Date Built, Builder:**     c.1796

**Ship's Master:**          Goodill

---

On Thursday 16th December 1841 this vessel became a total loss when off Beachy Head.

*Ref: SIBI*

# ELIZABETH

| | |
|---|---|
| **Date:** | 10.1.1842 |
| **Wreck Location:** | Ashore opposite Seaford |
| **Description of Vessel:** | |
| **Vessel Type -** | British sailing brig |
| **Cargo:** | Ballast |
| **Home Port:** | Sunderland |

---

On the night of Monday 10th January 1842 the *Elizabeth* and the *Dunn* (see next page) were both driven ashore in Seaford Bay. The *Elizabeth* came ashore opposite the town of Seaford and an unsuccessful attempt was made to re-float the vessel. However, it is not known if any later attempts were successful.

*Ref: SIBI; SE 15.1.1842*

# DUNN

| | |
|---|---|
| **Date:** | 10.1.1842 |
| **Wreck Location:** | Ashore under the cliff at Seaford |
| **Description of Vessel:**<br>**Vessel Type -** | British sailing brig |
| **Cargo:** | Timber |
| **Home Port:** | Arundel |

On the night of Monday 10th January 1842 the *Dunn* and the *Elizabeth* (see previous page) were both driven ashore in Seaford Bay. The *Dunn* and its cargo of timber came ashore under the cliff at Seaford, but due to its situation and its heavy cargo it was doubtful that the vessel could be re-floated.

*Ref: SE 15.1.1842*

# JOHN & ELIZA

**Date:**                                      00.3.1842

**Wreck Location:**                 Near Beachy Head

**Description of Vessel:**
**Vessel Type -**                      British sailing vessel

**Voyage:**                               London to Shoreham-by-sea

---

In March of 1842 the *John & Eliza* became a total loss.

*Ref: SIBI*

# WATTS

| | |
|---|---|
| **Date:** | 25.10.1842 |
| **Wreck Location:** | Ashore opposite the Sea Houses, Eastbourne |
| **Description of Vessel:** | |
| **Gross Tonnage -** | 500 approx. |
| **Vessel Type -** | British sailing barque |
| **Cargo:** | Timber |
| **Home Port:** | Plymouth |
| **Number of Crew:** | 6 and 1 boy |

The crew of the *Watts* when it came ashore at Eastbourne on Tuesday 25th October 1842, was not the original crew of the vessel. The six men and the boy had been part of a crew on another vessel sailing westward out in the Atlantic ocean when their vessel came across the *Watts* drifting. There was no sign of life on the *Watts* when they boarded it. On inspection it was found that there was no more than 4ft/1.2m of water in the hold and so the six men and boy volunteered to sail the *Watts* into a port. However, their voyage was not without its hardships as the provisions on board were extremely meagre.

On the afternoon of Tuesday 25th October 1842 a very strong south-westerly gale blew up and forced the *Watts* and its volunteer crew onto the Boulder Bank, off Eastbourne, after earlier losing the rudder. After beating for some time the vessel lost the fore and main masts and drifted off the Boulder Bank towards the shore, finally running aground opposite the Sea Houses.

The local lifeboat was made aware of the predicament of the *Watts*, and under Coxswain Samuel Knight a crew of 12 men launched and without loss of life safely rescued all those on board the vessel.

Over the following days much of the timber cargo was removed from the *Watts*. On Monday 31st October, with the vessel now much lighter, it was pulled off the shore and taken in tow by a steam tug to Portsmouth.

Although not directly related to the *Watts,* there was an incident during this period that demonstrated the unforeseen risks of being a Coastguardsman. Edward Banks was a Coastguardsman stationed at Crowlink and had occasion to fire a musket, which unfortunately exploded on him. His left hand and arm were so badly damaged that he had to have the arm amputated below the elbow. The successful operation was performed by Mr. Richard Geere, a surgeon of Seaford. Banks was told that he was unlikely to receive any compensation from the Crown for his injury.

*Ref: SELB; SE 29.10.1842 & 5.11.1842*

# MANUEL

| | |
|---|---|
| **Date:** | 29.11.1842 |
| **Wreck Location:** | Ashore 1 mile/1.6km west of Newhaven harbour |
| **Description of Vessel:** | |
| **Gross Tonnage -** | 30 |
| **Vessel Type -** | French sailing smack |
| **Cargo:** | Apples |

---

On the afternoon of Tuesday 29th November 1842 the *Manuel* was driven ashore 1 mile/1.6km west of Newhaven harbour. However, the vessel came to rest a short distance from the beach and two local Coastguardsmen, Haydon and Driver, managed to swim through the heavy surf and get onboard. Their aim was to give the crew what assistance they could. However, once on board they found no signs of any of the crew or what could possibly have become of them. One can only surmise they were all drowned. There was also little gear on the vessel and only a few apples in the hold.

The following incoming tide smashed the vessel to pieces.

During the previous day the brig *Louisa*, of Newhaven, saw a vessel on her beam ends drifting 4 miles/6.4km off Beachy Head. There was a quantity of apples floating about the vessel and is believed to have been the *Manuel*.

*Ref: SE 3.12.1842; LL 8964 2.12.42*

# JOHN & WILLIAM

| | |
|---|---|
| **Date:** | 13.1.1843 |
| **Wreck Location:** | Ashore Bearside near Newhaven |
| **Description of Vessel:** | |
| **Vessel Type -** | British sailing schooner |
| **Home Port:** | Newhaven |
| **Voyage:** | Great Yarmouth to Newhaven |
| **Date Built, Builder:** | c.1835 |
| **Number of Crew:** | 2 |

This vessel was wrecked near Newhaven on Friday 13th January 1843, with both crew drowning as soon as the vessel run aground. One of the crew was a young man named Smyth from Barcombe, whose body was washed ashore at Birling Gap on 3rd February. As the body had been in the water such a long time it was only possible to identify it from some of the clothing. The body was later interred in the churchyard at Newick.

*Ref: SIBI; SE 11.2.1843*

# UNIONE

| | |
|---|---|
| **Date:** | 28.1.1843 |
| **Wreck Location:** | Ashore at Cow Gap |
| **Description of Vessel:** | |
| **Vessel Type -** | Italian sailing brig |
| **Cargo:** | Wine, fresh fruit, rape seed |
| **Home Port:** | Ancona |
| **Voyage:** | Trieste to Dunkirk |
| **Ship's Master:** | Mariano Probej |
| **Number of Crew:** | 11 and pilot |

On the morning of Saturday 28th January 1843 the *Unione* (also referred to as the *L'Urrione Fortunata*), was trying to get round Beachy Head in a terrific gale. Unfortunately due to the horrendous weather and heavy sea the vessel was not responding to the helm and was consequently blown ashore near Cow Gap. As soon as the vessel struck land she started to go to pieces, so the crew quickly took to the jolly-boat in an attempt to reach the shore. Sadly, the jolly-boat quickly sank with the loss of eight of the Italian crew including a young cadet. Also lost was the pilot, Thomas Burton of Cowes, who had boarded the vessel at the Isle of Wight.

Eleven Coastguardsmen under the command of Lieutenant Gilson managed to launch a boat in this extremely dangerous sea and to rescue four other members of the crew who were hanging onto a piece of the wreck. Lieut. Gilson was to later receive a silver medal for his skill and courage in this rescue.

The rescued men were taken to the Holywell Coastguard Station and there placed in the care of Lieutenant Conduit who treated them for their exhaustion and injuries. Lieut. Conduit was also the agent for the Shipwrecked Fishermen and Mariner's Benevolent Society, and was responsible for clothing the seamen and giving them sufficient money to travel to the Italian Consulate in London.

Four of the bodies were later recovered, including the master and cook, and buried in the local church yard at Eastbourne. The bodies of the other five missing men were not found, including that of the pilot, whose two sons had offered a reward of £10 for the recovery of their father's body.

A person who went to look at the remains of the wreck the following day saw a number of drunken fishermen along the beach. They had been on board the *Unione* and sampled part of the wine cargo!

*Ref: SIBI; SELB; SE 4.2.1843 & 11.2.1843; SWA 7.2.1843; EG 21.3.1888 & 28.3.1888*

# AUST

| | |
|---|---|
| **Date:** | 5.2.1843 |
| **Wreck Location:** | Near Beachy Head |
| **Description of Vessel:** | |
| **Vessel Type -** | British sailing vessel |
| **Home Port:** | Bristol |
| **Ship's Master:** | Hart |

The *Aust* became a loss off Beachy Head on Sunday 5th February 1843.

*Ref: SIBI*

# TWEE CORNELISSEN

| | |
|---|---|
| **Date vessel sank:** | 27.12.1845 |
| **Wreck Location:** | Ashore near Martello Tower 55, Pevensey Bay |
| **Description of Vessel:** | |
| **Gross Tonnage -** | 860 |
| **Length -** | 123½ft/37.6m |
| **Beam -** | 22ft/6.7m |
| **Vessel Type -** | East Indiaman* |
| **Cargo:** | Coffee, sugar, indigo |
| **Home Port:** | Amsterdam |
| **Voyage:** | Batavia, Java to Amsterdam |
| **Date Built & Builder:** | c.1831 by S.R. Boelen, De Haan, Amsterdam |
| **Owner:** | Harsten Bros. & Co. |
| **Ship's Master:** | H.D. Van Wyck |
| **Number of Crew:** | 27 |
| **Number of Passengers:** | 3 |

It was about 1am on Sunday 28th December 1845 that tragedy struck this vessel. She had been 92 days out from Batavia for Amsterdam and at anchor in Pevensey Bay awaiting a pilot. It was while at anchor that a fierce south-westerly gale sprang up and, with the accompanying seas, drove the vessel aground. It soon became apparent that the vessel would have to be abandoned, and 18 of the 31 people on board managed to reach the shore in the vessel's longboat.

The Eastbourne lifeboat, being aware of the plight of the *Twee*

*Cornelissen*, was taken to Langney Point and launched under the command of Coxswain Samuel Knight, at about 10.30am. However, before the lifeboat reached the *Twee Cornelissen* a small pleasure boat, the *Rebecca* had put off from Wallsend, Pevensey, to try and assist. The boat was manned by Thomas Pierce and Thomas Woods, who were both pilots, and three Coastguardsmen, Oliver, Wornell and Flemming. Unfortunately they did not manage to get alongside the vessel before the lifeboat due to the terrible conditions.

On reaching the *Twee Cornelissen*, the lifeboat found that the remaining crew on board, which included the master and mate, had taken to the rigging of the mizzen mast. This was the only place of safety as the huge waves were now breaking right across her decks. Due to the conditions, coxswain Knight positioned the lifeboat to the stern and from this position managed to take off the master and the rest of the crew, who slid down a rope to the lifeboat.

When all were safely ashore it was noticed that one person was still hanging to the rigging. The *Rebecca* returned to the *Twee Cornelissen* but found the man was already dead. The severe seas on the days following the incident broke the vessel up.

In recognition of the Eastbourne lifeboat's rescue, the entire crew were presented with silver medals and certificates by the South Holland Lifeboat Society.

* The term 'Indiaman' was first coined in the 16th century when the Dutch East India Company (or VOC – Verenigde Oostindische Compagnie) built a number of ships for trade to the Dutch East Indies. However, the company ceased in 1799, but the term for such ships carried on. Hence the term seemed to refer to a defensively armed fully rigged three masted merchantman with one or two decks, that normally plied the trade routes, for a number of northern European countries between the Caribbean in the west (West Indiaman) and Asia in the east (East Indiaman).

*Ref: SIBI; SELB; BHB; SWA 30.12.1845 & 13.1.1846; SE 3.1.1846*

# LA FAYETTE

| | |
|---|---|
| **Date:** | 29.12.1848 |
| **Wreck Location:** | Ashore opposite the Buckle Inn, Seaford |
| **Description of Vessel:** | |
| **Vessel Type -** | Swedish sailing schooner |
| **Cargo:** | Salt |
| **Home Port:** | Uddewalla |
| **Voyage:** | St. Ubes to unknown destination |
| **Number of Crew:** | 6 |

At the height of a terrific storm early on Wednesday 29th December 1848, the *La Fayette* made a critical navigational error: the master and his 6 crew mistook the light at Newhaven for the light at Dover. This, coupled with the conditions, caused the vessel to come ashore in Seaford Bay opposite the Buckle Inn, with the loss of two lives, one of whom was a man named Nicholas Nelson. With the vessel now aground, and with the mountainous seas continually breaking over her, it was obvious she would go to pieces.

The Chief Boatman at the Blatchington Coastguard Station, Abraham Hart Young, was soon on the scene, and at great risk to his own life waded into the turbulent surf towards the stricken vessel. He finally reached the the ship and held on to part of the vessel's bulwark where he became trapped and badly injured by the pounding sea. However, the five remaining crew threw Young a rope, and despite his injuries he managed to reach the shore and secure the rope in order that the remaining crew could be rescued.

For his bravery in effecting this rescue, Abraham Hart Young was awarded his fourth silver medal from the Royal Humane Society, and £3. Two of his colleagues, Richard Paddy and Jeremiah Nagle, were awarded the sum of £1 each for the part they also played in this rescue.

*Ref: CNMM; SELB*

# SEA FLOWER

**Date:**                                    00.6.1849

**Wreck Location:**                          Boulder Bank west of Eastbourne

**Description of Vessel:**
**Vessel Type -**                            British sailing vessel

**Cargo:**                                   Granite blocks

---

The *Sea Flower* became a total loss in June 1849.

*Ref: SIBI*

# AGNES

| | |
|---|---|
| **Date:** | 14.2.1850 |
| **Wreck Location:** | Off Beachy Head |
| **Description of Vessel:** | |
| **Vessel Type -** | British sailing schooner |
| **Home Port:** | Glasgow |
| **Date Built, Builder:** | c.1846 at Bowling Bay |
| **Owner:** | McGill & Co |
| **Ship's Master:** | W. Scott |
| **Number of Crew:** | 4 |

The *Agnes* was lost off Beachy Head on St. Valentine's Day 1850.

*Ref: SIBI*

# DEFIANCE

| | |
|---|---|
| **Date:** | 7.7.1850 |
| **Wreck Location:** | Off Beachy Head |
| **Description of Vessel:** | |
| **Gross Tonnage -** | 107 |
| **Vessel Type -** | British sailing schooner |
| **Home Port:** | Cardigan |
| **Voyage:** | Liverpool to Dordt |
| **Date Built, Builder:** | c.1832 at Blyth |
| **Owner:** | Thomas Davies, Cardigan |
| **Ship's Master:** | T. Davies |
| **Number of Crew:** | 5 |

It was on Sunday 7th July 1850 that the *Defiance* became a total loss.

*Ref: SIBI*

# FIFE

| | |
|---|---|
| **Date:** | 5.5.1851 |
| **Wreck Location:** | 20 miles/32km west-south-west of Beachy Head |
| **Description of Vessel:** | |
| **Vessel Type -** | British sailing schooner |
| **Cargo:** | Ballast |
| **Home Port:** | Seaton, Exeter |
| **Voyage:** | Seaton to Newcastle-upon-Tyne |
| **Owner:** | Mr. Head, Seaton |
| **Ship's Master:** | Henry Dare |
| **Number of Crew:** | 5 |

At 2.30am on Monday 5th May 1851, the *Fife* was in ballast sailing up the Channel in a moderate northerly breeze. However, the master, Henry Dare, was asleep in his cabin. Sailing in the opposite direction and on a collision course with the *Fife* was a brig of unknown identity. The crew of the *Fife* altered course but for unknown reasons the oncoming brig made no alteration to her course and struck the port bow of the *Fife*.

The effect of the collision was that the bowsprit of the *Fife* was smashed and her anchor was torn off, dropping into the sea and pulling out about 100 fathoms/185m of chain cable. Once the anchor hit the seabed it held and brought the *Fife* to a standstill, but due to the damage caused by the collision it rapidly filled with water. The brig that was the cause of the collision made no attempt to stop or assist the *Fife* or its crew.

It took the master and his five crew twenty minutes to get the jolly-boat ready and to leave their stricken vessel. No sooner had they left than the *Fife* sank bow first in about 20 fathoms/37m of water. Having seen their vessel go down the crew started to row their boat north, but with the wind still coming from that direction it made progress very difficult. Fortunately it was not long before the *James,* under the command of Thomas William Burrows and twenty two days out from Bermuda for London, came across the jolly-boat. The *James* took the six men on board and landed them at Hastings at 11am the same morning. The jolly-boat was given to the master of the *James* for rescuing the crew. It transpired that the *James* nearly came to a similar fate from the same brig, soon after the *Fife*.

The crew lost almost everything they had including £6 in money and about £14 worth of property belonging to the master. However, the Shipwrecked Mariners Society did what they could for Dare and his men. Mr. Talbot, the Hastings Station Master of the South Eastern Railway Company, gave the crew free tickets to London, as was the usual custom by most of railway companies, when they departed on the 5pm train.

*Ref: SIBI; HN 9.5.1851*

# DIVINIA

**Date:** 2.10.1852

**Wreck Location:** Off Beachy Head

**Description of Vessel:**
**Vessel Type -** British sailing snow

**Cargo:** Coal

**Home Port:** Sunderland

**Date Built, Builder:** c.1825

---

This vessel became a loss when off Beachy Head on Saturday 2nd October 1852.

*Ref: SIBI*

# METROPOLITAN

| | |
|---|---|
| **Date:** | 18.10.1852 |
| **Wreck Location:** | Off Beachy Head |
| **Description of Vessel:** | |
| **Gross Tonnage -** | 340 |
| **Vessel Type -** | British steamship |
| **Voyage:** | Glasgow to London |
| **Date Built, Builder:** | c.1851 at Glasgow |
| **Owner:** | David Sloan |

---

At 3am on Sunday 18th October 1852 the *Metropolitan* was in collision with *Zollvarein,* a Prussian sailing brig en route to Danzig from Bristol. The *Zollvarein* stood by the *Metropolitan* and took all the crew off, as it was inevitable that she would sink from the damage of the collision. Three and half hours after the impact the *Metropolitan* went down.

The *Zollvarein* later landed the rescued crew at Portsmouth.

*Ref: SIBI*

# BRENDA

| | |
|---|---|
| **Date:** | 26.8.1853 |
| **Wreck Location:** | East of Newhaven harbour entrance |
| **Description of Vessel:** | |
| **Vessel Type -** | British sailing brig |
| **Cargo:** | Timber |
| **Home Port:** | London |
| **Voyage:** | Quebec to Newhaven |
| **Date Built, Builder:** | c.1849 in Prince Edward Island |
| **Owner:** | T. Petley |
| **Ship's Master:** | Buckle (or D. Keith) |
| **Number of Crew:** | 10 |

On the night of Thursday 25th August 1853, shortly after 11pm, a south-westerly storm blew up, accompanied by driving rain, and by morning the wind had reached hurricane strength. A number of vessels along the Channel and elsewhere were to become casualties of this storm including the *Brenda*.

On the morning of Friday 26th August, the *Brenda,* under the command of the master Mr. Buckle (although some records show it to be Mr. D. Keith), was nearing the end of its voyage from Quebec with good quality timber for Messrs. Chatfield & Sampson of Lewes. Throughout the voyage the vessel had leaked considerably and in these terrible conditions became almost waterlogged. The condition of the vessel caused much apprehension among the crew that it would founder before reaching Newhaven. However, in trying to make for the port it ran ashore just east of the eastern pier of the harbour.

The Blatchington Coastguard Station were already aware that the

*Brenda* was in distress, and were soon on the spot with their rocket apparatus under the command of Lieutenant Ryves. The surf was far too severe for any boat to reach the wreck. They quickly fired a line onto the stranded vessel and a cradle was sent aboard for the 11 crew, who were pulled to safety.

*Ref: SIBI; SWA 30.8.1853; SE 3.9.1853*

# BENEVOLENT

| | |
|---|---|
| **Date:** | 2.9.1853 |
| **Wreck Location:** | 7 miles/11.3km south-east of Beachy Head |
| **Description of Vessel:** | |
| **Vessel Type -** | British sailing brig |
| **Cargo:** | 140 tons of Iron |
| **Home Port:** | Plymouth |
| **Voyage:** | Cardiff to Hamburg |
| **Owner:** | Martin Hitchins, Sutton Wharf, Plymouth |
| **Ship's Master:** | Breese |
| **Number of Crew:** | 6 |

The last voyage of the *Benevolent* was to be quite an eventful one, starting on Thursday 25th August 1853 when the vessel was then off St. Catherines, near Plymouth. The vessel was struck by heavy seas causing damage that necessitated the vessel putting into Portsmouth for repairs. It took a week to do the repair work with the *Benevolent* leaving Portsmouth to continue its voyage early on Friday 2nd September, the day it was to become a wreck.

At 11pm that same night the *Benevolent* was 7 miles/11.3km south-east of Beachy Head in very stormy conditions. The wind was blowing from the north with heavy showers and poor visibility. Suddenly, as if from nowhere, a brig appeared out of the gloom, ran into the *Benevolent* and disappeared just as quickly. This collision caused serious damage to the *Benevolent* and the crew had just enough time to get the jolly-boat out, before the vessel went down within ten minutes of the collision. So sudden and unexpected was this event that four of the crew who were below had no time to get dressed. With the crew safely in the jolly-boat, they pulled away from the wreck just as the vessel went down, and were very lucky not to have also been drawn down by the vortex of the sinking vessel.

There was much despair among the crew as they were in terrible weather conditions, in an open boat at night and a considerable distance from land. Fortunately the *Hope,* a lugger from Deal under the command of George Heather, came across them and took them on board. Some five hours after the collision the crew of the *Benevolent* were safely landed at Hastings, by which time the four crew without clothes were suffering considerably from the conditions they had been exposed to.

The crew were cared for by William Phillips and Nicholas Wingfield of the Shipwrecked Mariners Society who arranged with the Hastings station master Mr. Kennett for their transport to the London offices of the society. The crew, one of whom by the name of Gabriel Watson was born in Westfield near Hastings, were granted free second class transport by the South-Eastern Railway Company and left Hastings for London on the 2.25pm train that same afternoon.

*Ref: SIBI; HN 9.9.1853*

# DALHOUSIE

| | |
|---|---|
| **Date:** | 19.10.1853 |
| **Wreck Location:** | 16 miles/25km west by south-west of Beachy Head |
| **Description of Vessel:** | |
| **Gross Tonnage -** | 800 |
| **Vessel Type -** | British full-rigged sailing vessel |
| **Cargo:** | General |
| **Voyage:** | London to Sydney |
| **Date Built, Builder:** | c.1848 at Moulmein |
| **Owner:** | J. Allan, Leadenhall Street, London |
| **Ship's Master:** | John Butterworth |
| **Number of Crew:** | 46 |
| **Number of Passengers:** | 13 |

This vessel, owned by J. Allan of London, was on charter to Fry & Davison, Fenchurch Street, London as one of the 'White House Line of Australia' passenger ships. On the morning of Wednesday 19th October 1853, whilst on its voyage to Australia, the vessel was to sink in 20 fathoms/37m of water, with the loss of all those on board except one.

The *Dalhousie* started its fateful journey at the East India Docks at Blackwall, London, a week earlier on 12th October. When the vessel left Blackwall under tow of a steam tug, there were 46 crew under the command of the master John Butterworth, 32 of whom were described as Lascars*, having come from Calcutta on the *Dalhousie's* last voyage.

On reaching Gravesend, the vessel took on board 13 passengers namely Mr. John Underwood (45 years of age), his wife, and their children Catherine (16yrs), Frederick (14yrs), Alfred (14yrs), and a family friend

Miss Radford from Essex. The other passengers were Mrs. Simpson and three children, and the master's wife Eliza and two sons. Mrs. Butterworth's plan was to leave the vessel when it put in at Plymouth to take on board further passengers. On leaving Gravesend the vessel proceeded to the Downs, arriving at 7am on Saturday 15th October. The pilot went ashore at Deal together with the elder of the master's sons so that the latter could return to school near the town. The *Dalhousie* remained at anchor in the Downs because of adverse weather conditions until 7am the following Tuesday, when it left to continue its voyage down the Channel in a fresh north-westerly breeze.

At 7pm that evening when the *Dalhousie* was about 10 miles/16km to the west of Dungeness, the wind had shifted to a freshening south-easterly wind. Within three hours the wind had increased considerably and all the topsails had been reefed. The Beachy Head light could now be seen about 8 miles/13km to the starboard of the vessel by the helmsman, 22 year old Joseph Reed, who was to be the lone survivor. At 4am with the wind increasing to gale force and the sea becoming ever more violent, the main sail was double reefed and the mizzen sail was stowed. The vessel was now starting to labour in these conditions, rolling, lurching and going broadside on to the troughs between the waves. The waves themselves were constantly breaking over the vessel and had already carried away the starboard boat. Joseph Reed was to say later it felt as though the vessel was water-logged, although up to 8pm the previous night there was no water in the hull. By 5am with the vessel in serious difficulty the master decided that the water-casks, sheep pens and other cargo on the deck had to be jettisoned.

The crew had started to throw the deck cargo overboard as instructed by Butterworth, when the vessel made a violent lurch to the starboard. At the same time a huge wave swept over the vessel, washing away the vessel's longboat which was full of live stock. The weather continued to get worse and at 5.30am the *Dalhousie* lurched and rolled right over on her starboard side, such that the mast head was in the sea, and stayed there. The vessel was now being completely swamped by the sea which had washed away the port side longboat. Many of the crew took refuge in the rigging, but the sole survivor, Joseph Reed, took refuge on the weather quarter of the vessel, together with the master, chief mate, second mate and a number of other crew members. The crew also managed to drag John Underwood, his wife and their two sons through the gallery window and on to their refuge. Unfortunately no sooner had they done so than all four were knocked into the sea by a large wave, never to be seen again. A similar fate was to befall four of the crew members in the rigging, who also were washed away from their refuge by the horrendous seas. John Underwood's daughter Catherine, who had been in the poop cabins, was pulled from the water and lashed to a spar by Reed and James Burley, another crew member. It was clear to all that the *Dalhousie* would not stay afloat much longer.

John Butterworth and Reed then saw a schooner about ½ mile/805m away heading towards them. The schooner was later found to be the *William* under the command of her master Richard Milman. Butterworth knew that his vessel was doomed and told everybody to do what they could to save themselves. Reed cut away the lashings holding the girl Catherine to the spar in order to give her some chance of survival. The spar drifted away with the girl still clinging to it. The master, Mr. Finch the second mate, a son of the passenger Mrs. Simpson and a couple of the Lascars jumped from the vessel and also hung onto the same spar. Many of the crew and passengers had by this time been washed away by the sea and drowned. About 10 minutes after the master had left the vessel for the spar, the *Dalhousie* started to sink bow first, which must have been seen by the approaching schooner. There were still a few survivors hanging onto debris, struggling to stay alive. All the time the *William* was getting nearer to the wreck. When at about 100yds/91.4m away, Reed called out to the schooner to drift in towards him so that he and the others in the water could be rescued. Unfortunately, the reply from the *William* was for him to swim towards the vessel, which in the conditions was totally impossible as the schooner was drifting faster than a man could swim. Reed was to later state that the schooner stayed in the area for about 2 hours before sailing away without taking any steps to try and rescue any of those still struggling in the sea. However, this was later denied by the master of the *William*.

Throughout the rest of the morning of Wednesday 19th October the remaining survivors saw a number of vessels going up and down the Channel, but none came to their aid. One by one the survivors died in what were still gale force winds and high seas. Joseph Reed was finally alone in the water when at 4pm he saw the brig *Mitchel Grove,* under the command of Mr. Rawson. Reed was totally exhausted from his ordeal but waved his handkerchief as best as he was able, fortunately being seen by the crew of the brig, who came alongside him and hauled him onboard. He was found to be totally exhausted and suffering from exposure after being in the sea for over ten hours. The *Mitchel Grove* finally arrived off Dover at 4pm the following afternoon where Reed was put ashore.

Those who perished included the steward, a man named Brotherton aged 45yrs from Deptford; James Burley, the youngest assistant sail-maker; 14 year old James Marcus Harris the son of an east London clergyman and on his first voyage; William Hartshorn, another young man, the son of an army Captain of 3, Ontario Close, Rathmines, Dublin, also on his maiden voyage; Edward Saxon Kendle, on his second voyage for the vessel's owner; John Henry Sturkman, the son of a wealthy family; and a man named Ward who had been wrecked on a previous occasion in a vessel called *Barbara Gordon*. The passenger John Underwood who perished had worked for many years for Messrs. Brittle & Co, Wood Street, Manchester, and was going to Sydney intending to start up the business there. His own goods and the 180 cases belong to Messrs. Brittle & Co. were insured for £10,000. The ship and cargo were insured for £70,000.

The actions of the schooner the *William* as related by Reed were disputed by its master Richard Milman. His version of the events was that he first saw the *Dalhousie* at 7am on the morning of Wednesday 19th October with her starboard side in the water. He approached her from the leeward side and when a about 1 cable/185m away, the *Dalhousie* sank. Milman said he had great difficulty in controlling the *William* in the terrible conditions with the sea breaking over his small 119 ton vessel. The conditions made it almost impossible to get near the *Dalhousie* although all his crew had lead lines and cork fenders in readiness to rescue any of those still in the water. He remained in the vicinity of the sunken vessel for about an hour and a half but was slowly drifting towards the shore. Milman discussed the situation with the rest of his crew and a decision was made to sail away as there was little else they could do, and to save their own vessel. Milman denied anybody on his vessel called out to Joseph Reed that he should swim towards his vessel. He said that in those conditions and at that distance away from the *Dalhousie* a voice would not be heard. Joseph Reed maintained his version of events was correct.

One of the boats washed from the deck of the *Dalhousie* during this tragic event was washed ashore at Cuckmere on the Friday after. It was 25ft/7.6m long and fitted to take six oars and two sails.

The body of Eliza Butterworth, wife of the master, was found the following Monday by William Spice, a fisherman from Hastings. It was at about 2pm and 2 miles/3.2km off Lovers Seat, near Hastings, that one of his crew of six men and a boy called out, '*Here's another pig*' believing he could see a hog. The previous day they had found two hogs floating in the sea. As they approached they could see it was the body of a woman, laying face down in the water. They pulled the body from the water and returned to Hastings, where Inspector Campbell of the local Police took charge of the body and two rings found later by the crew in the bottom of their boat. It was found that the initials 'E.B.' were on some of her clothing.

At 2pm the following day, Tuesday 25th October, an inquest was held at Hastings Town Hall before the Deputy Coroner John Phillips. The jury then examined the body of Mrs. Butterworth and returned to the Town Hall to hear the evidence. The first witness was William Spice who gave evidence of finding the body. The next witness was Joseph Pain of 2 Park Terrace, Old Ford Road, London, a silk weaver and the brother of Eliza Butterworth. He gave evidence of identification that the deceased was his 34 year old sister and wife of the master of the *Dalhousie*. He also stated that the two rings found by Spice's crew in their boat were those of his sister. After summing the evidence up the jury returned a verdict of 'Found drowned'.

During the days following the wreck of the *Dalhousie* a large amount of articles from the vessel were washed ashore along the coast. Among the items found was a case of spy glasses, a writing desk with a brass lid plate with the name 'John Kay' engraved on it, and a parchment trunk marked 'T.R. Thomas, surgeon, Ship Dalhousie'.

The total number of passengers on the *Dalhousie*, i.e. 13, does not seem to be in doubt. However, the vessel's total complement does seem to vary as records show it to be the master and 59 crew, whereas sole survivor Joseph Reed reported the vessel's complement as being the master and 46 crew.

* A Lascar is a native East Indian seaman.

*Ref: SIBI; SWA 25.10.1853; HN 28.10.1853; SE 29.10.1853*

# WILLIAM

**Date:**                              00.00.1854

**Wreck Location:**                    Ashore under the Belle Tout Light

**Description of Vessel:**
**Vessel Type -**                      Sailing barque

**Cargo:**                             Wine

---

This vessel was driven ashore, its fate unknown, but it is believed to have become a total wreck without loss of life.

*Ref: SIBI; EG 20.6.1888*

# AGENORIA

| | |
|---|---|
| **Date:** | 29.1.1854 |
| **Wreck Location:** | Off Beachy Head |
| **Description of Vessel:** | |
| **Vessel Type -** | British sailing sloop |
| **Cargo:** | Pipe clay |
| **Home Port:** | Wisbech |
| **Voyage:** | Poole to Lee |

This vessel was abandoned by its crew off Beachy Head after having sprung a leak. They were later safely landed at Deal, presumably having been picked up by another vessel.

*Ref: SIBI*

# NAVARIN

**Date:**                                   6.8.1854

**Wreck Location:**                         Off Beachy Head

**Description of Vessel:**
**Length -**                                59ft/17.93m
**Beam -**                                  15ft/4.54m
**Vessel Type -**                           British sailing dandy

**Cargo:**                                  Ballast

**Home Port:**                              Shoreham

**Voyage:**                                 Harwich to Shoreham

**Date Built, Builder:**                    c.1828 at Lymington

**Owner:**                                  G. Griggs, Shoreham

**Ship's Master:**                          James Taylor

**Number of Crew:**                         2

---

The *Navarin,* an oyster fishing vessel, was lost on Sunday 6th August 1854 off Beachy Head. The fate of the master, James Taylor, and his crew are not known

*Ref: SIBI*

# JANE BEALE

| | |
|---|---|
| **Date:** | 27.2.1855 |
| **Wreck Location:** | 26 miles/42km south-east of Beachy Head |
| **Description of Vessel:** | |
| **Gross Tonnage -** | 75 |
| **Vessel Type -** | British sailing schooner |
| **Cargo:** | Stone (for road mending) |
| **Home Port:** | Weymouth |
| **Voyage:** | Guernsey to London |
| **Ship's Master:** | S. Beale |

At 6am on Tuesday 27th February 1855, the *Jane Beale* was found abandoned and drifting about 26 miles/42km south-east of Beachy Head, by two Dover vessels, the *Twins,* a cutter under the command of David Axford, and the pilot cutter *Gulnare.* The two cutters took the abandoned vessel in tow and brought it safely into Newhaven harbour at about 6.30pm the same day. Once in harbour, a check was made of the vessel that revealed both masts were missing, having broken close to the deck, as well as a considerable amount of water in the hold.

It was later established that all the *Jane Beale's* crew had safely arrived at Eastbourne that same day. They had abandoned their vessel the previous Saturday when they encountered a serious gale off the French coast which had caused the loss of both masts. The crew had also believed the vessel was in danger of sinking due to the amount of water they found in the hold.

*Ref: HC 7.3.1855; HN 9.3.1855; LL 12769 28.2.53; LL 12770 1.3.55*

# ANDRE

| | |
|---|---|
| **Date:** | 1.3.1855 |
| **Wreck Location:** | Ashore west of Seaford |
| **Description of Vessel:** | |
| **Vessel Type -** | Austrian sailing barque |
| **Cargo:** | Linseed |
| **Voyage:** | Constantinople to Antwerp |
| **Ship's Master:** | Sussannich |
| **Number of Crew:** | 12 |

The *Andre* left Constantinople on 9th November 1854 with her cargo of linseed bound for Antwerp. The vessel put in at Falmouth on the 18th February 1855, leaving four days later to continue her voyage.

On the night of Thursday 1st March the *Andre* was off Newhaven in very dense fog, which was to be the cause of her running aground to the west of Seaford at about 1am the following morning. Fortunately the crew all managed to reach the safety of the shore. As the day progressed the weather steadily deteriorated from the south-west with increasing winds. The steamer *Paris* attempted to take the *Andre* in tow but due to the strengthening wind and heavy seas this was unsuccessful. The vessel was left to the elements and by 10pm that night she went totally to pieces in the south-westerly gale that blew up, with the loss of the cargo of linseed valued at £6,000. However, the broken hull and other articles that were salvaged were sold at auction by Mr. R. Verrall the following Thursday.

*Ref: HC 7.3.1855; HN 9.3.1855; SE 10.3.1855; LL 12772 3.3.55; LL 12773 5.3.55*

# JOYEUSE

| | |
|---|---|
| **Date:** | 29.1.1856 |
| **Wreck Location:** | Off Newhaven |
| **Description of Vessel:** | |
| **Gross Tonnage -** | 140 approx. |
| **Vessel Type -** | French sailing schooner |
| **Cargo:** | Flour (bagged) |
| **Home Port:** | St. Malo |
| **Voyage:** | Spain to Dunkirk |
| **Date Built, Builder:** | c.1855 |
| **Number of Crew:** | 4 and 1 boy |

The *Joyeuse* was first seen drifting bottom uppermost off Newhaven by two Shoreham steam tugs who towed it Shoreham harbour on Friday 1st February 1856. Although the true facts of how this nearly new vessel became a loss is not known, it is believed to have encountered a storm soon after leaving Spain about six weeks earlier.

The cargo was found to be sacks of high quality flour, much of which was damaged. However, that was not all that was found when the vessel was checked: the body of a 15 year old boy was found in the forecastle.

*Ref: SIBI; SE 9.2.1856*

# TETI

| | |
|---|---|
| **Date:** | 14.7.1856 |
| **Wreck Location:** | Ashore between Beachy Head and Cow Gap |
| **Description of Vessel:** | |
| **Vessel Type -** | Spanish sailing brigantine |
| **Cargo:** | Dried fish |
| **Home Port:** | Barcelona |
| **Voyage:** | Aalsund to Barcelona |
| **Ship's Master:** | Salazar |

The *Teti* came ashore between Beachy Head and Cow Gap during the evening of Monday 14th July 1856, in very thick fog. The crew fortunately all managed to get ashore safely but the vessel eventually became a total wreck.

*Ref: SIBI; SE 19.7.1856*

# MATILDA

| | |
|---|---|
| **Date:** | 22.2.1857 |
| **Wreck Location:** | Off Eastbourne |
| **Description of Vessel:** | |
| **Gross Tonnage -** | 70 |
| **Vessel Type -** | Dutch Sailing schooner |
| **Cargo:** | Oil, white lead |
| **Ship's Master:** | Laarman |
| **Number of Crew:** | 4 |

The vessel is also known as the *Mathilde*.

During the night of Saturday 21st February 1857 the *Matilda* was in collision with H.M. steam frigate *Bulldog* off Eastbourne. At the time the *Bulldog* was towing another frigate, the *Melampass,* to Portsmouth. It appears that the *Bulldog* took the *Matilda* in tow but the casualty struck the Boulder Bank at low water and capsized. As the *Matilda* was not too badly damaged she was successfully righted and taken into Newhaven on the morning of Monday 23rd February for repairs.

*Ref: SIBI; SE 28.2.1857; HC 18.3.1857*

# YOURNAMA

| | |
|---|---|
| **Date:** | 00.3.1857 |
| **Wreck Location:** | Off Eastbourne |
| **Description of Vessel:** | |
| **Vessel Type -** | Sailing barque |
| **Voyage:** | Portsmouth to unknown destination |
| **Number of Crew:** | 10 |

---

The date of this collision in March 1857 is not stated. However, it is known that the *Yournama* was sailing up the Channel in thick fog when it collided with the *Queen of Plymouth*. It sank within a few minutes of the collision, but all the crew were rescued by the *Queen of Plymouth* and taken into Eastbourne.

*Ref: SIBI; EG 28.3.1888*

# OCEAN

| | |
|---|---|
| **Date:** | 8.10.1857 |
| **Wreck Location:** | Ashore east of Newhaven harbour |
| **Description of Vessel:** | |
| **Vessel Type -** | British sailing schooner |
| **Cargo:** | Coal |
| **Home Port:** | Llanelly |
| **Voyage:** | Newcastle to Plymouth |
| **Ship's Master:** | Edwin Bentley |
| **Number of Crew:** | 7 |

In the early hours of the morning of Thursday 8th October 1857 a terrible south-westerly gale was blowing in the Channel, causing much havoc to shipping. One of the vessels caught in this gale was the *Ocean,* under the command of Edwin Bentley, which had lost its head-masts and was running before the wind for Newhaven harbour. As the *Ocean* approached the harbour at about 7am, it ran aground just east of the entrance. It was low tide so the vessel was in a perilous situation with mountainous seas and an imminent flood tide. Those ashore first saw the *Ocean* when she was about 3 miles/4.8km south-west of the harbour and watched her approach towards the port. Bearing in mind the state of the tide, it was evident to the onlookers that she would run aground.

Mr. White, the chief mate of the steamship *Orleans*, which was in the safety of the harbour, realised what had happened and lowered the ship's lifeboat with a crew of four volunteers. The lifeboat went down river where it was hauled out of the water and taken over land to a point nearer the stranded *Ocean*. This lifeboat, together with the Newhaven lifeboat, were then launched into the horrendous surf. After much difficulty the crew in the *Orleans* lifeboat succeeded in rescuing four of the crew from the *Ocean* with the Newhaven lifeboat rescuing Edwin Bentley, the mate and the remaining crew members. The rescued crew were taken to the local Coastguard station where they were cared for.

The *Ocean* finally went to pieces about 2pm that afternoon having taken a terrible battering from the sea. The coal cargo was washed out of the vessel and strewn along the coastline. Many local people were later seen collecting the coal from the beach in readiness for the oncoming winter.

*Ref: SE 10.10.1857; HC 14.10.1857; LL 13578 8.10.57; LL 13582 13.10.57*

# PAULINE

| | |
|---|---|
| **Date:** | 10.10.1857 |
| **Wreck Location:** | 7 miles/11.3km south-west of Newhaven Harbour |
| **Description of Vessel:** | |
| **Gross Tonnage -** | 200 approx. |
| **Vessel Type -** | Polish sailing schooner |
| **Cargo:** | 200 tons of brandy, wines, nuts |
| **Home Port:** | Stettin |
| **Voyage:** | Bordeaux to Stettin |
| **Ship's Master:** | C.F. Wenke |

On Saturday 10th October 1857, a lugger from Deal came into Newhaven harbour with the news that she and another vessel had come upon the upturned hull of the *Pauline* 7 miles/11.3km south-west of the harbour. They requested that a steamship give assistance in recovering the *Pauline* and so the *Alar* from Shoreham arrived on the scene the next day. However, she was unable to move the upturned *Pauline* because the chains had run out from her. The *Dieppe* was then summoned to assist and with great difficulty managed to tow the *Pauline* between the two piers at Newhaven on Wednesday 14th October.

When the tide ebbed the name of the vessel was established and the cargo it was carrying discovered. The vessel's masts were found to have been broken close to the deck, but otherwise there was little damage. The fate of the crew is not known but it is assumed that they all perished. However, found in the vessel was a label bearing the name 'C.F. Wenke' and this is assumed to be the master.

*Ref: SE 24.10.1857; LL 13581 12.10.57; LL 13585 16.10.57*

# PELICAN

| | |
|---|---|
| **Date:** | 18.10.1857 |
| **Wreck Location:** | Off Newhaven |
| **Description of Vessel:** | |
| **Vessel Type -** | French Man-of-war steamship |
| **Ship's Master:** | Martin |

---

On the afternoon of Sunday 18th October 1857 the steamship *Pelican* was towed stern first into Newhaven harbour by the French steamship *Paris and London* and a Dover cutter. The *Pelican* had earlier been in collision with the barque *Malabar* from London and had suffered considerable damage in that the bow had been completely cut off and the foremast lost. After the collision the *Malabar* took the *Pelican* in tow until they fell in with the *Paris and London* under the command of M. Le Gros.

The *Malabar* did not escape unscathed in this encounter, and had to return to London for repairs to the extensive damage she also sustained.

*Ref: SE 24.10.1857; LL 13581 12.10.57*

# COASTGUARD VESSEL (UNNAMED)

| | |
|---|---|
| **Date vessel sank:** | 17.1.1859 |
| **Wreck Location:** | Off Pevensey |
| **Description of Vessel:** | |
| **Vessel Type -** | Four-oared galley |
| **Cargo:** | Flags, pennants |
| **Voyage:** | Tendering off shore |
| **Owner:** | Pevensey Coastguard Station |
| **Ship's Master:** | Dennis Perrin |
| **Number of Crew:** | 5 |

This is an occasion where the rescuers themselves needed to be rescued. This four-oared galley belonged to Pevensey Coastguard Station and at the time of this unfortunate event was ferrying some old flags and pennants from the Coastguard Station to a Coastguard cutter named the *Active*.

The Chief Officer of the Station, Lieutenant Mansel, had given orders the previous evening that once the *Active* came into view, the station's galley was to put to sea with its cargo of flags and pennants and take them to the *Active*. At 10am on the morning of Monday 17th January, Michael Russell of the Coastguard Station was the first to see the *Active*. At the time there was a violent sea running and an ebbing tide. At about 12.45pm, when the *Active* was almost a mile/1.6km from the shore, the Coastguard vessel finally set off for the cutter. The crew consisted of Dennis Perrin (acting as Coxswain), William Hutchings, William Bricknell, William Cook and Michael Russell.

There was a stiff breeze blowing which was freshening all the time. The vessel got alongside the *Active* without any great difficulty and the cargo of flags was put aboard her. As the Coastguard vessel made to return to the shore, Perrin appeared to have the vessel under control until it reached the breaking waves and surf. Then, instead of waiting for the calm patch of sea after the 'third wave' and running the boat in stern first, he kept the boat bow first into the surf. The vessel suddenly broached, throwing most of the crew into the sea. Three of them managed to hang onto the stern. The vessel was now filling with water but was still afloat and drifting eastwards. Lieutenant Mansel realised that this could be a potential disaster and so sent a member of his detachment, William Dent, to fetch the Coastguard's Chief Boatman and his boat. However, the Chief Boatman, named Munday, would not launch the boat because it was impossible to get her through the sea, especially as the vessel in distress was much the same type of boat. By coincidence Dent should have been one of the crew of the galley but was five minutes late arriving and so missed the launch. Michael Russell went in his place. Mansel, having given this order to Dent, stripped off and headed into the sea with the intention of saving the vessel's crew. He managed to get hold of the only survivor, Michael Russell, who was floating quite close to the shore and hauled him to safety.

Three of the dead crewmen had families. Perrin and Cook both had five children all under fifteen years of age, with Cook's youngest only being eight weeks old. Hutchings was also married with five children.

Cook's body was found at low water by James Balcombe, a labourer employed by Major Vidler, a local Surveyor, at about 5pm the same day. As a result an Inquest into his death was held at the Sluice Inn, Pevensey before Hastings Borough Coroner Mr. R. Growse and Jury. Captain Gough, R.N. Commander of the Coastguard district, attended as an observer. The rescued man, Russell, did not attend the hearing as he was still too unwell to give evidence.

During the hearing the Chief Officer of the Station, Lieutenant Mansel, said that he had been in the service nearly two years and had been stationed at Pevensey about eight months. In his evidence to the Coroner he said that he did not think it was too rough to send the boat out, although he had not sent it out before except for the one occasion he himself went out in it. Under questioning Mansel said that the crew did not practice at the station and that they had not been out on exercise since he had been there. Although the Chief Boatman, Munday, had been at the station for seven years, Mansel considered his own judgement and knowledge of the sea to be superior to that of the Chief Boatman. He accepted that none of the crew had been provided with cork jackets or life-belts. The Coroner felt that had the crew been provided with these there may well not have been a loss of life. He told the Jury that there was no doubt that Cook's death had been caused by accidental drowning but it was for the Jury to decide whether there was any criminal conduct on the part of Lieutenant Mansel, even though the

Coroner believed there was none. If there was any misconduct on his behalf, then it was for his senior officers to take the necessary action.

The Jury agreed with the Coroner and formally returned a verdict of 'Accidental Drowning'. They also made the recommendation that the Coastguard should be provided with the proper life saving equipment when going to sea in rough conditions and that the gallant conduct of Lieutenant Mansel after the tragedy be brought to the attention of his senior officers.

On Saturday 22nd January the body of Hutchings was found among the rocks opposite the Hastings Fishmarket by an 11 year old boy, John Chatfield, who was searching for whelks at low tide. The body was embedded in the sand face down with only part of the legs and heels showing above the surface. The body of Perrin was also found the same day but near Galley Hill. The inquests into Hutchings death was held on the morning of Monday 24th October and the inquest into Perrin's death was held in the afternoon of the same day.

The inquest into the death of 44 year old William Hutchings was held at Hastings Town Hall before the same Coroner who enquired into the death of William Cook. He decided to call no additional evidence, other than for identification and that of the youth Chatfield who found the body. He made this decision because the Jury had read the report of the previous Inquest and therefore thought it unnecessary. However, in answer to a question from Mr. Stevenson, a member of the Jury, who asked the Commander of the Coastguard, Capt. Gough, was it not a trifling reason to send a boat out in such conditions, Capt. Gough said that had nothing to do with it, as the boat had not been out for a long time and the crew needed the practice, transporting stores was a good excuse. He said the task should have taken about an hour but the sea can change dramatically in 30 minutes. Capt. Gough confirmed to the Inquest that he had left orders that the boat was only to go if practicable. He said that it was the duty of Lieutenant Mansel to use his discretion as to allowing the boat to go and he had subsequently told Lieut. Mansel that he was not fit to command a station. The Jury returned a verdict of 'Accidental Drowning' and expressed a view that greater caution should be exercised before sending boats off.

The Inquest into the death of Perrin was held at the Bell Inn, Bexhill, before Mr. N.P. Kell, the Coroner for the Rape* of Hastings on the afternoon of the same day. At this hearing the rescued man, Russell, was fit enough to attend and give evidence. He said that he had two war medals, one for the coast of Syria and the other for the Baltic. He said that once the boat had broached he was thrown into the sea. When he had recovered himself he found he had an oar in his hand which he handed out to Perrin who was still in the waterlogged boat. He asked Perrin to pull him aboard but before he could do this, a wave had washed him away from the boat. He said that he also found one of the seats from the vessel and with the oar he had swum for the beach to be met by Lieutenant Mansel. He stated that he was so exhausted that had Mansel not been there then he would surely have drowned. Once the sea washed him away from the vessel he did not see any of the crew again. Although he had not been out in such a boat as this in such rough weather he did not object to doing so. He had been in similar seas in the West Indies but had been in eight and ten-oared boats.

* The County of Sussex was divided into six divisions, each called a Rape.

*Ref: HC 19.1.1859 & 26.1.1859; HN 21.1.1859 & 28.1.1859*

# VIZCAYA

**Date:** 2.2.1859

**Wreck Location:** Off Beachy Head

**Description of Vessel:**
**Vessel Type -** Spanish sailing barque

**Cargo:** Ballast

**Home Port:** Bilboa

**Voyage:** London to Bordeaux

**Ship's Master:** Jose Francisca Urquiola

---

On the night of 1st/2nd February 1859, the *Vizcaya*, was in collision off Beachy Head with a Dutch vessel, the *D'Elmira,* bound for Rotterdam, in a south-westerly gale and heavy seas. The *Vizcaya* sustained considerable damage with all the rigging smashed, boats smashed, and sides stoved in. However, the crew all managed to get aboard the *D'Elmira* which was so badly damaged in the collision that a distress cannon was fired when the vessel was off Shoreham. This was answered by the tug *Don*, who took the vessel under tow to Portsmouth. The crew of the *Vizcaya* later returned to Newhaven by rail.

On the morning of Wednesday 2nd February the *Vizcaya* was seen drifting westward down the Channel about 4 miles/6.4km off the coast at Brighton. Both the Brighton lifeboat and the Newhaven lifeboat, *Friend in Need*, together with a four-oared Coastguard galley from the Greenway Station at Rottingdean put off to investigate. However before leaving, the coastguard sent a message to Newhaven requesting a steamship join them as soon as possible to give assistance. The Coastguard galley was the first to arrive and on boarding her found the vessel totally deserted. The coastguardsmen, with help from the lifeboat crews, managed to anchor the vessel to await the assistance they had requested from Newhaven. It was to be the railway steamer *Lyons* that was to respond to their request and, by the afternoon, had the *Vizcaya* safely in Newhaven harbour.

At a subsequent hearing of the Admiralty Court £250 was awarded to the *Lyons*, £150 to the Rottingdean Coastguard, and £100 to the Newhaven lifeboat.

The wreck of the *Vizcaya,* which was armed with six guns, was later bought and re-rigged by J. Robinson of Littlehampton. It unfortunately was lost on the Yorkshire coast in 1893.

*Ref: SNLB; CNMM; SE 8.2.1859; HN 11.2.1859; HC 16.2.1859; LL 13992 7.2.59*

# ARIADNE

**Date:**                               25.10.1859

**Wreck Location:**                     Near Newhaven

**Description of Vessel:**
**Vessel Type -**                       British sailing cutter

**Home Port:**                          Isles of Scilly

**Date Built, Builder:**                c.1841 at Sandgate, Kent

**Owner:**                              Bluett & Co

---

The *Ariadne* became a total loss near Newhaven on Friday 25th October 1859.

*Ref: SIBI*

# ONDINE

| | |
|---|---|
| **Date:** | 19.2.1860 |
| **Wreck Location:** | Off Beachy Head |
| **Description of Vessel:** | |
| **Vessel Type -** | British steamship |
| **Cargo:** | General |
| **Home Port:** | Waterford |
| **Voyage:** | Dublin to London |
| **Date Built, Builder:** | c.1852 |
| **Ship's Master:** | James Hunt |
| **Number of Crew:** | 24 |
| **Number of Passengers:** | 50 |

February 1860 was not the first time the steamship *Ondine* had been involved in a collision. The previous occasion was on 7th August 1859 when the *Ondine* was in collision with the Dover collier *Robert Garden* while off South Foreland. Of the nine people on board the *Robert Garden,* 4 of them including the pilot were to drown.

Six months later at 3am on Sunday 19th February 1860 the *Ondine*, off Beachy Head in a force 4 wind, collided with the sailing schooner *Heroine* of Bideford. The impact was so severe that the *Ondine* sank within 20 minutes.

It was apparent to the crew, after the impact, that the *Ondine* was in a desperate state and would soon sink, so they set about getting the boats off. Unfortunately the port lifeboat had been smashed in the impact, and the starboard lifeboat was damaged in getting it launched. This damage was such that it caused the lifeboat to fill with water up to its thwarts, so the second mate Richard Burke got two buckets to bale the water out. When he returned with the buckets he found that twelve men, three women and two children who were all passengers, sitting in the lifeboat. Burke quickly pushed the lifeboat away from the *Ondine* for fear of being pulled down in the vortex when the vessel sank. As he do did so he looked back towards the stricken vessel to see the master and a large number of passengers, mainly women and children, as well as soldiers who were returning from leave, still on the sinking vessel.

All those in the lifeboat were sitting in water up to their waists, and the only thing keeping it afloat was the cork buoyancy. Burke took an oar to the bow to steer the drifting boat, as he was unable to go to the stern because the women and children had gathered there. Although there were four oars on the lifeboat they were of no use because of its partial submersion. The perilous condition of the lifeboat was not enhanced by the fresh north-west breeze and waves continually breaking over it. About half an hour after leaving the *Ondine* Burke looked back towards her to see the bows raise up and the vessel sink stern first.

The conditions in the lifeboat were quite desperate with sea continually breaking over it and those on board having to deal with the bitterly cold wind. One by one, they slowly succumbed to the conditions and were washed away. A woman passenger, Mrs. Marsh, was the first to be washed away still holding one of her young children. Each time a passenger was washed away it lightened the lifeboat and improved the rescue chances of the remainder. Sadly, there were to be only three survivors from this lifeboat, Burke and two other male passengers, who were picked up later the same day by the London and Mediterranean Navigation Company's steamship, *Thetis*, under the command of H.S. Machin.

The *Heroine,* although suffering considerable structural damage, rescued sixteen crew and four passengers from the *Ondine*, and put them into Dover later that day. Those rescued by the *Heroine* were: Edward West (chief mate); Francis Le Brand (boatswain); William McKay, George Elvish, John Dench (seamen); William Dench (boy); Edward O'Brien (cabin boy); John Miller (cook); Thomas Hewston (chief steward); William Cummins (second steward); W.H. Dickenson (second engineer); Richard Lynch, Patrick Kelly, Benjamin Buckingham, John Sherlock, Patrick Rouke (firemen); John Wood, Francis Cross, Private Alfred Gentry, Private Edward Mahony (passengers).

The only other survivor was the ship's carpenter, Alexander McLean, who was picked up by the brig *Salem* en route from Le Havre to Blyth. The remaining 51 people on board the *Ondine* including the master, James Hunt, were never found.

*Ref: SIBI; HG 25.2.1860; HN 24.2.1860*

# CHRISTEL

| | |
|---|---|
| **Date:** | 2.6.1860 |
| **Wreck Location:** | Off Beachy Head |
| **Description of Vessel:** | |
| **Vessel Type -** | German sailing schooner |
| **Cargo:** | Wheat |
| **Home Port:** | Oldenburg |
| **Voyage:** | Danzig to Dublin |
| **Ship's Master:** | Tschernitz |

---

On the afternoon of Saturday 2nd June 1860 there was an horrendous south-west gale which was to catch a number of vessels out along the Channel. The *Christel* was to be one of them and the others are recorded over the following pages.

The weather earlier in the day had been slight rain showers in a very strong south-east wind which caused a number of smaller vessels to take refuge wherever they could. However, by noon the weather started to decrease and by 2pm there was total calm which lasted for two hours. The wind then started to get up again but this time from the south-west until it became a hurricane. It was in this gale when off Beachy Head that the *Christel* capsized. Fortunately for the crew the *Lively* was nearby and rescued them from the sea landing them at Deal two days later. A large amount of debris from the *Christel* was later washed up along the beach at Hastings including a chest bearing the name Wilhelm Schluter.

*Ref: SIBI; HC 6.6.1860*

# ANNE

| | |
|---|---|
| **Date:** | 2.6.1860 |
| **Wreck Location:** | Ashore east of Newhaven harbour |
| **Description of Vessel:** | |
| **Gross Tonnage -** | 250 approx. |
| **Vessel Type -** | British sailing collier brig |
| **Cargo:** | Ballast |
| **Home Port:** | Shoreham |
| **Voyage:** | Portsmouth to Newcastle-upon-Tyne |
| **Owner:** | Merrick |
| **Ship's Master:** | Merrick |
| **Number of Crew:** | 7 |

As stated on the previous page, on the afternoon of Saturday 2nd June 1860 there was an horrendous south-west gale which was to catch a number of vessels out along the Channel. The weather earlier in the day had been slight rain showers in a very strong south-east wind which caused a number of smaller vessels to take refuge wherever they could. However, by noon the weather started to decrease and by 2pm there was a total calm which lasted for two hours. The wind then started to get up again but this time from the south-west until it became a hurricane that was to last right into the following day. The vessels *Anne, Woodside* (see page 199), *Margaret* (see page 200), *Eliza Jones* (see page 201), *Jeune Henri* (see page 202), *John Whiteman* (see page 203), *Endeavor* (see page 204) and the *Wonder* (see page 205), were all to become casualties on the same stretch of shore.

The *Anne* was the first of these vessel to be driven ashore whilst at anchor trying to ride out the storm off Newhaven. At about 8pm on the Saturday evening she parted from both anchors and started to drift towards the beach, finally coming ashore to the east of the harbour entrance. All the crew got safely off the vessel with the use of the Manby's rocket apparatus by the Blatchington Coastguardsmen under the command of Lieutenant Wollaston, R.N. The last to leave the vessel was the 62 year old master who, when he reached the shore, was found to be totally exhausted. It was not long after that the vessel started to go to pieces from the action of the sea with the wreckage strewn all along the beach. Fortunately the *Anne* was insured for almost its full value with the Shoreham Shipowners Mutual Society.

The sail of another vessel could be seen a long way off making for the harbour. The vessel, which transpired to be the *Woodside,* was riding the weather and the tremendous seas quite well until she was about ½ mile/ 800m off, when an absolutely huge wave swept over her. The vessel was totally lost from sight and everybody watching feared it had been lost, but moments later the vessel righted herself and continued to make for the harbour. It was, however, obvious to those watching that the crew were not in control and it was drifting eastward before the weather. The *Woodside* finally run aground at 6.45pm with the waves continually pushing her further onto the shore.

Except the master, all the crew got safely ashore by tying a rope to their waists and being pulled through the surf by those on the beach. Unfortunately, the master was lost when instead of tying the rope around his waist that was being used to haul the crew ashore, he tied himself to a loose rope. He then jumped into the sea expecting to be hauled ashore. Edward Mewett who was ashore noticed what had occurred and dived into the raging sea in an attempt to save the man, but he was too far out for Mewett to rescue him.

Although all the rigging and superstructure of the *Woodside* was severely damaged the hull was relatively unscathed, so as soon as the tide had receded the cargo was unloaded.

Gunner Charles Leese and Mr. F.R. Tothill, Mayor of Seaford, both received awards from the National Lifeboat Institution for the parts they played in rescuing the crews from these two vessels.

The next vessel to become a casualty to this storm was the *Margaret*, and again it was driven ashore by the weather to the east of the harbour entrance. It was fortunate that the crew were quickly got off the vessel when they struck the shore, because the *Margaret* rolled over on it's side with the hull splitting into two parts; one half being embedded into the beach and the other half being carried ½ mile/800m further eastward. A strange aside to this wreck is that, although laden with coal, not one piece was washed ashore.

The schooner *Eliza Jones* was the next of these eight vessels to be driven ashore. As it came towards the shore in the huge waves, the crew could be seen in the rigging with the mate, Benjamin Thomas, on the bowsprit. He was saved from the vessel almost as soon as it struck, but it took a little longer for the others, because the master, two crew and a boy were on the weather side of the vessel, and it took nearly three hours before a line could be got to them. When the boy was finally got ashore he was suffering from exhaustion and together with the rest of the crew he was taken on board the steamship *Lyons* where they were all cared for.

The uninsured cargo of wheat was washed out of the vessel and strewn along the beach. The vessel itself was insured at Bangor.

The *Jeune Henri* was the next to come ashore and, like all the others, was trying to make for the safety of the harbour. However, due to the horrendous hurricane force winds all the vessel's sails had been torn to shreds making the vessel almost unmanageable. The result was that it drifted past the harbour entrance but as it did so, let go the anchor close to the east pier. Unfortunately the anchor would not hold in these conditions and the *Jeune Henri* continued to drift eastward until it ran aground. The vessel was pushed further and further up the beach with each wave that struck. All 15 of the crew were safely rescued. It was later found that the vessel had sustained surprisingly little damage from the ordeal.

The next vessel to be driven ashore by the hurricane this night was the *John Whiteman*. Like the others, it was running for the harbour when it not only lost all the sails but became water-logged when a huge wave broke over the vessel. In this water-logged state it was safer to run for the shore which the *John Whiteman* did close to where the others had come ashore. However, once the vessel hit the shore the sea turned it broadside on to the beach, though considering the circumstances it suffered little damage. All the crew then managed to get ashore safely.

Daylight of the following day, Sunday 3rd June, was to reveal further scenes of tragedy. All along the shore to the east of the harbour were strewn nets and other debris from the Hastings fishing lugger *Endeavour*. She had been yet another casualty of the hurricane, having come ashore at about 9pm the previous evening with the loss of the entire crew consisting of the owner/master Edward Pomphrey, his son, William White, William Sutton, Mann, Brett, and S. Spice. The destruction of the vessel was so complete that it was described as 'matchwood'. There is an even more melancholy side to this wreck in that one of the crew had only been married on Monday 21st May, just under two weeks earlier.

Daylight also revealed one further casualty, that of the *Wonder,* a collier of Hastings. All the timbers of this vessel were found absolutely smashed to pieces along a ¼ mile/400m stretch of beach. On further inspection of these timbers it was found that they were rotten, which may account for why the vessel went to pieces. Fortunately, all the crew reached the shore safely.

On Thursday 8th June 1860 two labourers, Richard Simmons and Charles Potter, appeared before Mr. H. Simpson and Mr. F.R. Tothill at Seaford Court. Mr. Tothill being the town's Mayor and involved in the rescue of the crews from the *Anne* and the *Woodside*, as mentioned above. Simmons and Potter had been charged by Police Constable Selmes with stealing from the wrecked vessels. They were convicted and sentenced to pay 19s. 0d (95p) or one months imprisonment at Lewes prison in default.

*Ref: SIBI; SNLB; SE 5.6.1860 & 12.6.1860; HC 6.6.1860; HN 8.6.2860*

# WOODSIDE

**Date:** 2.6.1860

**Wreck Location:** Ashore east of Newhaven harbour

**Description of Vessel:**
**Vessel Type -** British sailing schooner

**Cargo:** Coal

**Home Port:** Southampton

**Ship's Master:** H.G. Dench

**Number of Crew:** 3

---

See *Anne* page 195.

*Ref: SIBI; SNLB; SE 5.6.1860 & 12.6.1860; HC 6.6.1860; HN 8.6.2860*

# MARGARET

| | |
|---|---|
| **Date:** | 2.6.1860 |
| **Wreck Location:** | Ashore 1 mile/1.6km east of Newhaven harbour |
| **Description of Vessel:** | |
| **Vessel Type -** | Sailing brigantine |
| **Cargo:** | Coal |
| **Voyage:** | Shields to Poole |
| **Owner:** | Walker |
| **Ship's Master:** | Walker |

See *Anne* page 195.

*Ref: SIBI; SNLB; SE 5.6.1860 & 12.6.1860; HC 6.6.1860; HN 8.6.2860*

# ELIZA JONES

| | |
|---|---|
| **Date:** | 2.6.1860 |
| **Wreck Location:** | Ashore east of Newhaven harbour |
| **Description of Vessel:** | |
| **Vessel Type -** | British sailing schooner |
| **Cargo:** | Wheat |
| **Home Port:** | Carnarvon |
| **Voyage:** | Harwich to Dublin |
| **Ship's Master:** | James Jones |
| **Number of Crew:** | 3 and 1 boy |

See *Anne* page 195.

*Ref: SIBI; SNLB; SE 5.6.1860 & 12.6.1860; HC 6.6.1860; HN 8.6.2860*

# JEUNE HENRI

| | |
|---|---|
| **Date:** | 2.6.1860 |
| **Wreck Location:** | Ashore east of Newhaven harbour |
| **Description of Vessel:** | |
| **Vessel Type -** | French fishing *chasse maree* |
| **Home Port:** | Dieppe |
| **Number of Crew:** | 15 |

See *Anne* page 195.

*Ref: SIBI; SNLB; SE 5.6.1860 & 12.6.1860; HC 6.6.1860; HN 8.6.2860*

# JOHN WHITEMAN

| | |
|---|---|
| **Date:** | 2.6.1860 |
| **Wreck Location:** | Ashore east of Newhaven harbour |
| **Description of Vessel:** | |
| **Vessel Type -** | British sailing lugger |
| **Home Port:** | Hastings |
| **Ship's Master:** | Clark |
| **Number of Crew:** | 6 |

See *Anne* page 195.

*Ref: SIBI; SNLB; SE 5.6.1860 & 12.6.1860; HC 6.6.1860; HN 8.6.2860*

# ENDEAVOUR

| | |
|---|---|
| **Date:** | 2.6.1860 |
| **Wreck Location:** | Ashore east of Newhaven Harbour |
| **Description of Vessel:** | |
| **Vessel Type -** | British sailing lugger |
| **Home Port:** | Hastings |
| **Ship's Master:** | Edward Pomphrey |
| **Number of Crew:** | 6 |

See *Anne* page 195.

*Ref: SIBI; SNLB; SE 5.6.1860 & 12.6.1860; HC 6.6.1860; HN 8.6.2860*

# WONDER

| | |
|---|---|
| **Date:** | 2.6.1860 |
| **Wreck Location:** | Ashore east of Newhaven harbour |
| **Description of Vessel:** | |
| **Vessel Type -** | British sailing schooner |
| **Cargo:** | Coal |
| **Home Port:** | Hastings |

---

See *Anne* page 195.

*Ref: SIBI; SNLB; SE 5.6.1860 & 12.6.1860; HC 6.6.1860; HN 8.6.2860*

# MARY WYLIE

| | |
|---|---|
| **Date:** | 21.12.1860 |
| **Wreck Location:** | Off Beachy Head |
| **Description of Vessel:** | |
| **Vessel Type -** | British sailing brig |
| **Cargo:** | Roofing slates |
| **Home Port:** | Beaumaris |
| **Voyage:** | Bangor to Sunderland |
| **Date Built, Builder:** | c.1837 at Kincardine |
| **Owner:** | R. Dawber |
| **Ship's Master:** | Roberts |
| **Number of Crew:** | 6 |

The *Mary Wylie* became a wreck when in collision with the *West Indian* which was under the command of Vautier en route from London to Barbados, on Friday 21st December 1860. The result of the impact between these two vessels caused the *Mary Wylie* to sink, although all the crew were rescued by the *West Indian* and put ashore at Dover three days later. The *West Indian* suffered structural damage and the loss of anchor and cable.

*Ref: SIBI*

# LEVERET

| | |
|---|---|
| **Date:** | 00.00.1861 |
| **Wreck Location:** | Off Beachy Head |
| **Description of Vessel:** | |
| **Vessel Type -** | British fishing sailing smack |
| **Cargo:** | Oysters |
| **Home Port:** | Jersey |
| **Voyage:** | Jersey fishing and return |

Details of the date this vessel became a wreck are not known other than the year. What is known is that the vessel was laden with oysters when it was caught in a storm off Beachy Head. The *Leveret* weathered the storm for a while but eventually her rudder was ripped away which left the vessel at the mercy of the wind and sea, causing her to drift onto rocks off Beachy Head. Fortunately all the crew were safely rescued.

*Ref: SIBI; EG 28.3.1888*

# RENOVATION

| | |
|---|---|
| **Date:** | 18.3.1861 |
| **Wreck Location:** | Off Beachy Head |
| **Description of Vessel:** | |
| **Vessel Type -** | British sailing snow |
| **Cargo:** | Coal |
| **Home Port:** | North Shields |
| **Voyage:** | N. Shields to Gibraltar |
| **Date Built, Builder:** | c.1810 at Bideford |
| **Owner:** | Mary Young & Co. |
| **Ship's Master:** | J. Butler |
| **Number of Crew:** | 10 |

Information is limited as to how this vessel became a wreck other than on Monday 18th March 1861, the *Renovation,* whilst en route to Gibraltar from North Shields, was wrecked on the rocks off Beachy Head.

*Ref: SIBI; EG 28.3.1888*

# FALCON

| | |
|---|---|
| **Date:** | 30.7.1861 |
| **Wreck Location:** | Off Beachy Head |
| **Description of Vessel:** | |
| **Vessel Type -** | British sailing brig |
| **Cargo:** | Coal |
| **Home Port:** | Scarborough |
| **Voyage:** | Newcastle-upon-Tyne to Brest |
| **Ship's Master:** | Vint |

On the evening of Tuesday 30th July 1861, when off Beachy Head, the *Falcon* sprung a leak and sank. All the crew were saved.

*Ref: SIBI*

# DRUID

| | |
|---|---|
| **Date:** | 11.1.1862 |
| **Wreck Location:** | Ashore at Eastbourne |
| **Description of Vessel:** | |
| **Vessel Type -** | British sailing barque |
| **Cargo:** | Coal |
| **Home Port:** | Sunderland |
| **Voyage:** | Sunderland to Naples |
| **Number of Crew:** | 9 |

---

During a severe gale and heavy seas on Saturday 11th January 1862, the *Druid* dropped anchor in the Eastbourne Roads, flying a signal of distress. Part of the vessel's sails had been blown away and the cargo had shifted. The Royal National Lifeboat Institution's lifeboat at Eastbourne was launched and fought its way through the surf to the *Druid* coming alongside at 5pm. The crew of the *Druid* wanted to leave immediately but the vessel's master would hear none of this and kept the lifeboat alongside all night, with the crew of the lifeboat assisting with the vessel's pumps.

At about 8am the following morning, Sunday, a steam tug from Newhaven came to the assistance of the *Druid* which allowed the lifeboat to return to its station. However, the tug was eventually compelled to beach the vessel off Marine Road, Eastbourne as it was becoming so unmanageable and quickly filling with water. The lifeboat was again summoned and launched at 5pm but this time, when alongside, it took all nine crew off and brought them safely ashore.

The following Tuesday morning, 100 tons of cargo was thrown overboard to make the vessel lighter and it was not long before local men and boys were at the scene collecting the discarded coal. The steam tug from Newhaven took the *Druid* in tow again safely arriving at Newhaven harbour.

*Ref: SELB; SE 18.1.1862*

# RUBY

**Date:**                        16.4.1862

**Wreck Location:**         Newhaven Bar

**Description of Vessel:**
**Vessel Type -**             British sailing smack

**Home Port:**              Grimsby

**Voyage:**                  Grimsby fishing and return

---

This vessel became a loss when stranded on the sand bar off Newhaven Wednesday 16th April 1862.

*Ref: SIBI*

# RESIDENT VAN SAN

**Date:**                   27.5.1862

**Wreck Location:**       Ashore between Newhaven & Seaford

**Description of Vessel:**
**Vessel Type -**         Dutch sailing vessel

**Ship's Master:**         Jacob William Butner

---

There are a number of spellings of this vessel's name recorded including *President Van Son* and *Resident Von Son*.

Having become a wreck on Tuesday 27th May 1862 on the shore between Seaford and Newhaven, the vessel and its cargo were placed in the care of Capt. Knight, stationmaster and the local Lloyd's agent. He subsequently arranged for many of the articles to be removed from the vessel and stored at a warehouse owned by Richard Hoare, a local sail maker. Among the items was a cabinet that the vessel's master was taking home as a present for his wife, and valued at £50.

Two days after the vessel ran aground, Julius Ryke Vandenberg, son and secretary to the Dutch Consul at Portsmouth, attended the scene. His father was also Counsel to 14 or 15 other governments. It was during his period of attending the wreck that he said the cabinet, intended as a present for the master's wife had gone missing. The first person approached about this was Richard Hoare who denied stealing the cabinet although when the master later went to his house he found it in the back parlour.

There was subsequently a very acrimonious trial where the accused Hoare was represented by Mr. Barrow and Mr. Hawkins Q.C and the prosecution were represented by Police Sergeant Ballantine and Mr. Merrifield. Throughout the trial it was suggested that Vandenberg was only interested in getting Hoare in trouble and that the allegation was false. Eventually Hoare was found not guilty of stealing the cabinet and there was much public celebration in Newhaven on hearing of the acquittal, with flags being flown in the town and on the vessels in the harbour.

*Ref: SE 5.8.1862 & 9.8.1862*

# JEUNE ALBERT

| | |
|---|---|
| **Date:** | 17.10.1862 |
| **Wreck Location:** | Ashore near Buckle Inn, Seaford – 1½ miles/2.4km east of Newhaven harbour |
| **Description of Vessel:** | |
| **Gross Tonnage -** | 190 |
| **Vessel Type -** | French sailing brigantine |
| **Cargo:** | Zinc ore |
| **Home Port:** | Bordeaux |
| **Voyage:** | Requejada, Spain to destination not known |
| **Owner:** | George Mainard and others |
| **Ship's Master:** | George Mainard |
| **Number of Crew:** | 3 and 1 boy |

This vessel is also referred to as the *Jean Albert*.

On Friday 17th October 1862 there was a violent south-westerly storm accompanied by huge seas and torrential rain. Throughout the morning the *Jeune Albert* had been struggling against these elements which finally tore her sails to pieces, making her almost impossible to handle in these conditions. Eventually the storm drove the *Jeune Albert* ashore near the Buckle Inn, Seaford at 12.30pm.

About an hour before the vessel was driven ashore the lookout at Blatchington Coastguard Station had already seen it was in difficulty and informed the station commander, Lieutenant Wollaston R.N. He immediately gathered his men together with the Manby's rocket apparatus and set out for the shore. They arrived just before the *Jeune Albert* ran aground. A shot was soon fired with a line from the rocket apparatus across the stranded vessel. One of the coastguardsmen, Richard Mallett, was the first man into the sea with a line which he managed to get on board the vessel. The crew of five were then safely brought ashore with the assistance of the Coastguard and men from the local Royal Artillery Barracks. The crew had no time to collect any of their possessions and within an hour the wind had shifted to the north-west and by 2.30pm the vessel had completely gone to pieces.

As a result of Richard Mallett's actions he was recommended for promotion to the rank of Chief Boatman.

*Ref: SMLH; SE 21.10.1862 & 25.10.1862; HN 24.10.1862; LL 15143 18.10.62*

# WESLEYAN

| | |
|---|---|
| **Date:** | 17.10.1862 |
| **Wreck Location:** | Cuckmere Bay, 5 miles/8km off Beachy Head |
| **Description of Vessel:** | |
| **Vessel Type -** | British sailing schooner |
| **Cargo:** | Stone |
| **Home Port:** | Goole |
| **Voyage:** | Portland to London |
| **Ship's Master:** | Green |
| **Number of Passengers:** | 7 |

---

The *Wesleyan* was caught in the same storm on the morning of Friday 17th October 1862 as the *Jeune Albert* (see page 213) and coupled with having sprung a leak she was always going to have difficulties. It was early afternoon that the vessel started to sink but fortunately for all on board there were two fishing smacks, the *Wave* and the *Harlequin*, close by. By the time they reached the *Wesleyan* the passengers, which were the master's wife and his six children the youngest of which was only 6 months old, were huddled in the cabin in 3 feet/0.9m of water. The passengers and crew were safely removed from the sinking vessel, which was abandoned but only after fruitless further attempts had been made to pump the water out.

*Ref: HN 24.10.1962; LL 15144 20.10.62*

# CESTRIAN

| | |
|---|---|
| **Date:** | 31.8.1863 |
| **Wreck Location:** | Ashore east of Newhaven Harbour |
| **Description of Vessel:** | |
| **Gross Tonnage -** | 99 |
| **Vessel Type -** | British sailing schooner |
| **Cargo:** | Fertiliser/Superphosphate of lime |
| **Home Port:** | Chester |
| **Voyage:** | London to Plymouth |
| **Owner:** | Jones and others |
| **Ship's Master:** | Jones |
| **Number of Crew:** | 4 |

The schooner *Cestrian* was at 3am on Monday 31st August 1983 struggling down the Channel on a port tack against a south-westerly gale off Newhaven when a wave broke over it. The water got into the cargo of fertiliser causing it to liquefy. The master, Mr Jones, then put the vessel on a starboard tack which caused the liquefied cargo to shift across and forward in the vessel making the bow of the *Cestrian* exceptionally heavy. In this state the vessel was almost unmanageable. Mr. Jones decided that they were in a perilous state and decided that to save himself and the crew he would have to run for the shore. He managed to get the vessel to go before the wind and made a run towards Newhaven harbour. The master was aware that it was low water and also of the bar near the harbour entrance. However he believed that if he got stranded on the bar, the next high tide would lift him free and he could then get into the harbour safely.

As the *Cestrian* approached Newhaven it did in fact get stuck on the bar to the west of the harbour entrance. A small harbour boat put off and managed to get alongside her, and the master asked that they return and arrange for a steam tug to come and tow him in the moment he re-floated. The *Cestrian* remained on the bar until 9pm when the Newhaven lifeboat *Thomas Chapman* put off under the command of coxswain, E. Mewett.

This was the one and only time this lifeboat had to answer a service call in the four years it was stationed at Newhaven between 1863 and 1867.

The *Thomas Chapman* got close enough to the stranded vessel to get a line between her and the pier head. It was while they were getting a large hawser secured to effect the crew's rescue, the incoming tide started to raise the *Cestrian*, putting the line already on the vessel under tremendous strain. The inevitable result was the line snapped leaving the vessel to drift eastward. The vessel was bound to drift ashore so the lifeboat took the master and his crew off taking them into Newhaven. As the lifeboat entered the harbour it was forced against the east pier and narrowly became a casualty itself, but for the expert seamanship of the coxswain.

The *Cestrian* was driven ashore just east of the harbour and by high tide had been forced onto its starboard side with the waves slowly breaking the vessel to pieces. Capt. Knight, the local Lloyd's agent, took charge of the wreck. The cargo, of now liquified fertiliser, was totally washed out of the vessel.

*Ref: SNLB; SE 1.9.1863; LL 15410 31.8.63*

# GENERAL HAVELOCK

**Date:** 7.10.1863

**Wreck Location:** 6 miles/9.7km off Beachy Head

**Description of Vessel:**
**Gross Tonnage -** 120
**Vessel Type -** British sailing schooner

**Cargo:** Coal

**Home Port:** Portsmouth

**Voyage:** Hartlepool to Ryde

**Owner:** Messrs. Fairall, White, H. Sewell

**Ship's Master:** H. Sewell

**Number of Crew:** 4

---

The collision between this vessel and the *Nelson* (see page 220) took place at about midnight on Wednesday 6th /Tuesday 7th October 1863. It was a very stormy night and after the impact both crews abandoned their respective vessels and took to one of the boats of the *General Havelock*. The two crews in their small boat stayed in the area for a short time before rowing towards Eastbourne where they came ashore at Seaside.

After the two crews had left, a London barge and a smack came across the *General Havelock* drifting off Eastbourne without a crew. They took the vessel in tow to Newhaven where it was found she was little damaged. However the same could not be said for the *Nelson* because this vessel sank as a result of the collision impact.

Once ashore at Eastbourne, the two crews sought assistance from Mr. S. Hall, the local honorary agent of the Shipwrecked Mariners Society. He arranged for the *General Havelock* crew to travel to Newhaven to rejoin their vessel, and for the crew of the *Nelson* to get to Portsmouth, by courtesy of the local railway company. The *General Havelock* finally left

Newhaven on Thursday 9<sup>th</sup> October for its home port of Portsmouth.

A sum of £150 was awarded as salvage to the vessels that took the *General Havelock* in tow.

*Ref: SIBI; CNMM; SE 10.10.1863; HC 14.10.1863; LL 15444 9.10.63*

# NELSON

**Date:**       7.10.1863

**Wreck Location:**    6 miles/9.7km off Beachy Head

**Description of Vessel:**
**Gross Tonnage -**    160
**Vessel Type -**     British sailing brigantine

**Cargo:**      Pipe clay, mail

**Home Port:**     Bridport

**Voyage:**      Poole to London

**Date Built, Builder:**  c.1825 at Cork

**Owner:**      Jacob Simes

**Ship's Master:**    Jacob Simes

**Number of Crew:**   5

---

See the *General Havelock* page 218.

*Ref: SIBI; CNMM; SE 10.10.1863; HC 14.10.1863*

# ARTHUR LEARY

| | |
|---|---|
| **Date:** | 8.11.1863 |
| **Wreck Location:** | Ashore near Martello Tower, Seaford |
| **Description of Vessel:** | |
| **Vessel Type -** | British sailing vessel |
| **Cargo:** | Coal and general |
| **Home Port:** | London |
| **Voyage:** | London to Gibraltar via Lisbon |
| **Ship's Master:** | William Charles Owen |
| **Number of Crew:** | 7 |
| **Number of Passengers:** | 4 |

---

This vessel left Gravesend on Sunday 1st November 1863 under the vessel's master, Collinridge, reaching the Downs two days later. It was here for some unknown reason that Collinridge left the vessel in the care of the vessel's mate, William Charles Owen. Before leaving, Collinridge gave written instructions as to how to get to Lisbon and told Owen that he would rejoin the vessel there.

The *Arthur Leary* left the Downs the following Friday in hazy conditions and with a moderate north-westerly breeze and made down the Channel. Almost as soon as Collinridge had left the vessel, Owen got drunk and remained more or less in this condition throughout the voyage until the vessel ran aground on the Sunday, leaving it in the charge of John Bigmore.

John Bigmore was only 20 years of age and had joined the vessel as boatswain. However, he only had 3 years experience at sea and no navigation certificate or certificate to allow him to be in charge of such a vessel.

At 2pm on Sunday 8th November, when off Newhaven, the passengers on board pleaded with Bigmore to put in at the port and report Owen's behaviour to the vessel's owner. Bigmore agreed to this and when the vessel was anchored off Newhaven, the local coastguardsmen came aboard to assist. No sooner were they aboard than the anchor chain snapped and the vessel was driven ashore. All those on board were safely got off, but by the following Thursday the vessel had gone completely to pieces.

The tons of coal that were the vessel's cargo were washed all along the foreshore which was readily collected by the local people in readiness for the winter.

*Ref: SIBI; SE 14.11.1863*

# MI MI

| | |
|---|---|
| **Date:** | 12.2.1864 |
| **Wreck Location:** | Ashore near Langney Point |
| **Description of Vessel:** | |
| **Vessel Type -** | Danish sailing fishing smack |
| **Home Port:** | Flensburgh (possibly) |
| **Owner:** | H.H. Peterson (part owner) |
| **Ship's Master:** | H.H. Peterson |
| **Number of Crew:** | 6 |

This Danish fishing smack had earlier put into Newhaven and taken on board two local men to help the vessel's Danish crew fish the local oyster beds. It was while they were out fishing that the *Mi Mi* was to become a complete wreck. The vessel had previously been used to transport timber but lately had turned to oyster fishing, mainly off the French coast.

At 6pm on Thursday 11th February 1864 the vessel was anchored off Eastbourne to commence work but by 11.30pm a fierce southerly gale had blown up with driving rain. It was decided to up anchor but in the process the chain broke so the *Mi Mi* sailed further out to sea to prevent being blown ashore. This was successful until 5am the following morning, when the weather worsened. Although the crew could just see the lights of Eastbourne through the weather it was 30 minutes later that the vessel ran aground near Langney Point. It was not until then that they realised they were so close to land. Fortunately the crew and the stores were saved before the vessel became a complete wreck at the hands of the violent waves on the shore.

*Ref: EG 17.2.1864*

# BRECHIN

| | |
|---|---|
| **Date:** | 16.2.1864 |
| **Wreck Location:** | Ashore at Seaford Head |
| **Description of Vessel:** | |
| **Vessel Type -** | British sailing brigantine |
| **Cargo:** | Coal |
| **Home Port:** | Whitby |
| **Voyage:** | Llanelly to London |

---

This vessel is also referred to as the *Brechin Castle* or *Breckin Castle*.

This vessel came ashore in thick fog at about midnight on 16th/17th February 1864 in a strong south-westerly wind near the cliff at Seaford. However, when rescuers arrived they found that the vessel had been abandoned except for two dogs. It later transpired that the crew had been taken off and landed at Dover.

On the following tide the vessel was smashed to pieces.

*Ref: SS; LL 15552 13.2.64; LL 15553 15.2.64*

# FLENSBURG

**Date:**                                    12.11.1864

**Wreck Location:**                 Ashore near Beachy Head

**Description of Vessel:**
**Vessel Type -**                      Danish sailing barque

---

This vessel is also referred to as the *Frensberg*.

On Saturday 12th November 1964 the *Flensburg* was in too close to shore in a prevailing gale and as a result ran aground near Beachy Head.

*Ref: SIBI; EG 28.3.1888*

# WAVE

| | |
|---|---|
| **Date vessel sank:** | 27.1.1867 |
| **Wreck Location:** | Ashore 3 miles/4.8km east of Seaford |
| **Description of Vessel:** | |
| **Gross Tonnage -** | 431 |
| **Length -** | 124ft/37.94m |
| **Beam -** | 28ft/8.44m |
| **Vessel Type -** | British sailing barque |
| **Cargo:** | Barley, peas |
| **Home Port:** | South Shields |
| **Voyage:** | New York to London |
| **Date Built & Builder:** | c.1869 by Pickersgill at Sunderland |
| **Owner:** | G. Lawson & Son |
| **Ship's Master:** | Henry Henderson |

The cause of this vessel becoming a wreck was the master's incorrect belief that his compass showed a half point error to the south.

The *Wave* left New York on Wednesday 19th December 1866 having a fairly uneventful return voyage, arriving off the Lizard on Friday 25th January 1867. It was here that Henry Henderson, the master, took a bearing of the Pole Star and in his calculations took into account his believe in the half point error in his compass. As a result of that he steered a course further north than was usual up the Channel. The inevitable result of this error was that in the south-westerly gale and heavy seas that prevailed in the early hours of Sunday 27th January, the *Wave* ran aground 3 miles/4.8km east of Seaford near the Crowlink Coastguard Station. All the crew were safely got ashore.

At 12 noon the same day the steam tugs *Victoria* of Newhaven and the

*City of London* of London, attended the scene with the intention of trying to pull the vessel free. Having surveyed the scene on their arrival they decided not to make an attempt to get her off. However, the cargo was removed by hauling it up the cliff and loading it into carts to be carried to Newhaven.

A week or so later the wreck was still in this same position when, at 7.45pm on Wednesday 6th February, three Police Constables, Gladman, Creasy and Cox, were on duty near the site of the wreck. They saw James Robinson, a coastguardsman, walking up the cliff towards them from the direction of the wreck. The Officers asked Robinson what he was doing and he replied that he had lost his cap. P.C. Gladman was not happy with his explanation and followed Robinson up the cliff and in the light of his lamp, saw him throw down a quantity of copper, which had come from the wreck. Robinson was detained and when they searched his home the Officers found more copper from the wreck with a total weight of 62½lbs/ 28.4kg.

*Ref: SIBI; SE 29.1.1867; EC 9.2.1867*

# SOUVENEER VANSWICTON

| | |
|---|---|
| **Date:** | 2.2.1867 |
| **Wreck Location:** | Ashore at Beachy Head |
| **Description of Vessel:** | |
| **Gross Tonnage -** | 340 |
| **Vessel Type -** | Dutch sailing brig |
| **Cargo:** | Hides, tallow, wool |
| **Home Port:** | Rotterdam |
| **Voyage:** | Buenos Aires to Antwerp |
| **Ship's Master:** | Singer |
| **Number of Crew:** | 13 |

This vessel is also referred to as the *Governor Nan Swieten* and *Gouverneur Van Swieten*.

The *Souveneer Vanswicton* left Corvo in the Azores about seven days prior to the vessel becoming a wreck.

It was at low tide at 4am on Saturday 2nd February 1867 and in very thick fog, that the *Souveneer Vanswicton* ran ashore on the rocks off Beachy Head known as 'The Ledge'. It was not until the vessel struck the rocks that the crew were aware of how close to the shore they were. As the tide came in it pushed the vessel further onto the rocks, but the crew managed to get off the vessel safely in their boat. Once ashore the crew were taken care of by Mr. S. Hall, the honorary agent of the Shipwrecked Mariners Society, who provided them with a free pass to London on the railway. The London and Brighton Railway Company, like many other railway companies, allowed shipwrecked crew to return to their home towns free of charge. However, one of their number was very ill and when examined by Mr. Colgate, the medical officer of the Eastbourne Union, was found to be suffering from bronchitis and was detained in hospital.

On the following Monday's high tide the vessel broke up completely and the cargo washed out of the vessel. The wool literally covered the beach, although a lot of it was still in bales. During Monday afternoon there was considerable activity on the beach by men with horses collecting up the wool and hides and hauling it to the foot of the cliffs. Notices were put up warning those collecting the cargo that it must be taken to Mr. Henderson at the Coastguard Station at Seaside, Eastbourne, where they would receive salvage.

The remains of the vessel's hull, spars and rigging, which were littered along the beach, were sold on the Tuesday to Mr. Fidler and Mr. G. Adams, on the condition that all such parts that lay on the beach between the vessel and Langney Point were included in the price of £67. These same two men also bought the anchors and cables for a further £27.

The recovered cargo was sold by auction a week later on Wednesday 13th February at Diplocks Assembly Rooms in Eastbourne. There were 161 lots consisting of 200 bales of Argentine wool averaging ½ ton/508kg each, 30 casks of tallow, 350 ox and cow hides, and 417 goat hides. When the sale got under way the prices for the wool ranged between 3½d to 7½d per pound (approximately 1p to 3p per ½kg). The hides fetched an average price of 12s./60p with the majority of them being purchased by Messrs. Lamb, Wanklin and Co. of London. The tallow being sold at average price of 4d per pound (approximately 1½p per ½kg). It was said that the vessel's Underwriters were very pleased with results of the sale.

*Ref: HC 6.2.1867; EC 9.2.1867 & 16.2.1867; SE 9.2.1867*

# DILIGENCE

| | |
|---|---|
| **Date:** | 24.1.1868 |
| **Wreck Location:** | Ashore at Seaside, Eastbourne |
| **Description of Vessel:** **Vessel Type -** | British sailing sloop |
| **Cargo:** | Cement |
| **Home Port:** | Cowes |

On Friday 24th January 1868, the *Diligence* was on the beach at Seaside, Eastbourne discharging its cargo of cement which was required for the building of the nearby Cavendish Hotel. As was the case with all vessels that discharged their cargo on the beach, they had to wait for the next high tide to get off again. However, before the *Diligence* could get to sea a severe southerly gale blew up while she was still on the beach. As the tide rose in the gale it soon turned the vessel broadside to the sea and quickly filled with water causing considerable damage to the hull.

As the vessel was old no attempt was made to salvage it. Fortunately all the crew got safely ashore.

*Ref: SE 28.1.1868*

# ALBION

| | |
|---|---|
| **Date:** | 22.8.1868 |
| **Wreck Location:** | 4 miles/6.4km south-east of Eastbourne |
| **Description of Vessel:** | |
| **Vessel Type -** | British sailing brig |
| **Cargo:** | Coal |
| **Date Built, Builder:** | c.1816 |
| **Ship's Master:** | |
| **Number of Crew:** | 7 |
| **Number of Passengers:** | 3 |

The afternoon high tide on Saturday 22nd August 1868 was one of the particularly high tides of the year and accompanied by a severe south-westerly gale. Due to the time of year there were many visitors in the town of Eastbourne who were to witness a terrible sight.

At 2pm the *Albion,* which was under tow from a steamer, was off Eastbourne struggling with the horrendous sea and weather conditions. The passengers on board were the master's wife and two children. One of the *Albion's* masts had already fallen down and this, together with other damage sustained earlier, had made the vessel leak, making it unmanageable. Suddenly the tow line between the two vessels parted leaving the *Albion* at the mercy of the sea. It drifted to off the town pier where in view of the gathered visitors the vessel sank with the loss of all those on board except one of the crew who was rescued by a steamer.

There were two theories as to what caused the tow line to part. One was that it broke under the strain of towing a leaking vessel, and the other was that the master of the steamer cut the rope to save his own vessel and crew.

*Ref: SIBI; EG 26.8.1868*

# GARIBALDI

| | |
|---|---|
| **Date:** | 12.2.1869 |
| **Wreck Location:** | Ashore 880yds/804m west of Beachy Head |
| **Description of Vessel:** | |
| **Gross Tonnage -** | 147 |
| **Length -** | 85ft/26.39m |
| **Beam -** | 21ft/6.45m |
| **Vessel Type -** | British sailing schooner |
| **Cargo:** | Coal |
| **Home Port:** | Colchester |
| **Voyage:** | Swansea to London |
| **Owner:** | Harvey |
| **Ship's Master:** | D. Harvey |
| **Number of Crew:** | 3 and 2 boys |

By Friday 12th February 1869 the *Garibaldi* had been at sea for three months on its voyage from Swansea with its coal intended for London, having encountered terrible conditions en route. At 5.15am in fog and drizzling rain the *Garibaldi* ran aground on a ledge of rocks between the Belle Tout Lighthouse and Beachy Head. The crew did not realise exactly where they were due to the darkness and not being able to see the Belle Tout Lighthouse due to the poor visibility. At the time the master, who was a cousin of the owner, was at the wheel. The impact was so sudden and unexpected that he was thrown forward with such force that he sustained considerable bruising.

The instant the *Garibaldi* ran aground the rudder was carried away and the crew realised that they had to abandon the vessel as soon as possible. Fortunately for them the tide was low, enabling them to get ashore safely in their jolly-boat. However, this was not without its problems because before getting ashore two planks of the jolly-boat were stove in and several inches of water taken in.

As the tide rose the actions of the waves smashed this very old vessel to pieces and by 9.30am it's planking and timbers were drifting past Eastbourne. Nothing of the cargo or other items on board were saved.

The crew, consisting of the master, mate, two seamen and two boys, were cared for by Mr. S. Hall, the local agent of the Shipwrecked Mariners Society, who arranged for them to have a free pass to London on the railway.

*Ref: SIBI; SWA 16.2.1869; ES 16.2.1869; EG 17.2.1869; HC 17.2.1869*

# DIAMOND

| | |
|---|---|
| **Date:** | 11.9.1869 |
| **Wreck Location:** | Off Newhaven |
| **Description of Vessel:** | |
| **Gross Tonnage -** | 220 |
| **Length -** | 86ft/26.26m |
| **Beam -** | 21ft/6.27m |
| **Vessel Type -** | British sailing brig |
| **Home Port:** | London |
| **Voyage:** | Shields to Portsmouth |
| **Date Built, Builder:** | c.1828 at Hastings |
| **Owner:** | T. Elkin |
| **Number of Crew:** | 8 |

This vessel sank with the loss of all those on board.

*Ref: SIBI*

# COUNTESS OF LEICESTER

**Date:** 11.9.1869

**Wreck Location:** Off Beachy Head

**Description of Vessel:**
**Gross Tonnage -** 172
**Length -** 80ft/24.38m
**Beam -** 21ft/6.45m
**Vessel Type -** British sailing brig

**Cargo:** Stone

**Home Port:** Guernsey

**Voyage:** Guernsey to London

**Date Built, Builder:** c.1874 at Wells-next-the-Sea, Norfolk

**Ship's Master:** J. Gearing

**Number of Crew:** 6

---

On Saturday 11th September 1869, when off Beachy Head, the *Countess of Leicester* sank having developed a leak in a southerly force 9 gale.

*Ref: SIBI*

# ONEIDA

| | |
|---|---|
| **Date:** | 12.9.1869 |
| **Wreck Location:** | Ashore 300yds/275metres west of Langney Point |

**Description of Vessel:**

| | |
|---|---|
| **Gross Tonnage -** | 200 |
| **Length -** | 102ft/31.24m |
| **Beam -** | 24ft/7.46m |
| **Vessel Type -** | British sailing brig |
| **Cargo:** | 360 tons of iron railway track |
| **Home Port:** | Aberystwyth |
| **Voyage:** | Hull to Trieste |
| **Date Built, Builder:** | c.1866 by Douse at Prince Edward Island, Nova Scotia |
| **Ship's Master:** | Edward Morris |
| **Number of Crew:** | 5 and 1 boy |

The *Oneida* left Hull on Monday 6th September 1869 with its cargo of iron railway track from the Parkgate Iron Company and was off Beachy Head by Thursday of the same week. However the vessel returned to just off Dungeness and remained there until Saturday afternoon when the *Oneida* once again set off down the Channel in a tremendous south-westerly gale, believed to be a hurricane. By 2am the following morning, Sunday 12th September, the wind was to continue to increase in strength, although the weather was very clear.

After about 2 hours the vessel was off Eastbourne in a gale that had continuously increased in strength throughout this time and in mountainous seas. As the strength of the gale increased it slowly ripped the sails to pieces until they were totally destroyed. The *Oneida* would not now respond to the mate, David Davies, who was at the helm, making the vessel totally unmanageable.

The crew, realising that they were in serious difficulties, took to the rigging. The master and the one of the crew, believed to be the cook, climbed into the fore-rigging while the four remaining crew, David Davies, Richard Wells, Peter McMaster and George Carter, took to the main rigging, except for the cabin boy. He was very ill and had been below throughout and was never seen again.

The vessel, being totally at the mercy of the gale and high seas, was soon driven ashore to the west of Langney Point stern first. The violence with which the vessel struck, coupled with the effects of the huge seas, threw the master and the cook, John 'Jack' Nicholson, who were in the fore-rigging, into the sea and they drowned. Similarly, the four remaining crew in the main rigging were tossed into the sea, except they were fortunate enough to be thrown towards the shore and managed to get through the surf safely. Having reached the shore they made their way to Eastbourne where Mr. S. Hall, the local agent of the Shipwrecked Mariners Society, provided them with clothing and food together with a free rail pass to London. However, the mate stayed on and attended the subsequent Inquests. As soon as the vessel was driven aground the heavy seas turned it broadside to the shore and within 30 minutes the *Oneida* broke up.

At 6.30am the same day the body of the cook, John Nicholson, who was only known as Jack, was found on the beach at Pevensey by Samuel Olive a local fisherman. The body was laying face down and about 2 to 3 miles/3.2 to 4.8km from the wreck. The Inquest was held that afternoon at Wallsend before the High Bailiff of Pevensey Mr. W. Adams, acting as the Coroner. However, because the main witness, the mate David Davies had already travelled to Hastings to attend another Inquest, it was adjourned to 6pm the following day. On that day Davies told the hearing what had happened to the vessel and that the cook who was 21 years of age, came from Howth near Dublin, and had been with the *Oneida* for about three weeks, having joined the vessel in Hull.

At 6.15pm on the Sunday, the body of Edward Morris, the master, was found washed ashore at Marina, St. Leonards by Edward Gillam a blacksmith of 4 Old Market, St. Leonards. The Inquest was held the following day at the Fountain Inn, Bo-Peep, St. Leonards before the Hastings Borough Coroner Mr. F. Ticehurst. There were three witnesses, the first being David Davies who identified the deceased as the master of the *Oneida*, followed by Edward Gillam. The third and final witness was Police Sergeant Raymond who said that he had assisted in removing the body to the Fountain Inn and when he searched it found 17s. 2d. (85p approx.), a pocket handkerchief and a key. He also told the Inquest that the clothes were marked 'E.M.' The Inquest Jury returned a verdict of 'Found Drowned'. At the completion of the hearing the body was placed in a coffin and returned to his home town of Aberystwyth by rail.

On Tuesday 14th September the remains of the wreck were sold at auction by Mr. J.C. Towner at Eastbourne and realised the price of £64. It was hoped that the cargo of railway track would be salvaged and be sold on behalf of the underwriters.

*Ref: SIBI; SWA 14.9.1869; EG 15.9.1869; HN 17.9.1869; EC 18.9.1869; HO 18.9.1869*

# MYRTLE

| | |
|---|---|
| **Date:** | 5.12.1869 |
| **Wreck Location:** | Newhaven Harbour |
| **Description of Vessel:** | |
| **Vessel Type -** | British sailing vessel |
| **Cargo:** | Stone |
| **Home Port:** | Weymouth |
| **Voyage:** | From unknown port to London |
| **Owner:** | Name not known, but is known to also be the master |

---

At 3am on Sunday 5th December 1869, the *Hope* of Portsmouth, under the command of James Dyer, came across the crew of the *Myrtle* in a small boat. They had decided to leave their vessel, despite their exhaustive efforts with the pumps, when they found that they were losing the battle against the rising water level after the *Myrtle* sprung a leak.

Having taken the crew on board, the *Hope* went in search of the *Myrtle* which was found and brought safely into Newhaven harbour. James Dyer received £60 for the salvage of the *Myrtle*.

*Ref: EC 11.12.1869*

# SERAPHINA

| | |
|---|---|
| **Date:** | 16.12.1869 |
| **Wreck Location:** | Ashore between the Martello Tower and cliff at Seaford. |

**Description of Vessel:**

| | |
|---|---|
| **Gross Tonnage -** | 241 |
| **Length -** | 96ft/29.59m |
| **Beam -** | 26ft/7.89m |
| **Vessel Type -** | British sailing brig |
| **Cargo:** | Stone |
| **Home Port:** | Sunderland |
| **Voyage:** | Caen to Swansea |
| **Date Built, Builder:** | c.1859 Lister, Sunderland |
| **Owner:** | J. Hastie |
| **Ship's Master:** | Langris |
| **Number of Crew:** | 7 and a boy |

---

There are a number of things that have been differently reported in respect of this vessel. The first being the name, which has also been said to be *Seraphine* or *Seraphim*. The second thing was doubt as to whether the vessel was in ballast or carrying stone. The third and final difference was the confusion as to whether the vessel's home port was Sunderland or Marseilles. However, this may well have been fuelled by the fact that the vessel had a French crew, consisting of the master Langris, the mate Runguard, and crew Octamori, Silvade, Forriere, Romani, Locture, Maran and a boy whose name is not known (though it is known he came from a respectable family near Caen).

The morning of Thursday 16th December 1869 started pleasantly enough with a calm sea until about noon when the wind began to freshen. As the afternoon progressed the wind increased considerably and by 7.30pm it was gale force with driving rain and huge seas. In these conditions, off Seaford, was the *Seraphina* attempting to make for the safety of Newhaven harbour. However, as it approached, the conditions made the vessel almost unmanageable, driving it past the mouth of the harbour and ashore to the east. The state of the tide and the ferocious sea pushed the vessel more than halfway up the beach.

Prior to the vessel going ashore a local fisherman, George Green, had seen the difficulties the *Seraphina* was experiencing and feared that the vessel would in fact be driven ashore. As a result he raised the alarm and many people from Seaford, who lived nearby, were soon on the scene. It was fortunate that there was a bright moon despite the weather, since this enabled those ashore to see the predicament of the crew. However, due to the condition of the sea none of those present was able to get close enough to the vessel to help the crew.

Richard Mallett, a chief boatman with the coastguard stationed at Blatchington arrived, and by chance had a small boathouse close-by which he used as a store for fishing gear. Mallett soon had a quantity of rope from his boathouse and had tied one end of the rope around his waist. He then went into the raging surf, with the other end of the rope being held by those ashore. He took a line with him which he managed to throw onto the vessel and then remained in the sea close to the hull to help the crew. Then, one by one, the crew used this line to get themselves ashore. It then came the turn of the boy who had only been at sea a few days, this being his maiden voyage. As he made his way along the line, hand-over-hand like the rest of the crew, he suddenly lost his grip among the surf. At the same time as he lost his grip a large wave came round the stern of the vessel and carried the boy away before Mallett could do anything about it. The boy was seen to throw his arms into the air two or three times and then seen no more. He was to be the only loss of life from the *Seraphina*.

The rescued crew were taken to the New Inn Hotel where the owner, Mrs. Simpson, gave them dry clothing before they were taken care of by Mr. Walter Towner, the secretary of the local Shipwrecked Mariners Society. The crew had lost everything they possessed including a box containing 3,000 francs in bank notes belonging to the master. Mr. P. Black, the vice consul at Brighton, and Mr. Dolan, the Receiver of Wrecks at Newhaven, arranged for the crew, with the exception of the master, to be taken to Newhaven on Saturday 18th December, where they boarded a vessel bound for France. The following day what remained of the vessel was sold at auction by Messrs. Verrall & Son of Lewes.

For Richard Mallett's endeavours in the rescue of this crew he was awarded the Royal Humane Society's bronze medal and a gold medal first class by the French Government. He was also presented with a watch and chain paid for from a collection locally supervised by Mr. Henry Blyth. The balance of the collection, which amounted to £8.7s.11½d (£8.38p), was distributed among the others that were on shore that night and who assisted Mallett in the rescue.

*Ref: SIBI; SS; SE 21.12.1869; SWA 21.12.1869; EC 25.12.1869*

# ELLEN RADFORD

| | |
|---|---|
| **Date:** | 20.12.1869 |
| **Wreck Location:** | 6 miles/9.7km south-east of Beachy Head and lies with its head south east x east |

**Description of Vessel:**

| | |
|---|---|
| Gross Tonnage - | 318 |
| Length - | 135ft/41.25m |
| Beam - | 24ft/7.37m |
| Vessel Type - | British sailing Barque |

| | |
|---|---|
| **Cargo:** | Saltpetre |
| **Home Port:** | Liverpool |
| **Voyage:** | Mexillones to Newcastle-upon-Tyne |
| **Date Built, Builder:** | c.1855 at Shaldon |
| **Owner:** | Radford |
| **Ship's Master:** | J. Evans |
| **Number of Crew:** | 10 |

---

The *Ellen Radford* left Queenstown on Friday 17th December 1869 for Newcastle under the command of the master, J. Evans and his crew of 10. At about 9.30pm the following Monday, when the vessel was off Beachy Head, it was in collision with another vessel in a south-westerly force 6 wind. Although the name of the other vessel is not known it is believed to be a steamer as soon after the collision one was seen nearby.

At the moment of impact the sole survivor, Charles B. Howard, was asleep in his berth. The noise of the collision woke him up and he ran up on deck to see a full-rigged vessel under the bows of the *Ellen Radford*. The *Ellen Radford* instantly started to sink, bow first, and within five minutes had completely submerged. This was not enough time for the crew to get the boat off. It would seem that as the vessel went down Howard went down with it because the next thing he was aware of was floating in the sea, alone, clinging to part of the rigging debris.

At 8am the following morning, about 10½ hours after the collision, the *Falmouth,* a Dockyard Lighter, found Howard alive and totally exhausted, still clinging to a part of the rigging. He was taken on board and by the time the *Falmouth* arrived in Portsmouth the next day he had recovered considerably from his ordeal.

Charles B. Howard from Cork, was the only survivor from the total vessel's complement of 11 men. Those who died were the master, Evans from Cheshire; the mate Lewis from Liskeard; the quartermaster McLean from Shields; the cook Hall from Yarmouth; the carpenter William Bontron from Dysart; and seamen John Sowely from Kirkcaldy, Henry Johnson whose home town was not known, Thomas Prendergast from New Ross, Benjamin S. Tait from Dublin and Edward Pisk also from Dublin.

On Wednesday 29th December Reuben Wood, an Eastbourne boatman, together with some friends, set off to try and trace the wreck *Ellen Radford.* Their search was successful, finding one of the vessel's mast and sail sticking out above the level of the sea. The vessel was laying with her bow towards the south-east. Mr. Wood subsequently informed Lloyds of the whereabouts of the vessel as a warning to other shipping as it was clearly a hazard.

*Ref: SIBI; HO 25.12.1869; EG 5.1.1870; LL 17381 30.12.69*

# YOUNG LOUISA

| | |
|---|---|
| **Date:** | 30.12.1869 |
| **Wreck Location:** | Ashore near Cuckmere Coastguard Station |
| **Description of Vessel:** | |
| **Vessel Type -** | British sailing brigantine |
| **Cargo:** | Stone |
| **Home Port:** | Jersey |
| **Voyage:** | Chatham to unknown destination |
| **Ship's Master:** | Jasper |

During the early part of Thursday 30th December 1869, the *Young Louisa* encountered a severe gale whilst in the Channel which resulted in the vessel being dismasted. As the storm subsided the vessel drifted and eventually came ashore on rocks near the Cuckmere Coastguard Station at 10pm that same day. Fortunately at the time of running aground there was a very slight sea which enabled the crew to remain aboard until daylight the following morning, when all the crew got safely ashore together with their possessions.

Due to the heavy cargo of stone the vessel soon filled with water becoming a complete wreck.

*Ref: EG 5.1.1870; EC 8.1.1870*

# ELIZA

| | |
|---|---|
| **Date:** | 5.1.1870 |
| **Wreck Location:** | Off Newhaven |
| **Description of Vessel:** | |
| **Length -** | 46ft/14.19m |
| **Beam -** | 13ft/3.86m |
| **Vessel Type -** | British sailing cutter |
| **Home Port:** | Shoreham |
| **Date Built, Builder:** | c.1852 at Cherbourg |
| **Owner:** | J & H Stilling, Shoreham |

The *Eliza* became a loss when off Newhaven on Wednesday 5th January 1870.

*Ref: SIBI*

# AUGUSTE STRALSUND

**Date:**                                  22.2.1870

**Wreck Location:**              Off Eastbourne

**Description of Vessel:**
**Vessel Type -**                    Prussian sailing vessel

**Voyage:**                            From unknown port to Leith

---

This vessel sank in the Channel on Tuesday 22<sup>nd</sup> February 1870 with only three of the Prussian crew surviving. They were picked up and taken to Eastbourne.

*Ref: SIBI; EG 28.3.1888*

# CHARLTON

| | |
|---|---|
| **Date:** | 16.1.1871 |
| **Wreck Location:** | Ashore east of Newhaven harbour |
| **Description of Vessel:** | |
| **Gross Tonnage -** | 500 approx. |
| **Vessel Type -** | British iron steamship |
| **Cargo:** | Sugar, biscuits |
| **Home Port:** | Sunderland |
| **Voyage:** | London to St. Nazaire, France |
| **Date Built, Builder:** | c.1869 |
| **Number of Crew:** | 27 |

During the night of Sunday 15th/Monday 16th January 1871 the *Charlton* was caught in a severe gale that swept along the Sussex coast. The vessel encountered her first problem during the Sunday night when she was off the Owers Light, near Selsey Bill. The gale was so severe that the steamship was having extreme difficulty coping with it and so decided that, with the assistance of both sail and steam, it would try and keep up wind. However, such was the ferocity of the wind that the sails were ripped to shreds. The ever-increasing seas started to break over the vessel and managed to get into the engine room and extinguish two of the engine boiler fires.

This now left the vessel at the mercy of the storm. All the master could do was to drop the anchors and hope the cables would hold in these conditions, but alas that was not to be the case, because the cables snapped under the strain. The vessel was now drifting and the master did all that he could to try and make for Newhaven harbour. Meanwhile, the crew were working up to their waists in water in the engine room trying to keep as much steam as possible but it was insufficient and the vessel continued to drift slowly eastward.

At 6.15am on the Monday, with the tide ebbing, the *Charlton* finally ran aground to the east of Newhaven harbour pier, bumping along the sea-bed until it came to rest, with the waves constantly sweeping over the vessel. Once the *Charlton* grounded the crew set about securing the cargo and removing the rigging to make the vessel as stable as possible.

The local coastguard had been made aware of the vessel's predicament and were on the beach very quickly, together with the local Lloyds agent, Captain Knight. Using the Manby's rocket apparatus, the coastguard soon had a line on the *Charlton*. This enabled three of the crew to get off the vessel but the remainder, although being constantly battered by the sea, decided to remain on board as the beach was reasonably sheltered.

The ebbing tide left the *Charlton* broadside to the sea but high and dry, which allowed all the remaining crew onboard to get safely ashore. A later inspection of the hull found it to be little damaged and it was hoped that steam tugs from London would be able to tow the vessel off.

*Ref: CNMM; HO 21.1.1871; LL 17707 17.1.71*

# UNNAMED

| | |
|---|---|
| **Date:** | 1.4.1871 |
| **Wreck Location:** | 2-3 miles/3.2-4.8km off Eastbourne |
| **Description of Vessel:** | |
| **Length -** | 19ft 6ins/6m |
| **Beam -** | 6ft 6ins/2.02m |
| **Vessel Type -** | British sailing oyster fishing vessel |
| **Cargo:** | Oysters |
| **Home Port:** | Eastbourne |
| **Voyage:** | Eastbourne fishing and return |
| **Ship's Master:** | George Henry Manser |
| **Number of Crew:** | 1 |

---

At 7am on Saturday 1st April 1871 George Henry Manser, a 31 year old fisherman from Eastbourne, went fishing for oysters in his boat, together with Dennis Breach. Manser had been accustomed to the sea for most of his life, not only as a local fisherman but from being an Able Seaman in the Royal Navy for 10 years, (he had been discharged due to deafness).

The two men sailed about 2-3 miles/3.2-4.8km off Eastbourne and started dredging for oysters. They were not alone as there were about 5 or 6 other boats in the same area. During the course of the dredging, Breach suggested to Manser that he slacken the foresheet, and as he was in the process of doing this a gust of wind caught the sail and the vessel heeled over. It sank immediately, stern first in 8 to 9 fathoms/14.5 to 16.5m of water. At the time the vessel had a foresail, mizzen and jib sail up, which was not considered to be excessive in the prevailing conditions.

As soon as the vessel heeled over both of the crew were thrown into the water but fortunately for Dennis Breach, Joseph Huggett, who was in one of the other boats and about 200yds/182m away, had seen what had happened. He made his way towards the sunken vessel and managed to rescue Breach but was unable to save Manser, whose body was recovered later.

The Inquest into Manser's death was held on Tuesday 4th April at the Victoria Inn, before the Coroner Mr. L.G. Fullagar and a jury, who heard evidence from both Breach and Huggett. The only other person to give evidence was Robert Colegate, a surgeon, who said that he had made a post-mortem examination of the deceased and from this there could be no doubt George Henry Manser died from drowning. The jury returned an appropriate verdict.

*Ref: SE 8.4.1871*

# OSPREY

| | |
|---|---|
| **Date:** | 13.1.1872 |
| **Wreck Location:** | Ashore on Sandacre shoal between Beachy Head and Eastbourne |
| **Description of Vessel:** | |
| **Length -** | 99ft/30.35m |
| **Beam -** | 22ft/6.65m |
| **Vessel Type -** | British sailing schooner |
| **Cargo:** | 270 tons of coal |
| **Home Port:** | Ipswich |
| **Voyage:** | Sunderland to Poole |
| **Date Built, Builder:** | c.1861 by Read at Ipswich |
| **Owner:** | Mann, Brackenbury & Co., Kirby near Colchester |
| **Ship's Master:** | William Jennings |
| **Number of Crew:** | 6 |

---

On New Years Day 1872, the *Osprey* left Sunderland with her cargo of 270 tons of coal, the property of J. Brackenbury & Co., of Kirby near Colchester. The vessel was bound for Poole and on Saturday 13th January encountered a very strong gale in foggy and rainy conditions off Eastbourne. The master, William Jennings, could see the lights of Eastbourne but thought they were the lights of Hastings. He also did not realise how close in land he was until he found himself among the surf, but while trying to sail out of the surf the vessel ran aground at about 6pm.

The vessel had come ashore at low tide on the shoal between Beachy Head and Eastbourne known as the Sandacre. The crew immediately made distress signals by burning a fire with whatever they could find to burn.

Fortunately the look-out at the nearby Holywell coastguard station saw their signal and acknowledged it with a blue lamp. The master and crew stayed with their vessel until 8.30pm when there was about 9ft/2.7m of water in the hold before deciding to abandon the *Osprey* in their own boat.

When he saw the distress signals of the *Osprey*, the coastguard look-out immediately sent a message to the lifeboat coxswain, Joseph Huggett at Eastbourne, who soon mustered his crew. Initially the lifeboat was to be launched from the boathouse at the Wish but it was then decided to take the lifeboat to the east of the town. A team of horses was obtained and they pulled the lifeboat to Holywell and down on to the beach. There were by now a number of spectators and these together, with the lifeboat crew, dragged the lifeboat along the shingle for about ½ mile/800m. When they arrived with the lifeboat it was found that the crew from the *Osprey* had managed to get ashore opposite the Burlington Hotel, Eastbourne, using their own boat

Once the crew of the *Osprey* had landed they were taken to Samuel Hall, the local agent of the Shipwrecked Mariners Society, who provided them with food and accommodation at the Workmen's Hall. On the following Monday the crew returned to London on the London, Brighton and South Coast Railway, free of charge where Mr. F. Lean, secretary of the Shipwrecked Mariners Society, received the crew and arranged for their onward journey home.

The lifeboat not now being required, arrangements were made to get it back to the lifeboat station with the help of additional horses borrowed from Mr. Tomes, Mr. Arkcoll, Mr. Gorringe and Mr. Wickham. In total 17 horses were gathered to get the lifeboat and its carriage, back up the slope from the beach. However, the strain of the incline was far too great and the chains connected to the carriage kept breaking. After a number of attempts it was decided to leave the lifeboat in-situ and try again the following day. However, the next morning it was decided not to take it back on the carriage but to re-float the lifeboat and row it back to the lifeboat house, where it arrived at 11am.

The Board of Trade ordered that the remains of the vessel, together with its cargo, be sold. On Thursday 18th January it was all sold by Mr. J.C. Towner.

**Ref: SIBI; EG 17.1.1872; EC 20.1.1872**

# HAWK

**Date:**                              29.11.1872

**Wreck Location:**            4 miles/6.4km off Newhaven

**Description of Vessel:**
**Vessel Type -**                 Thames sailing barge

**Cargo:**                           Oil, coal tar

**Home Port:**                    Rochester

**Voyage:**                         Shoreham to London

**Date Built, Builder:**       c.1842

**Owner:**                          H. Wickenden

**Ship's Master:**               J. Riley

**Number of Crew:**          1

---

This vessel sank in a force 6 south easterly wind when 4 miles/6.4km off
Newhaven with the loss of one crew.

*Ref: SIBI*

# UNION

| | |
|---|---|
| **Date:** | 16.12.1872 |
| **Wreck Location:** | Ashore opposite Blatchington Coastguard Station at Seaford |
| **Description of Vessel:** | |
| **Gross Tonnage -** | 2000 |
| **Vessel Type -** | American sailing vessel |
| **Cargo:** | Tins of pineapple, sewing machine parts, barrels of lamp black, toys, wheat, flour. |
| **Voyage:** | New York to London |
| **Ship's Master:** | Delano |
| **Number of Crew:** | 26 |

---

The *Union* is also referred to as the *American Union*.

The *Union* left New York on Friday 22nd November 1872 bound for London, under the command of the master, Delano, and his crew of 26. The voyage was fairly uneventful until the vessel reached the Channel.

During the night of Monday 16th December 1872, the *Union* was off Newhaven in a strong south-westerly wind, but nothing gave the vessel any concern as she was under little sail. The visibility, however, was very poor, due to the mist and rain, and was one of the causes of the vessel going aground at about 11pm between the high and low water marks, almost opposite the Blatchington Coastguard Station. Another, and the most significant cause, being that the master believed he was in mid-Channel.

It was the *Union's* lookout who first saw land but by this time the vessel was very close in. As it was under little sail, the order was given for more sail with the intention to tack and sail out to sea away from the shore. Unfortunately it was too late, and before anything could be done the vessel ran aground rolling over broadside, with the deck towards the sea.

The coastguard watch at the Blatchington Station had already seen that the vessel was in too close and informed the officer in charge, Mr. Scott, of the possibility that the vessel would go aground. Scott mustered his men and together with the rocket apparatus were quickly on the scene and soon had a line on board the stricken *Union*. Then, by the use of the line and the basket, 16 of the crew were soon brought ashore. The remainder stayed with the vessel until the falling tide left her high and dry allowing them to get ashore safely. The crew was taken to the Blatchington Coastguard Station and cared for until arrangements could be made for their travel to the American Consul in London.

By mid-day the returning high tide, together with a strong wind, started to break up the vessel, which was insured for £8,000. It was believed that both the vessel and the cargo were underinsured.

With the sea breaking over the *Union* at high tide, it soon washed the £25,000 worth of cargo out of the holds and along the beach towards Seaford. One amusing aside to this was that part of the cargo consisted of flour and lamp-black compound in barrels. The action of the sea smashed open some of these barrels causing a large black damp cloud to drift in shore on the wind. On the beach by now were a large number of spectators and officials who suddenly found themselves black from head to toe. It was reported that this black cloud was seen between 1-2 miles/1.6-3.2km in land.

During the day a number of other officials arrived on the scene including officers from the East Sussex Constabulary together with the Deputy Chief Constable, Mr. Peacock, a contingent of the Naval Reserve, and Excise officials under Mr. Dolan. All were there to protect and collect the cargo and wreckage.

On the following day, Tuesday 17th December, men were employed to recover anything of value from the wreck, including the copper from the vessel's hull as it was anticipated that one more high tide would completely smash the vessel to pieces. At this time the sea was already flowing straight through the vessel. For two hours men worked trying to salvage as much as possible to beat the incoming tide, while others were engaged in recovering as much as possible of the cargo that had been washed along the beach.

The cargo strewn beach looked more like an emporium, including barrels of flour, oat cake, resin, casks of vegetable black, boxes of clothes pegs, timber, sewing machines, brooms, hogsheads* of tobacco leaf, tins of paint, tins of fruit, and casks of biscuit. Although some of the barrels, casks, boxes etc. were intact, the majority had been broken. Apart from the above list, by far the largest part of the cargo was several thousand bags of wheat, which were entirely lost. The sea caused the wheat to swell, bursting the bags, which then sank to the bottom forming a carpet on the seabed several inches thick, which became visible at low tide.

Throughout the Tuesday and subsequent days men continued their work of collecting the cargo from the beach, all of which was taken to a yard at the Royal Artillery Battery. To transport the cargo, the authorities had requisitioned nearly every horse and cart from the neighbourhood. However, the local population did not mind because the extra income just before Christmas was most welcome.

* Hogshead of tobacco is 12 to 18cwt/609.6 to 914.4kg

**Ref: EC 21.1.1872; LL 18304 18.12.72**

# ST. PETER

| | |
|---|---|
| **Date:** | 22.10.1873 |
| **Wreck Location:** | Off Beachy Head |
| **Description of Vessel:** | |
| **Vessel Type -** | British sailing brig |
| **Cargo:** | 185 tons of coal |
| **Home Port:** | Liverpool |
| **Voyage:** | Llanelly to Dieppe |
| **Date Built, Builder:** | c.1832 |
| **Number of Crew:** | 5 |

---

The *St. Peter* became a loss on Wednesday 22nd October 1873.

*Ref: SIBI*

# CARRIE M

| | |
|---|---|
| **Date:** | 4.9.1874 |
| **Wreck Location:** | 15 miles/24km west of Beachy Head |
| **Description of Vessel:** | |
| **Gross Tonnage -** | 200 |
| **Length -** | 90ft/27.63m |
| **Beam -** | 23ft/6.9m |
| **Vessel Type -** | British sailing brigantine |
| **Cargo:** | 120 tons of coal |
| **Home Port:** | Cowes |
| **Voyage:** | Shields to Cowes |
| **Date Built, Builder:** | c.1862 at Prince Edward Island |
| **Owner:** | W. Woodnutt & Co, Newport |
| **Ship's Master:** | Charles Odell |
| **Number of Crew:** | 4 and 1 boy |

This vessel also referred to as the *Carrieme*.

At 6pm on Thursday 3rd September 1874 the brigantine *Carrie M* was off Eastbourne going down the Channel in a south-easterly wind. However, by 11pm the wind had changed to a gale from the south-west, with the sea becoming exceptionally heavy. It was the strain of these conditions that caused the to vessel develop a leak.

At 12.30am the following morning when 15 miles/24km west of Beachy Head, the crew decided to abandon the vessel because she was taking in too much water. They managed to lower their boat just before the *Carrie M* went down, and started to row towards Eastbourne. At 7.30am they arrived at Eastbourne totally exhausted from their seven hour row in such terrible conditions.

Mr. Samuel Hall, the local agent of the Shipwrecked Mariners Society, attended to their needs while Captain Dolan, the Receiver of Wrecks, took depositions from both the master and mate regarding their ordeal. The crew were given free rail passes to travel back to Cowes on the 4.55pm train.

A local collection was made for the crew by Mr. Rushton, Dr. Canton and Mr. Ferrers Guy, and raised £10.3s.0d./£10.15p for the crew who had lost all their possessions. The money was divided between the crew as follows: the master Charles Odell received £3.5s.0d./£3.25p, the mate received £2, three seamen received £1.6s.0d/£1.30p each, and the boy received £1 because this was his maiden voyage.

*Ref: SIBI; EC 5.9.1874; EG 9.9.1874*

# BLISS

| | |
|---|---|
| **Date vessel sank:** | 9.9.1874 |
| **Wreck Location:** | Ashore at Newhaven |
| **Description of Vessel:** | |
| **Vessel Type -** | British sailing sloop |
| **Cargo:** | Indian corn |
| **Home Port:** | Southampton |
| **Voyage:** | London to Southampton |
| **Ship's Master:** | Pearce |

This vessel is also referred to as the *Elizabeth* as result of an error in the original identification.

On Wednesday 9th September 1874, the *Bliss,* when off Beachy Head, suddenly sprung a leak and it was not long before the water was 2ft./60cm deep in the hold. The pumps were manned but quickly became choked and ineffective. Pearce, the ship's master, decided to run for the safety of Newhaven harbour, but with the extra weight of the water in the hold and the tide being at dead low water, the vessel struck the sand bar at the harbour entrance. The *Bliss* was then driven ashore at the back of the harbour east pier.

The coastguard were soon in attendance together with their rocket apparatus and after the second firing they had a line on the vessel and the crew were brought safely to the shore. Very soon after the vessel went to pieces and the cargo was lost.

*Ref: HI 11.9.1874; LL 18841 10.9.74; LL 18842 11.9.74*

# DELIGHT

| | |
|---|---|
| **Date:** | 11.12.1874 |
| **Wreck Location:** | Ashore between Blatchington Battery and Seaford |
| **Description of Vessel:** | |
| **Gross Tonnage -** | 150 approx. |
| **Vessel Type -** | British sailing schooner |
| **Cargo:** | Coal |
| **Home Port:** | Rye |
| **Voyage:** | Seaham to Southampton |
| **Owner:** | Hoad Bros., Rye |
| **Ship's Master:** | Thomas Groucher |
| **Number of Crew:** | 4 |

The *Delight* left Seaham for Southampton on Sunday 6th December 1874 and when off Brighton at 2am the following Friday, encountered a south-westerly gale with very heavy seas. The sea was so rough that the vessel's gangway and parts of the bulwarks and rigging were knocked away by the waves and started to fill with water. The crew had in fact been working the pumps for the previous couple of hours because the hull started to leak and was becoming water-logged. As a result of the adverse weather the vessel was slowly becoming unmanageable. As the *Delight* drifted towards Newhaven before the weather, the position was getting worse, so the crew hoisted distress signals.

As the vessel passed off Newhaven pier, local spectators saw the distress signals and ran along to the Newhaven Lifeboat House to raise the alarm. Fortunately the coxswain, Edward Mewett and the bow-man, Richard Lower, were in there at the time. They soon mustered their crew and launched the lifeboat *Elizabeth Boys*. Once launched the lifeboat crew encountered the same heavy seas but after rowing for 15 minutes managed to hoist their sail and make towards the *Delight*. The skill of the lifeboat crew enabled them to come alongside in the raging surf and take off the five man crew. It was just in time as by then the stricken vessel was getting extremely close to the beach with some 2ft/0.6m of water above the cabin floor. The crew were also totally exhausted from manning the pumps, desperately trying to keep the level of water down. No sooner had the lifeboat taken the crew off at 10am, than the *Delight* was driven ashore between the Blatchington Battery and Seaford. Within a very few minutes thereafter she was smashed to pieces. It was not long after that Captain Knight, the local Lloyds agent and Mr. Dolan, the Receiver of Wrecks, arrived at the scene.

While the lifeboat was effecting the rescue, the steamer *Alexander* and the tug *Victoria* had come out of Newhaven to render assistance but by the time they had arrived the *Delight* had already gone to pieces. However, the *Victoria* did tow the lifeboat back towards Newhaven letting her go to the west, so the lifeboat could enter the harbour.

The rescued crew were landed on the harbour pier where they were taken to the Hope Inn and tended to by Mr. Wellsted. He later took the crew to Mr. W.D. Stone, the local agent of the Shipwrecked Mariners Society, who arranged for them to be provided with clothes and food.

*Ref: SWA 15.12.1874; HO 19.12.1874; LL 18921 12.12.74*

# LIVONIA

| | |
|---|---|
| **Date:** | 24.1.1875 |
| **Wreck Location:** | 5 miles/8km off Beachy Head |
| **Description of Vessel:** | |
| **Gross Tonnage -** | 199 |
| **Length -** | 97ft/29.71m |
| **Beam -** | 23ft/7.11m |
| **Vessel Type -** | British sailing brig |
| **Cargo:** | 330 tons of coal |
| **Home Port:** | Guernsey |
| **Voyage:** | Shields to Jersey |
| **Date Built, Builder:** | c.1833 at Grangemouth |
| **Owner:** | R. Pennison & W. Bird & Co., Guernsey |
| **Ship's Master:** | R. Pennison |

---

The *Livonia* left Shields for Jersey on Sunday 17th January 1875 under the command of the master Pennison and his crew. At 8.30pm the following Saturday, 23rd January, the vessel was about 15 miles/24km off Beachy Head in a squally south-westerly wind with thick fog and rough seas. At this time the master was towards the bow and the mate, Mr. Bruce, was at the helm, when out of the fog they saw an unknown barque bearing down on them. The master gave the order to the helm, to go about, but it was too late and the barque struck the *Livonia* on the port bow. The impact was so violent that both the *Livonia's* masts collapsed and fell over board, although strangely there was no damage to the vessel's hull.

The mate and the crew that were all on deck at the time, jumped on to the barque, as they clearly thought the vessel was in imminent fear of sinking due to the collision. The master, however, went below deck to collect the box containing the vessel's papers and when he returned just a few seconds later, the barque was sailing away leaving him alone on his stricken vessel. The *Livonia* drifted before the wind and with the sea constantly breaking over it, was slowly filling with water. It was becoming more and more apparent to the lone Pennison that the craft would sink before he reached land or was rescued. He put on a life belt and tried to get his boots off but they were so wet he had to put his heels in the vessel's wheel to help prise them off. He then put a bag of clothing together with the vessel's papers and an axe, into the jolly-boat, which in turn was lashed inside the vessel's long boat, and waited for the vessel to go down. This it did about 5am the following morning, Sunday, when 5 miles/8km off Beachy Head.

As the vessel went down Pennison got into the jolly-boat and used the axe to cut the lashings holding it down. He floated clear of the sinking *Livonia*, however, as the vessel went down it started to pull the jolly-boat towards its vortex but Pennison managed to use an oar to push himself away and to safety. All that Pennison could do from thereon was to keep the jolly-boat before the wind and sea. Luckily he finally made shore at Seaside, Eastbourne at 7.30am. He was taken to the Workmen's Hall by Mr. S. Hall, the local agent of the Shipwrecked Mariners Society, where Mr. Powell the 'Hall Keeper' tended to his needs.

Mr. Pennison left Eastbourne the next day on the 1.55pm train for Southampton on his way back to Jersey. The fate of the crew is not known but it is assumed they were later put ashore.

*Ref: SIBI; EG 27.1.1875; HO 30.1.1875*

# JEANNE LOUISE

| | |
|---|---|
| **Date:** | 18.3.1875 |
| **Wreck Location:** | 5 miles/8km off Beachy Head |
| **Description of Vessel:** | |
| **Vessel Type -** | French sailing fishing trawler |
| **Home Port:** | Le Treporte |
| **Owner:** | Jean Lefor |
| **Ship's Master:** | Jean Lefor |
| **Number of Crew:** | 7 |

---

On 4.30am on Thursday 18th March 1875, the *Jeanne Louise* was trawling for fish about 8 miles/12.9km off Beachy Head. The vessel was showing lights which could not be said of the Swedish schooner *Johanna Mathilda* of Lehern, which was bearing down on them. It was impossible for the crew of the *Jeanne Louise* to get out of the path of the schooner as they had their nets out. All they could do was to call out to the schooner which was without any effect as it ran into them, cutting the *Jeanne Louise* to the water line.

On impact five of the trawler's crew managed to hang on to the schooner and were pulled on board, but the other 3, including the master, stayed on their own vessel and were never seen again. It is assumed they went down with it.

When off Shoreham the schooner *Johanna Mathilda,* signalled for a boat and the local fishing vessel *Rosy* answered the signal and came alongside. The five rescued crew were transferred on to the *Rosy* and landed at Brighton, where Mr. Powell the Chief Officer of the local coastguard, together with his colleagues Lieutenant Sutherland and Captain Fred Collins, looked after their immediate needs. However, they were later handed to the care of the local agent of the Shipwrecked Mariners Society, Mr. J.W. Jackson of 11 Ship Street, Brighton. He found them food and accommodation at Hunter's Coffee & Dining Rooms, 8 West Street.

On Friday morning the rescued crew set off for Newhaven to get a vessel back to France. They were Pierre Francois Biarre (whose father was one of those left on the *Jeanne Louise*), Duhermel Hippolite, Pierre Lamber, Pierre Poivoien and Ernest Villy.

*Ref: SIBI; HO 27.3.1875*

# LOUISA

| | |
|---|---|
| **Date:** | 30.8.1875 |
| **Wreck Location:** | Off Newhaven |
| **Description of Vessel:** | |
| **Vessel Type -** | British North Sea Pilot Boat |
| **Home Port:** | Dover |
| **Voyage:** | From Dover on patrol of the English Channel |
| **Number of Crew:** | 6 |

On Friday 27th August 1875 the North Sea pilot boat *Louisa* left Dover to patrol the Channel. At 1.40am on the following Monday she was run down and sunk by the steamship *Humboldt* bound for Genoa from Newcastle. Three of the crew were saved by the steamship but unfortunately the remaining three drowned.

The rescued crew were later transferred to the steam tug *Victor* and taken to Newhaven where the local agent of the Shipwrecked Mariners Society, Mr. W.D. Stone, tended to their needs and arranged for their transport back to Dover.

*Ref: SE 1.9.1875*

# RUBENS

| | |
|---|---|
| **Date:** | 17.1.1876 |
| **Wreck Location:** | Ashore near Beachy Head |
| **Description of Vessel:** | |
| **Gross Tonnage -** | 1266 |
| **Vessel Type -** | British steamship |
| **Cargo:** | Wool, hides |
| **Home Port:** | Liverpool |
| **Voyage:** | Buenos Aires to Antwerp |
| **Owner:** | River Plate Line, Messrs. Lamport & Holt of Liverpool. |
| **Ship's Master:** | Hugh Ferguson |
| **Number of Crew:** | 35 - 41 |

At 4pm on Monday 17th January 1876 the steamship *Rubens* ran aground under the Belle Tout Light in thick fog still sounding her whistle to warn others of her presence. Although there was a nasty sea running at the time the *Rubens* and her crew – reported to be between 36 to 42 in total – were in no immediate danger. The vessel and cargo was valued at about £150,000.

The coastguard from the Birling Gap Station, under the command of the Chief Boatman Mr. Heather, were soon on the scene. At the request of the master of the stricken vessel, Hugh Ferguson, the coastguardsmen remained on board all night while he made his way to Eastbourne to make contact with the owners of the vessel. The Newhaven lifeboat, *Elizabeth Boys,* was also launched and although eventually not required, stood-by for the next two days and two nights.

On the morning of 18th January it was found that a small hole had been made in the hull and she had taken in some 4 inches/10.2cm of water during the previous high tide. This tide had also pushed the vessel a further 24ft/7.3m further onto the rocks. During the morning two steam tugs from Newhaven arrived and tried to get the *Rubens* off the rocks but without success.

Soon after the vessel came ashore Mr. Dolan, the Collector of Her Majesty's Customs at Newhaven, requested that Captain Knight, the local Lloyds agent, send a representative to assess the situation with a view to recovering the cargo. The assessment was that it was possible to remove the whole cargo within 60 hours by the suggested use of tugs, barges and a number of men. These arrangements were agreed between Hugh Ferguson and Mr. Dolan. The removal of the cargo was started and only about 70 tons of wool, valued at about £3,000, had been loaded into Lighter* boats, when Ferguson, accompanied by Mr. Foster, a Lloyds agent of Latham & Co, Dover, demanded that this operation be halted. Mr. Foster said that it was on the instructions of the owners, Messrs. Lamport & Holt.

Captain Knight then gave a written opinion that the whole cargo could be salvaged within his time estimate of 60 hours but Mr. Foster produced a telegram from the owners stating that he was their agent and the unloading was to stop. However, to make the vessel lighter, 200 bales had already been thrown overboard before the work stopped.

On Tuesday night Messrs. Elphick & Son of Lewes received a telegram requesting them to send as many barges and assistance as possible to assist with removal of the cargo. The price offered for recovery of the wool was £2 per bale landed at Newhaven. They, together with Messrs. Newington & Co., duly dispatched men and barges but on arrival were told that, on instructions from the owners, the price on offer had dropped to 5s.0d/25p per bale landed. They refused to do it at this price as it was totally uneconomical and, after remaining idle all day, returned to Lewes. As a result other barge owners from Lewes were asked to assist but they refused because the owners of the *Rubens* refused to insure their barges. However, much of the cargo was later discharged by men from Newhaven who were to earn between £20 to £30, much to the chagrin of the Lewes barge owners. The *Rubens* was to be eventually towed to Southampton for repair.

A number of local fishermen from Eastbourne collected a large part of the cargo that had been thrown overboard, by tying ropes round their waists and going into the sea and rocks to collect it. The recovered bales were then taken back to Eastbourne, the fishermen knowing they would be able to claim salvage money on this cargo. These fishermen brought an action in the High Court which awarded George Hide and his crew £237, John Allchorn £75 and James Swain £55.

There was a peculiar incident on the cliff above the stricken vessel, when William Bannister of Westdean arrived on his horse. He left it in the charge of another person who walked to the edge of the cliff to look at the activity around the *Rubens*, drawing the horse with him. Suddenly the horse fell backwards down the 40ft/12.2m cliff to the beach below, remarkably sustaining very little injury.

* A large boat for unloading other vessels

*Ref: BH; SNLB; EC 22.1.1876; HC 26.1.1876*

# COONATTO

| | |
|---|---|
| **Date:** | 21.2.1876 |
| **Wreck Location:** | Ashore at Crowlink Gap |
| **Description of Vessel:** | |
| **Gross Tonnage -** | 633 |
| **Length -** | 166ft/48.83m |
| **Beam -** | 40ft/8.83m |
| **Vessel Type -** | British full-rigged sailing vessel |
| **Cargo:** | Copper, wool |
| **Home Port:** | London |
| **Voyage:** | Adelaide to London |
| **Date Built, Builder:** | c.1863, Thomas Bilbe, London |
| **Owner:** | Anderson & Co., London |
| **Ship's Master:** | John Eilbeck Hillman |

---

This vessel is also referred to as *Coonatte* or *Coonattee*, however *Coonatto* is correct, being a town in Australia, a country to which the vessel plied its trade from London. The *Coonatto* was very fast and the quickest time she had made this journey was 70 days. The master on this occasion was a Mr. Begg.

At 5am on Monday 21st February 1876 the *Coonatto* was on her way up the Channel returning to London, being 91 days out from Adelaide, when she ran into a south-westerly storm and thick fog off Beachy Head. It was these conditions that caused the vessel to be driven aground at high tide at Crowlink Gap, about ½ mile/804m west of Beachy Head in heavy seas.

With the alarm having been raised, Captain Knight the local Lloyds agent requested the attendance of the tugs *Victoria* and *Orleans* together with the Newhaven Lifeboat, *Elizabeth Boys*. The lifeboat was launched at 8.30am and made her way to the stricken vessel. On arrival at the scene the lifeboat stood by in case she was required, but by 3pm it was decided that there was no need of it and so returned to Newhaven. In the meantime the crew of the *Coonatto* had all been instructed to leave the vessel at low tide, which was safely done. They were later discharged on Wednesday, as the vessel was now entirely under the control of agents, returning to London on the 7.40pm train from Eastbourne.

On Tuesday despite the very heavy swell, the two tugs managed to get a line on the *Coonatto*. However the cable snapped when the tugs made an attempt to pull it free. Throughout, the stern of the vessel was constantly being struck by the sea, having the effect of pushing it further onto the rocks until it was within 50 yards/45.7m of the cliffs. It was therefore decided to leave any further attempt to get the vessel off the rocks until later, after some of the cargo had been removed to make it lighter.

During Wednesday and Thursday gangs of men dismantled the rigging of the *Coonatto* and working between the tides also removed the cargo and anything else that was salvageable. This work was not without its hazards. On Wednesday one of the workmen from Eastbourne named Ince was badly injured when a spar fell on him and was taken to Eastbourne Hospital where he was tended to by Mr. Colegate. On Thursday another man badly injured his hand. An Eastbourne Magistrate granted a special licence to Mr. Gardner of the Volunteer Inn, so that he could cater for the gangs working on this salvage operation.

To assist with this salvage work, on Friday, a steam driven derrick was taken to the edge of the cliff above the stranded vessel. Then with lines and pulley blocks the majority of the cargo was soon safely brought ashore which filled several rail trucks at Eastbourne railway station.

On Saturday night a gale blew up which persisted into Sunday, turning the vessel broadside to the sea. The combined effects of this and the swelling of the wool still on board, burst open some of the decking, causing the vessel to become a total wreck.

By a quirk of fate two of the partners who owned the vessel were staying at Eastbourne. One of them was staying with his family at Sydney House, Grand Parade and the other at Stafford House, Cavendish Place.

Poor navigation by the *Coonatto's* master John Eilbeck Hillman, was later found to be the cause of his vessel going aground and he subsequently had his master's certificate suspended for 3 months.

*Ref: SIBI; SNLB; R. Gilbert papers; HO 26.2.1876; HI 29.2.1876 & 7.3.1876;*

# NANCY'S PRIDE

**Date:**                        11.6.1876

**Wreck Location:**              ¾ mile/1.2km south-east of
                                 Eastbourne

**Description of Vessel:**
**Length-**                      22ft/6.7m
**Beam -**                       8ft/2.5m
**Vessel Type -**                British sailing fishing smack

**Home Port:**                   Eastbourne

**Voyage:**                      Local sailing

**Owner:**                       Samuel Huggett

**Ship's Master:**               Samuel Huggett

**Number of Crew:**              0

**Number of Passengers:**        11 and 1 boy

---

At 11.10am on Sunday 11th June 1876 the *Nancy's Pride* set off from the Redoubt at Eastbourne for a leisurely sail, under the control of Samuel Huggett. The 12 passengers on board were all young men except three year old John Thomas Groves, who was Samuel Huggett's nephew.

In a north-easterly wind the *Nancy's Pride* sailed off, with foresail and mizzen sails set, in a south-easterly direction for about ¾ mile/1.2km when they were suddenly becalmed in slightly rougher water. At this time Samuel Huggett was at the make-shift tiller, which had had been previously broken, and not holding the sheet, having earlier secured it to the vessel. The vessel had been becalmed for a few minutes when there was a sudden gust of wind which caused the *Nancy Pride* to heel to one side and take on some water. Most of the occupants, gripped by fear of the sudden movement of the vessel, inexplicably moved to the leeward side causing the vessel to capsize.

An additional contributory factor in the vessel capsizing, was undoubtedly the loose beach shingle ballast in the bottom of the boat. Had it been in bags then its movement in the bottom of the vessel would have been severely restricted and would not have been so violent when the vessel heeled over.

The only survivor of this tragedy, Richard Deen, was already on the leeward side when the vessel heeled over. He made the more wise decision, than the majority of the other occupants, as he moved to the windward side just as the vessel capsized. He then jumped into the water, clear of the vessel, and swam a short distance from the *Nancy's Pride* to prevent being sucked down. Having swum about 35ft/10.7m Deen looked back towards the capsized vessel and saw that it was still afloat. He swam back thinking that it may be possible to right the *Nancy's Pride* only to find a number of the other occupants clinging to it. Fearing that if he also took hold of the vessel it may not support them all, he swam away. As he did so two or three of the occupants who had not managed to get to the capsized vessel and were in imminent danger of drowning, grabbed his legs in desperation, pulling Deen under. He managed to release their grip and hold on to a floating oar when he was joined by another of the exhausted occupants. Deen told the man to hang on to the opposite end but the man's eyes rolled back and went under the water not to be seen again. It was then that Deen noticed that the *Nancy's Pride* had sunk taking all the passengers who were hanging on to it down as well.

Deen spent the remainder of his time in the sea astride the oar until he was picked up, having removed his boots and some clothing to improve his situation.

The capsize of the *Nancy's Pride* was seen from the shore by William Glidden, the coastguard on watch. He quickly arranged for three or four vessels to put off including the coastguard galley to attend the scene. When they arrived they soon picked up an exhausted Richard Deen and the unconscious body of Samuel Huggett's three year old nephew and returned them to the beach. Mr. Whitfield and Dr. Mundie attended to the young boy but all attempts to resuscitate him failed, whereas Richard Deen, after a short while, sufficiently recovered to walk back to his lodgings in Terminus Road. His watch had stopped at 11.16am.

Ten of the bodies were recovered during the rest of the day and the eleventh was found the next day. Their bodies were all taken to a large room at the Victoria Tavern, which was the scene of the Inquest. The unfortunate men who drowned were; Samuel Huggett, aged 29 years, the vessel owner from Eastbourne who had only been married a few months;

his nephew John Thomas Groves, aged 3 years and 4 months; Edward Parker, 22 years, a carpenter from Rotherfield; George Paine, 21 years, a carpenter also from Rotherfield; Frederick Wood, 25 years, a carpenter of Ashington near Pulborough; Edward Carpenter, 19 years, a porter with the London, Brighton and South Coast Railway from Bedhampton near Havant; William Rogers, 22 years, a blacksmith of Westham; Edwin Poole, 22 years, a labourer of Westham; Harry Russell, 21 years, a fireman from Chiddingly; his brother Alfred Russell, 18 years, a labourer; Jacob Baker, 36 years, a labourer from Eastbourne who left a wife and one child; and William Hammond, 22 years, also from Eastbourne. They were all single except Samuel Huggett and Jacob Baker.

At 2pm on Wednesday 14th June the funeral cortège for Samuel Huggett, Jacob Baker and the boy, John Thomas Groves, left the Victoria Tavern, Tower Street to make its way to the cemetery. The ¼ mile/400m long cortege was headed by sixty fishermen and boatmen wearing their blue Guernseys. There then followed Samuel Huggett's coffin, being carried by a group of sixteen married boatmen working in relays of four. Then came the body of John Groves carried in a sling by a group of eight boatmen working in a similar relay. They were followed by their relatives and friends in two coaches and several hackney carriages. Behind these came the body of Jacob Baker which was carried by fellow workmen from the company of his employer, Mr. Peerless, a builder. His coffin was followed by a coach and hackney carriage carrying his widow and relatives. Finally, at the rear of the cortège, were the hundreds of mourners who had lined the streets of the route and joined as the cortège passed. The other deceased were returned to their respective homes for interment.

*Ref: HC 14.6.1876; EG 14.6.1876; EC 17.4.1876*

# CLIO

| | |
|---|---|
| **Date:** | 5.7.1876 |
| **Wreck Location:** | 6 miles/9.7km south-east of Royal Sovereign Light |
| **Description of Vessel:** | |
| **Length -** | 111ft/34.07m |
| **Beam -** | 27ft/8.22m |
| **Vessel Type -** | British sailing barque |
| **Cargo:** | Iron, cattle fodder |
| **Home Port:** | London |
| **Voyage:** | Cabes to Newcastle-upon-Tyne |
| **Date Built, Builder:** | c.1845 at Sunderland |
| **Owner:** | Harrison of Whitby |
| **Ship's Master:** | F. Leng |
| **Number of Crew:** | 10 |

---

This vessel collided with the Austrian Steamship *Marentha* in a force 4 south-westerly wind.

*Ref: SIBI*

# ELSIE LINCK

| | |
|---|---|
| **Date:** | 10.11.1876 |
| **Wreck Location:** | 1 mile/1.6km south of Royal Sovereign Light |
| **Description of Vessel:** | |
| **Vessel Type -** | German sailing barque |
| **Cargo:** | Ballast |
| **Home Port:** | Danzig |
| **Voyage:** | London to Deboy |
| **Date Built, Builder:** | c.1866 |
| **Ship's Master:** | W. Pupp |
| **Number of Crew:** | 14 |

Soon after daylight on the morning of Friday 10th November 1876 with the weather fine, fishermen on the beach at Eastbourne heard the warning guns fired from the Royal Sovereign Light. On hearing this, two luggers from Eastbourne beach, one belonging to Mr. G. Hyde, the other belonging to Mr. Gausden, put off to see if they could assist with whatever the problem was. En route to the Royal Sovereign Light the two luggers came across the *Ben Lomond,* a steam tug, under the command of Mr. M.J. Hardy, who accompanied the two luggers on their search. At 11am, when about ¼ mile/ 400m south of the Royal Sovereign Light, they found the *Elsie Linck* which was slowly sinking bow first, in about 15 fathoms/27.8m of water. The crew of the tug boarded the *Elsie Linck* but found the crew had already left. It was later found that the vessel had collided with the German mail steam packet the *Euphrates*, who had taken on board the crew from the stricken vessel. The crew were later landed at Flushing.

The tug *Ben Lomond* put a line on the sinking vessel with the intention of salvaging it and towing it to shore. However, this was unsuccessful because by the time the tow was attempted the bow of the vessel was on the sea bed preventing the tug moving it. When the tug returned to Eastbourne, Mr. Hardy the Master, submitted a report to the local Lloyd's sub-agent Mr. T. Bennett, covering the above circumstances. For some days after this event, twenty feet of the stern of the *Elsie Linck* was still visible at low water.

*Ref: SIBI; HN 21.11.1876; EG 15.11.1876 & 11.4.1888; EC 18.11.1876; SEA 18.11.1876*

# JAMES GROVES

| | |
|---|---|
| **Date:** | 20.11.1876 |
| **Wreck Location:** | 4 miles/4.8km west x 880yds/800m south of Royal Sovereign Light |

**Description of Vessel:**

| | |
|---|---|
| **Gross Tonnage -** | 939 |
| **Length -** | 207ft/63.34.m |
| **Beam -** | 29ft/8.81m |
| **Vessel Type -** | British iron steamship |
| **Cargo:** | Barley |
| **Home Port:** | West Hartlepool |
| **Voyage:** | Sulina to Leith |
| **Date Built, Builder:** | c.1871 by Withy at Hartlepool |
| **Owner:** | J. Groves, West Hartlepool |
| **Ship's Master:** | J. Lundwall |
| **Number of Crew:** | 18 |

---

At 2am on the morning of Tuesday 21st November 1876, the Deal pilot lugger *Devastation* came upon the *Vale,* a Norwegian barque of Arendal, bound for London under the command of her master, Gundersen. The vessel had considerable damage to her bow. The *Devastation* offered the barque assistance which was refused in a very terse manner. However, they did learn from one crew member of the Norwegian barque that they had just recently been involved in a collision with a steamer off the Royal Sovereign Light. The *Vale* had to later put into Dover for repairs to the damage before continuing her voyage to London.

The *Devastation* duly made for the area of the Royal Sovereign Light, to find the top mast of the *James Groves* protruding above the sea. The vessel had gone down in about 18 fathoms/33.3m of water at low tide. Although there was no sign of the crew, the *Devastation* remained in the area for 2 hours, eventually going ashore at Eastbourne and reporting to Captain Henderson of the local coastguard. He in turn reported the wreck to the Trinity House authorities as its position was a danger to other shipping.

It later transpired that when the *James Groves* was run down by the Norwegian barque, they had asked for the barque's name and assistance as it was clear their vessel would not survive the impact. Both were refused, with the barque sailing away into the night. Although the *James Groves* sank within half an hour of the impact, the crew, many with facial injuries sustained from the collision, managed to take to their boats. Fortunately they were later picked up by the Dutch brig *Berndua* of Schiedam, under the command of her master J.D. Pater, who landed them at Folkestone at midday.

*Ref: SIBI; EG 22.11.1876; EC 25.11.1876; SE 28.11.1876*

# EMMA

| | |
|---|---|
| **Date:** | 30.11.1876 |
| **Wreck Location:** | 440yds/400m off Eastbourne |
| **Description of Vessel:** | |
| **Vessel Type -** | British fishing vessel |
| **Home Port:** | Eastbourne |
| **Voyage:** | Local angling trip |
| **Owner:** | Thomas Mitchell |
| **Ship's Master:** | Thomas Mitchell |
| **Number of Crew:** | 1 |

On the morning of Thursday 30th November 1876 the *Emma*, along with a couple of other vessels, had put off from the beach at Eastbourne to go fishing. In the craft were the owner, Thomas Mitchell, a man in excess of 60 years of age, and a similarly aged friend, Story Adams. By 4pm that afternoon most of the other vessels had returned to the beach as the wind had got stronger with ever increasing rough seas. However, *Emma* continued to fish until the light started to fade as the evening drew in, before starting to make back to the beach. The sea and the wind were by now quite severe.

The *Emma* set sail for the beach with her mizzen sail set. All was going well until about ¼ mile/400m from the shore when the vessel was completely swamped by a large wave. This filled the craft which sank very quickly leaving the two elderly occupants to hang on to the oars for buoyancy.

Fortunately the *Emma* was being observed by many people from the shore, and as soon as the vessel disappeared two craft on the beach put off to help. The first belonged to Arthur Matthews and he, together with his crew, Samuel Hide, Thomas Sayers, William Erridge and William Mitchell, were soon afloat. However, the sea was exceptionally rough and it was not long before they had to return for fear of themselves becoming a casualty. The second of the vessels, and the larger of the two that put off, was the *Guardian* belonging to George Hide but under the command of John Hide. His crew consisted of Charles Hide, James Collins, Jesse Huggett, Peter Waymark, George Gausden and John Prodger. The *Guardian* managed to get through the waves and surf to reach the crew of the sunken *Emma*. It was not a moment too soon for Mitchell, as he was totally exhausted when he was plucked from the sea.

The *Guardian* returned to the shore with both men, again through the very rough waves and surf. They all finally reached the beach safely but it was not without its worrying moments. Once ashore Adams was able to walk home but Mitchell was totally exhausted from the ordeal and had to be tended to by a doctor before he was allowed to go home some hours later.

During the course of the later part of that evening the *Emma* was washed ashore

*Ref: EC 2.12.1876; SE 2.12.1876*

# JOSEPH ET MARIE

**Date vessel sank:**                      7.2.1877

**Wreck Location:**                    20 miles/32km south-west of Beachy Head

**Description of Vessel:**
**Vessel Type -**                       French sailing smack

**Cargo:**                                Ballast

**Number of Crew:**                  7

---

This vessel and the *Bozzo* (see next page) were in collision 20 miles/32km off Beachy Head on Wednesday 7th February 1877. The crew of the *Joseph et Marie* managed to jump on board the *Bozzo* before their vessel went down but it was not long after that the *Bozzo* itself sank from the damage of the impact. Fortunately, nearby was another French fishing smack which managed to rescue three men from the *Joseph et Marie* crew, who were later put ashore at Newhaven. Thirteen crew of the *Bozzo* were rescued by the *Obla,* a Norwegian barque, who were also later put ashore at Newhaven.

*Ref: SIBI*

# BOZZO

**Date vessel sank:** 7.2.1877

**Wreck Location:** 20 miles/32km south-west of Beachy Head

**Description of Vessel:**
**Vessel Type -** Italian sailing vessel

**Cargo:** Ballast

**Voyage:** London to Baltimore

**Ship's Master:** C. Roggi

---

See the *Joseph Et Marie* on previous page.

*Ref: SIBI*

# ASTRO DE MER

**Date:**                             17.2.1877

**Wreck Location:**          20 miles/32.3km south off Newhaven

**Description of Vessel:**
**Vessel Type -**             French fishing smack

**Number of Crew:**         3

---

On Saturday 17th February 1877, while fishing, this vessel sank in a north-westerly force 5 wind after being in collision with the *Clyde* of Newcastle, Australia.

*Ref: SIBI*

# JAMES

| | |
|---|---|
| **Date:** | 20.2.1877 |
| **Wreck Location:** | 18 miles/29 km south-east of Beachy Head |
| **Description of Vessel:** | |
| **Gross Tonnage -** | 184 |
| **Length -** | 99ft/30.35m |
| **Beam -** | 24ft/7.18m |
| **Vessel Type -** | British sailing brigantine |
| **Cargo:** | 308 tons of coal |
| **Home Port:** | Faversham |
| **Voyage:** | Shields to Plymouth |
| **Date Built, Builder:** | c.1863 at Prince Edward Island, Nova Scotia |
| **Owner:** | J. Amos, Whitstable |
| **Ship's Master:** | Edward Alce |
| **Number of Crew:** | 6 |

Just before midnight on Sunday 19th February 1877 a severe west to north-west gale blew up when the *James* (official number 42,999) was off the Owers. Throughout the early hours of the following Monday morning the crew fought the horrendous weather and mountainous seas trying to make for Dungeness by daylight. However, when off Beachy Head, the strong winds turned northerly which made it more difficult to proceed up the Channel. In these increasingly difficult conditions the crew still managed to keep the vessel before the wind, until about noon on Monday when the vessel went down in what was a tremendous sea.

The crew managed to get the boat off before the *James* sank and five of them got into it leaving the master, Edward Alce, and the mate, Richard Bailey, still on board as she went down. The crew in their small boat were not in it long before the huge waves capsized the little craft throwing the occupants into the sea, never to be seen again.

When the *James* went down the master and the mate, Bailey, managed to find an oar and some wreckage to keep themselves afloat. Bailey called out to Alce that he had seen a French fishing smack just before the *James* went down and that it was making towards them. About five minutes later, Edward Alce was seen to turn over and disappear under the sea. The French fishing smack *No.72* soon picked up the sole survivor, Richard Bailey, who by then he had been hanging onto the oar for about an hour and a half.

The smack *No.72* of Trouville under the command of Joseph Croix made for Le Havre arriving at 4am on Wednesday morning, where Bailey was put ashore and tended to by the local English Consul. The Consul then made arrangements for him to return on the South Western Company's steamship *Alice* under the command of R.C. Mabb, from Le Havre to Southampton where he arrived the following morning, Thursday 23rd February, on the first leg of his journey home to Whitstable.

*Ref: SIBI; EC 24.2.1877*

# CHARLES

**Date:**                                 Autumn 1877

**Wreck Location:**              Ashore at Holywell

**Description of Vessel:**
**Vessel Type -**                     British sailing fishing lugger

---

One afternoon in the Autumn of 1877, the *Charles* was trying to deal with a storm and heavy seas not far off shore. On board the owner and his son were experiencing great difficulties in handling the craft in these conditions but eventually anchored just inside Eastbourne pier to weather the storm. The crew of the lifeboat had been made aware of the situation and were anticipating a launch to go to their aid. However the *Charles* started to drag her anchor and drifted quickly towards Holywell. On seeing this the lifeboat crew got into a carriage and also made for Holywell.

Just as the lifeboat crew arrived the wind drove the *Charles* across a groyne. The lifeboat crew dashed into the heavy surf at great risk to themselves and rescued the two crew members. The vessel very quickly went to pieces soon after.

*Ref: EG 2.5.1888*

# SINBAD

| | |
|---|---|
| **Date:** | 12.11.1877 |
| **Wreck Location:** | Ashore at Brickchurch, 1 mile/1.6km west of Cuckmere Coastguard Station |
| **Description of Vessel:** | |
| **Gross Tonnage -** | 1000 |
| **Vessel Type -** | Norwegian sailing barque |
| **Cargo:** | Ballast |
| **Voyage:** | London to Pensacola |
| **Date Built, Builder:** | c.1855 |
| **Owner:** | O. Nielsen, Sandejford |
| **Ship's Master:** | C. E. Anderson |
| **Number of Crew:** | 15 |
| **Number of Passengers:** | 1 |

On Sunday 11th November 1877, the *Sinbad* was coming up the Channel before a force 11 south-westerly gale. At about midnight, when the storm was at its height, the vessel lost all its sails and foremast, rendering it unmanageable in such violent wind and sea conditions. The *Sinbad* drifted before the weather being driven ashore at 1am Monday morning at Brickchurch, about half way between Seaford and Cuckmere. As it was a light vessel it bounced over the rocks breaking its back and losing the rudder, before being stuck fast a few yards from the base of the cliff. Fortunately, they were neap tides; if they had been spring tides the vessel would have been driven against the base of the cliffs with disastrous consequences.

Those on board the *Sinbad* all safely managed to get ashore by the use of ropes as the vessel was soon left high and dry by the tide. The crew then set about salvaging not only their personal belongings but as much as possible from the vessel itself. The crew were taken to Seaford where, the following day, they were treated to lunch at the Terminus Hotel. After the lunch, Mr. Sargent of the Shipwrecked Mariners Society, arranged for the crew to travel by train to London Bridge to start their journey home.

The wreck was sold the next day, Wednesday, by Mr. Verrall, the masts, rigging and copper having all been removed.

*Ref: SIBI; SE 13.11.1877; EG 14.11.1877; EC 17.11.1877*

# MIZPAH

| | |
|---|---|
| **Date:** | 6.12.1877 |
| **Wreck Location:** | 15 miles/24km south-west of Beachy Head |

**Description of Vessel:**

| | |
|---|---|
| **Gross Tonnage -** | 380 |
| **Length -** | 156ft/47.8m |
| **Beam -** | 22ft/6.85m |
| **Vessel Type -** | British iron steamship |
| **Cargo:** | 3,560 boxes of oranges |
| **Home Port:** | London |
| **Voyage:** | Seville to Leith |
| **Date Built, Builder:** | c.1875 by Softley & Co., South Shields |
| **Owner:** | T.S. Atkins & W. Crawthorn & Co., 28 Great Tower Street, London |
| **Ship's Master:** | Henry George Cram |
| **Number of Crew:** | 12 |

The steamship *Mizpah* left Seville on 26th November 1877 bound for Leith and then to Newcastle, with its cargo of oranges. It arrived off Portland at 11am on Wednesday 5th December and here the vessel lay at anchor for a short while before continuing her voyage up the Channel at 3.30pm the same afternoon. Little is known of the circumstances of the collision that was to later occur as the only survivor, a 20 year old steward named William Page, was in his berth at the time.

At 4.30am on the morning of Thursday 6th December, Page left his berth and went to the galley to make coffee for all the officers. About 30 minutes later he heard the mate shout out *"Hard-a-port"* followed by the collision. The *Mizpah,* in thick fog and a force 6 south-westerly wind, had been struck on the port bow by an unknown sailing vessel that was not showing any lights. It was clear to the master that the damage to the vessel was severe and so he gave instructions to the engineer to get the pumps working. However, this was not possible because water had got into engine room and extinguished the boilers as a result of the impact.

As the collision had carried away the lifeboat the master gave orders to get the punt ready, a small boat of some 14ft/4.3m in length with a beam of 5½ft/1.7m. The need to get the punt launched quickly became ever more urgent as the minutes went by because the *Mizpah* was rapidly going down. With the punt ready for launching, seven of the hands (including the survivor, Page) got on board while the master, first mate, and four crew lowered her from the sinking *Mizpah*. However, when the punt was released those in it failed to hand the painter to the master and the others still on the sinking vessel. The effect was that once in the sea the punt fell away from the *Mizpah* so the master and the others could not now get in it. The crew in the punt intended to row back to collect the master and the others, only to find that there was only one oar. They made what attempts were possible but after twenty minutes the *Mizpah's* bow suddenly raised up and the vessel went down stern first taking with her the master; first mate, John Thomas Bryant; Nicholl Gavangh, first engineer; able seamen J. Cram (the master's brother); W. Bell and another whose name is unknown.

With the sole oar the second mate Thomas Lewis steered the punt before the wind for three hours before they saw the Beachy Head Light although they believed it to be the Royal Sovereign Light. However just as it was getting light, they realised their mistake when they could see the cliffs. As they approached the shore they could see the tremendous surf breaking along the shore line. This caused much discussion in the punt as to whether to run for shore through this surf or stay off shore and wait for help. The consensus was to take the risk and run for shore. However, when 100yds/ 91.7m from the beach, the punt went broadside to the waves throwing all seven men into the raging surf as the punt capsized. The action of the surf soon washed ashore the only man in the punt to survive, William Page, who was wearing a life belt given to him by the master before the punt had been launched from the *Mizpah*.

At 8.30am that same morning Henry John Cooke, the lookout at the Cuckmere Coastguard Station, saw the upturned punt from the *Mizpah* 100yds/91.7m from the shore. He duly informed the officer in charge of the station, John Heather, who with the use of his telescope could see a body lying among the surf. He mustered all his men and they made their way to the upturned punt. On arrival they found Page, almost naked, crawling on his hands and knees up the shingle beach in weather that was now driving rain and sleet. Two of the coastguardsmen dragged him clear of the water and carried him to John Heather's home to be treated for exhaustion and exposure. Meanwhile, the other coastguardsmen recovered the punt together, with a chronometer and the *Mizpah's* cash box.

The six other men in the punt with William Page were the second mate, Thomas Lewis aged 42 years from London; James Pooley, aged 30 years from Ipswich, Patrick Law, aged 27 years from Newcastle, both able seaman; second engineer Charles Sbensfan, aged 25 years from Stockholm; fireman Edward Hall, aged 18 years from Newport; and engineer's steward Charles Thomas, aged 15 years from Bristol. It was clear that Page and Charles Thomas had become close friends because during Friday night Page became delirious, raving about his shipmates and in particular, Thomas

Throughout Thursday and Friday the bodies of five of the men in the punt were recovered from along the shoreline between Birling Gap and Seaford. On Saturday 8th December the Inquest into the death of three of them, Lewis the second mate, Patrick Murr an able seaman and the boy, Charles Thomas, was held. The Inquest was before the County Coroner Mr. L.G. Fullagar, at Exceat Farm, West Dean where three bodies were taken when recovered from the sea. The first witness was Mr. Thomas Saffery Atkins, half-owner of the *Mizpah* with William Crawthorn, from W. Crawthorn Company, who gave evidence of identification of the three men. He also told the Inquest that the master of the *Mizpah* had been employed by his company for the past year and was a very able master. There then followed coastguardsman John Heather who told the Inquest the events as outlined above including finding Lewis on the beach near where he had found Page. The next witness was John Pickford, a coastguardsman from the Crowlink Station who told the Coroner that he was patrolling the beach near Cliff End at 4.30am on the Friday morning when he found the deceased Patrick Murr and nearby the deceased Charles Thomas. The Inquest was then adjourned to enable William Page to attend to give his evidence.

Another Inquest was held at the Old Tree Hotel, Seaford the following Monday before Mr. W.W. Turner, the High Bailiff and Coroner, into the deceased Charles Sbensfan and James Pooley which William Page was able to attend. Atkins, the part owner, also attended this hearing and told the Coroner that only a month or so earlier the *Mizpah,* with Henry George Cram in command, had been caught in a storm when sailing from Swansea to Seville. On this occasion the vessel was blown by the storm 200 miles/ 321km off course out into the Atlantic Ocean. The other witness was the coastguardsman Cooke who had found both deceased on the shore.

The second mate of the *Mizpah*, Thomas Lewis, left a wife and five children. His wife travelled to Seaford on Sunday 9th December to take her husband's body home. A local collection arranged by Mr. Sargent of the Shipwrecked Mariners Society, raised £10 to assist her with this removal. He also arranged for the carriage of the body on the railway for a nominal charge of 2s.6d./12½p instead of the true cost of £3.

*Ref: SIBI; HI 11.12.1877; HC 12.12.1877; EG 12.12.1877; EC 15.12.1877*

# LONDON PACKET

| | |
|---|---|
| **Date:** | 7.3.1878 |
| **Wreck Location:** | 3 miles/4.8km north x north-east of Royal Sovereign Light |
| **Description of Vessel:** | |
| **Gross Tonnage -** | 69 |
| **Length -** | 58ft/17.62m |
| **Beam -** | 17ft/5.05m |
| **Vessel Type -** | British sailing schooner |
| **Cargo:** | 98 tons of wheat |
| **Home Port:** | Ipswich |
| **Voyage:** | London to Plymouth |
| **Date Built, Builder:** | c.1840, by Bayley of Ipswich |
| **Owner:** | Thomas Whalebone, Ipswich |
| **Ship's Master:** | Thomas Whalebone |
| **Number of Crew:** | 3 and a boy |

The *London Packet* left London on 26th February 1878, bound for Plymouth with her cargo of wheat. By the 5th March she was off the Sussex coast and in very strong westerly winds reaching force seven. Due to the conditions she was unable to make any progress much beyond Brighton, and spent the next three days between there and Hastings. It was while in this situation, at about 8.30pm on Thursday 7th March, that the ship's boy had occasion to go below only to find that the vessel was shipping water very rapidly. The last time anybody had been down below was at about 4pm for the customary four hourly testing of the pumps. At this time there was no sign of any leak in the vessel.

The speed at which the *London Packet* was filling with water meant that if something was not done soon, the vessel would quickly sink. It was apparent that the ship's pumps would not be able to keep pace with the level of water entering the vessel, so the Master decided that he would run for shore as quickly as possible. In the meantime the crew got the jolly-boat ready loaded with their belongings. At 10.30pm the water was coming over the vessel's rails and it was at this point that the decision was made to leave the *London Packet* so the crew manned the oars of the jolly boat and pulled away.

The *London Packet* was carrying a quantity of oil and the action of the waves caused this to spill out over the sea around the vessel. This was somewhat fortunate for the crew as it had the effect of calming the sea surface. The *London Packet* eventually sank in about five fathoms of water. Once the cargo of wheat came into contact with the water, it started to swell and this eventually forced out the sides of the vessel. This, coupled with the action of the sea, broke the vessel up into many pieces. It was insured for £300.

Luckily for the crew, the Master knew this part of the coast very well and decided to make for Hastings Pier. It was just as well that they did, because the sea was such that if they had attempted to land anywhere else at Hastings, their boat would have been smashed to pieces. It took the crew nearly three hours of great effort to arrive at Hastings Pier at 1.15am the following morning. They were met by the local Coastguard and taken to the Priory Coastguard Station under the care of the chief officer, Mr. Reed. They stayed until midday the following day when Mr. Moulton, Secretary of the Shipwrecked Mariners Society, gave them money and travel passes to return home.

The vessel's master sold the jolly-boat for £1 to a local fisherman.

*Ref: SIBI; HC 13.3.1878; FE 16.3.1878; HO 9.3.1878; HI 12.3.1878*

# JESSY

| | |
|---|---|
| **Date:** | 30.8.1878 |
| **Wreck Location:** | Ashore west of Newhaven harbour |
| **Description of Vessel:** | |
| **Vessel Type -** | British sailing ketch |
| **Cargo:** | 100 tons of bagged cement, 20 tons of machinery |
| **Home Port:** | Plymouth |
| **Voyage:** | London to Plymouth |
| **Date Built, Builder:** | c.1857 |
| **Owner:** | W. Wolland, Plymouth |
| **Ship's Master:** | J. Holten |
| **Number of Crew:** | 3 |

The *Jessy,* also referred to as the *Jesse* or *Jessie*, on the night of Thursday 29th August 1878 was running down the Channel making for Plymouth in a severe storm and very heavy seas. At 11pm, when 5 miles/8km west of Brighton, the vessel lost three of the mainmast shrouds which meant that it could not carry sufficient canvass to manage her properly. The master decided to try and make for the shelter of Newhaven harbour.

As the *Jessy* approached the harbour, early Friday morning, it was evident that without sail the master was not going to make it with safety, so he ran for the shore just west of the harbour and beached her without any loss of life. The crew remained on board until the tide had receded sufficiently for them to get ashore. They then set about getting most of the cargo off the *Jessy* before the following tide smashed the vessel to pieces.

*Ref: SIBI; SE 31.8.1878; HI 3.9.1878; HC 4.9.1878*

# NINA

| | |
|---|---|
| **Date:** | 2.1.1879 |
| **Wreck Location:** | Ashore near Langney Coastguard Station |
| **Description of Vessel:** | |
| **Gross Tonnage -** | 170 |
| **Vessel Type -** | British sailing brigantine |
| **Cargo:** | Ballast |
| **Home Port:** | Portsmouth |
| **Voyage:** | Portsmouth to Scotland |
| **Date Built, Builder:** | c.1875 in New Brunswick |
| **Owner:** | Messrs. J. Douglas, T. Douglas, Edward Savage. |
| **Ship's Master:** | Edward Savage |

At 3am on Thursday 2nd January 1879, when just off the Royal Sovereign Light, the steamship *Santander* of and from Newcastle and bound for Bilbao, collided with the starboard side of the *Nina* which was under full sail. Although it was later found that the damage caused to the *Nina* was slight, the crew abandoned her and were picked up by the *Santander* to be later landed at Dover.

At 4am the following morning the duty coastguard at Langney Coastguard Station saw the abandoned *Nina* approaching the shore with all sails set. At the time a south-westerly gale was blowing. The coastguard lookout believed the vessel to be in distress and raised the alarm informing the officer in charge, Mr. Smith. By the time Smith arrived on the beach with his men, the vessel had been driven ashore by the wind and turned broadside on to the beach. They found the vessel totally deserted and upon inspection found the slight damage to the starboard side caused by the

*Santander,* but no other reason as to why she should have been abandoned. The master's cabin was still locked although there were no boats on the deck. Not knowing what had happened earlier, this led the coastguard to believe the crew had left in the boats thinking that the *Nina* was about to immediately sink after a collision.

Mr. Smith gained entry to the master's cabin and took possession of the vessel's papers, the master's watch and charts as well as the crew's clothing. Later that afternoon his men removed the sails which were considerably damaged, together with the top mast and spars.

*Ref: HO 4.1.1879; SE 7.1.1879; LL 20184 4.1.79*

# MARIE

| | |
|---|---|
| **Date:** | 3.1.1879 |
| **Wreck Location:** | Off Newhaven |
| **Description of Vessel:** | |
| **Vessel Type -** | German sailing schooner |
| **Cargo:** | 150 tons of potatoes |
| **Home Port:** | Rostock |
| **Voyage:** | Stettin to Exeter |
| **Number of Crew:** | 15 |

During the morning of Thursday 2nd January 1879 the Italian barque *Tommasco* travelling from Philadelphia to Lynn under the command of the master Stagno, was in collision with the *Marie* off Beachy Head. The crew abandoned the *Marie* when she lost her mast as a result of the impact, but were picked up by the *Tommasco* and later put ashore at Deal, Kent.

At noon the following day the dismasted *Marie* was seen drifting off Newhaven and the alarm was raised. The lifeboat, *Michael Henry*, was launched under coxswain Richard Lower. He had only been made coxswain the previous July when his predecessor, Edward Mewett was drowned while sailing a barge down the river from Lewes to Newhaven.

Not only did the *Michael Henry* make for the *Marie*, but the steamer *Bordeaux* also went to assist. It took an hour for them to come alongside the drifting vessel only to find it totally abandoned. It was evident that the crew had left in great haste as their clothes and personal effects, including the master's watch, together with the vessel's papers, were still on board. The *Bordeaux* and the *Michael Henry* towed her safely to Newhaven. However the strain on the vessel had been too much and it started to break up in the harbour, so the cargo was quickly discharged. On boarding the vessel in Newhaven a dog and a pigeon were found still alive.

*Ref: SNLB; HC 8.1.1879; LL 20185 6.1.79*

# TRUE

| | |
|---|---|
| **Date:** | 13.1.1879 |
| **Wreck Location:** | Ashore at Portobello 4 miles/6.4km west of Newhaven |
| **Description of Vessel:** | |
| Length - | 104ft/31.69m |
| Beam - | 25ft/7.72m |
| Vessel Type - | British sailing brigantine |
| **Cargo:** | Coal |
| **Home Port:** | Faversham |
| **Voyage:** | Swansea to Newhaven |
| **Date Built, Builder:** | c.1866 by Simpson at Prince Edward Island, Nova Scotia |
| **Owner:** | C. Hoult, Whitstable |
| **Ship's Master:** | H. P. Coleman |
| **Number of Crew:** | 5 |

---

At about 7pm on the evening of Monday 13th January 1879 a patrolling coastguard on the cliff top at Portobello, about 4 miles/6.4km to the west of Newhaven, could hear voices below him. At the time, there was a strong south-westerly wind blowing and it was very foggy. On looking down he saw the *True* had been driven ashore and raised the alarm with a request for assistance at the scene.

The Newhaven lifeboat, *Michael Henry,* was launched and on arrival stood off her with the hope that the flood tide would lift the vessel clear and then be got off. However, this did not happen with the waves of the incoming tide breaking over the stranded vessel. At 2.45am the crew decided that they would have to leave the *True* and so the lifeboat was summonsed to come alongside and take the crew off. This was successfully accomplished with the lifeboat returning to Newhaven safely with all six men.

The following day the weather and seas had still not abated and with the *True* now full of water, it was slowly breaking up.

*Ref: SIBI; CNMM; HI 21.1.1879; EG 22.1.1879*

# OCEAN FLOWER

| | |
|---|---|
| **Date:** | 8.5.1879 |
| **Wreck Location:** | Ashore near Portobello Coastguard Station, Newhaven |
| **Description of Vessel:** | |
| **Vessel Type -** | British sailing lugger |
| **Cargo:** | Stone |
| **Voyage:** | Newhaven to Portobello |
| **Owner:** | E. Holder, Newhaven |
| **Ship's Master:** | William Martin |
| **Number of Crew:** | 2 |

On the evening of Thursday 8th May 1879, the *Ocean Flower* left Newhaven under the command of the master, William Martin, and two crew, Ted Gilham and Richard Wells. They had gone to collect boulders and by about 10.30pm had a cargo of about 5 tons.

The crew of the *Ocean Flower* were lifting the anchor and setting the sails for the return to Newhaven in the force 4 north-westerly wind when the vessel suddenly took a couple of large waves over the side causing it to sink about 60yds/18.4m from the shore. The three men on board managed to get the mast down with the intention of floating ashore on it, but another wave washed all three men off the vessel. William Martin and Ted Gilham managed to swim ashore but Richard Wells drowned with his body being found 7.30am the following morning by George Mantell.

The Inquest into the death of Richard Wells was held on Saturday at the Hope Inn, Newhaven, before the Coroner Mr. L.G. Fullagar. The first witness was David Stevens who was the master of the brig *Tagus*. He identified the deceased and told the Inquest that Richard Wells was 19 years of age and that they had both been on a ship together about a year ago. The second witness was William Martin who explained what happened on the *Ocean Flower*. The following witness was George Mantell who was himself a mariner. He told the Coroner that it was his belief that the deceased had managed to reach the shore alive because the body was to the east of the sunken vessel, whereas the tide would have taken him to the west of the *Ocean Flower*. The verdict returned was 'Accidental Drowning'.

*Ref: SIBI; SE 13.5.1879; HC 14.5.1879*

# GLANEUR

| | |
|---|---|
| **Date:** | 17.9.1879 |
| **Wreck Location:** | 15 miles/24km off Beachy Head |
| **Description of Vessel:** | |
| **Vessel Type -** | French sailing brigantine |
| **Home Port:** | Nantes |
| **Ship's Master:** | Jean Pepilist |
| **Number of Crew:** | 7 |

During the morning of Wednesday 17th September 1879 the *Glaneur* was run down by a large unknown steamship when about 15 miles/24km off Beachy Head. Two of the crew were found to be missing after the impact but it was not known if they managed to jump onto this unknown vessel or were lost at sea. The master and the remaining five members of the crew were fortunately picked up by a Welsh vessel and later transferred to the Deal fishing smack *Albert Victor* which put them ashore near the coastguard station at Seaside, Eastbourne. Later that day the rescued men were taken by Mr. Hall, the local Lloyds agent, to the French Consulate at Newhaven.

A few days after this incident some coastguardsmen found a long boat and oars from the *Glaneur*. On Friday 26th September this was sold by auction on the beach by Mr. J. Easter from the auctioneers and house agents Messrs. Easter & Wright, Terminus Road, Eastbourne.

*Ref; SIBI; EC 20.9.1879 & 27.9.1879; EG 24.9.1879*

# HARVEST HOME

| | |
|---|---|
| **Date:** | 25.6.1880 |
| **Wreck Location:** | 4 miles/6.4km south-east of Beachy Head and 3 miles/4.8km of Eastbourne. |
| **Description of Vessel:** | |
| **Gross Tonnage -** | 132 |
| **Length -** | 75ft/22.82m |
| **Beam -** | 21ft/6.49m |
| **Vessel Type -** | British sailing brig |
| **Cargo:** | Coal |
| **Home Port:** | Aberdeen |
| **Voyage:** | Sunderland to Portsmouth |
| **Date Built, Builder:** | c.1838 at Aberdeen |
| **Owner:** | W. Milburn, Sunderland |
| **Number of Crew:** | 4 |

The specific destination of the *Harvest Home* is not too clear as it is also recorded as being Jersey.

In the early hours of Friday 25th June 1880, when the vessel was off Shoreham, it developed a leak so severe that the pumps were unable to retard the rising water level. The vessel tried to make for Newhaven but the increasing level of water was making her more and more unmanageable.

There were two stories as to the cause of the leak. The first being that the *Harvest Home* had struck another sunken vessel, and the other story being that she was a 42 year old vessel and not very seaworthy. However, the vessel had been overhauled and recaulked after shipping her previous cargo. Whatever the cause, the crew had to leave the sinking vessel in their boat and start towards the shore in the force 6 north-westerly wind.

A local fisherman named Matthews noticed their plight and caused a fishing boat to put off to investigate and it found the crew of the *Harvest Home* and towed them into Eastbourne. As the rescued crew did not have time to collect any of their possessions or clothing from the *Harvest Home*, they were taken to Mr. Hall, the local agent of the Shipwrecked Mariners Society, who tended to their needs. He also arranged railway passes for them to travel that evening to the Shipwrecked Sailors' Home in London.

*Ref: SIBI; HC 30.6.1880; HT 3.7.1880;*

# LUNA NUEVA

| | |
|---|---|
| **Date:** | 16.7.1880 |
| **Wreck Location:** | 14 miles/22.5km south of Beachy head |

**Description of Vessel:**

| | |
|---|---|
| **Gross Tonnage -** | 300 |
| **Vessel Type -** | Spanish sailing barque |
| **Cargo:** | Brandy, whisky, rum, gin, iron rails |
| **Voyage:** | Antwerp to Havannah |
| **Date Built, Builder:** | c.1862 |
| **Owner:** | A. Sagasta & Co., Corcubion, Spain |
| **Ship's Master:** | J. A. Rodriguez |
| **Number of Crew:** | 10 |
| **Number of Passengers:** | 1 |

At about 2am on Friday 16th July 1880 in almost completely calm conditions the *Luna Nueva* was struck by lightening in a tremendous electric storm. The vessel's location at the time was described as 14 miles/22.5km south of Beachy Head by one account but 2 miles/3.2km west of the Royal Sovereign Light in another.

At the time of the lightening strike the crew were on deck watching the storm, together with the master's wife. The lightening was incredibly violent and it could be seen quite close to the vessel striking the sea. Suddenly one bolt hit the *Luna Nueva* causing the three masts to come crashing down. The lightening strike also demolished the wheel, with the helmsman having a lucky escape with his life, as well as the bulwarks which were extensively damaged along the full length of the vessel. The master, Rodriguez, mustered his crew to find that none had been injured, which in the circumstances was incredible. After the muster the crew was set to work clearing away the fallen masts, rigging and spar. The vessel was now totally unmanageable without both sails and steering.

During the course of removing the wreckage it was discovered that the vessel was on fire from the lightening strike. The crew had to divert from clearing the wreckage to trying to extinguish the fire, however, their fire fighting was having no effect. It was clear that the vessel would have to be abandoned so the crew, master's wife and the vessel's dog, got on board the vessel's jolly-boats and abandoned the *Luna Nueva*. Fortunately there were a number of other vessels nearby who had witnessed these events and they were quickly picked up by a steamer and then transferred to the Newhaven steam tug *Victor*.

The *Victor,* having taken the crew on board, also managed to get a line on the *Luna Nueva* and take her in tow bringing the vessel close inshore for the fire to burn itself out, opposite the Buckle Inn, Seaford. The rescued crew were landed at Newhaven and taken to the Bridge and Ship hotels to recover from their ordeal.

Late on Friday afternoon the vessel had burnt to the water line with continuous explosions and flames coming from the vessel as the barrels of spirits exploded one after another. It was in this condition that at high water that afternoon the *Luna Nueva* was towed nearer to the east pier at Newhaven harbour where she sank. On Sunday afternoon the hull fell in two going totally to pieces. At low water the only part of the cargo to be salvaged were the iron rails and the odd barrel of spirits.

*Ref: SIBI; SE 17.7.1880; EC 17.7.1880; HI 20.7.1880; HC 21.7.1880*

# SQUALE

| | |
|---|---|
| **Date:** | 12.11.1880 |
| **Wreck Location:** | 12 miles/19.3km south of Beachy Head |
| **Description of Vessel:** | |
| **Gross Tonnage -** | 68 |
| **Length -** | 69ft/21.18m |
| **Beam -** | 18ft/5.61m |
| **Vessel Type -** | British sailing schooner |
| **Cargo:** | Barley |
| **Home Port:** | Guernsey |
| **Voyage:** | St. Malo to London |
| **Date Built, Builder:** | c.1877 in France |
| **Owner:** | P. Gavey, Jersey, Channel Islands |
| **Ship's Master:** | A. P. Woods |
| **Number of Crew:** | 3 |

On Thursday 12th November 1880 in a force 6 westerly wind, the *Squale* sank after colliding with the German steamship *Silesia*.

*Ref: SIBI*

# APHRODITE

| | |
|---|---|
| **Date:** | 18.1.1881 |
| **Wreck Location:** | Ashore 200yds/182.9m west of Holywell Bank, Eastbourne |
| **Description of Vessel:** | |
| **Vessel Type -** | German sailing brigantine |
| **Cargo:** | 170 tons of coal |
| **Home Port:** | East Friesland |
| **Voyage:** | Newcastle-upon-Tyne to Bari, Italy |
| **Date Built, Builder:** | c.1867 |
| **Owner:** | R. W. Remmers & Co. Emden, Germany |
| **Ship's Master:** | Johann Dieu |
| **Number of Crew:** | 4 and a boy |

---

The *Aphrodite*, first registered in Munich on 6th March 1868 with the number 666, left Newcastle on Saturday 15th January 1881 bound for Bari, Italy with 170 tons of coal. Although not unduly heavily loaded the deck was only about 18ins./45.7cm above the surface of the water.

From the outset of her voyage the vessel encountered severe weather. From the North Sea to the English Channel the pumps were constantly manned as the vessel was shipping a great deal of water. Once in the Channel the vessel not only had the gale to contend with but also the accompanying snow.

At 4am on Tuesday 18th January, in these horrendous conditions, the master decided to make towards land to ascertain where they were, as the driving snow made this impossible to do out at sea. As they neared land they were able to see the lighthouse at Dungeness and the master decided that to save both crew and vessel they should put ashore at Holywell. He had a discussion with the crew who all agreed with this plan, except the mate Henrich Toben, who thought they should try and round Beachy Head before putting ashore. However, his suggestion was ignored and at 9.30am that morning the *Aphrodite* ran aground on rocks about 200 yards/182.9m off Holywell and within the hour it had gone to pieces. The crew, anticipating such an event, had already partly undressed in order that they could swim more easily once they were in the water as there were no life buoys on the vessel.

The mate, Toben, found himself in the water holding onto a piece of wreckage from the vessel with the vessel's boy, Wilhelm Goldberg. He held onto the boy for as long as was possible in the heavy seas and snow until through sheer exhaustion he had to let the boy go to save his own life. Unbeknown to Toben as he struggled in the water, his plight and that of the *Aphrodite,* had been witnessed from the shore and both the Coastguard and Lifeboat had been informed.

As soon as the lifeboat received the information they got their boat in readiness and were in the act of launching it when a large wave knocked the lifeboat off the carriage causing some damage. In view of this, at 10.50am, the following telegram was sent to Captain Gambier R.N., the Inspecting Commander for the Hastings District Coastguards, *"Ship ashore on Holywell Ledge. Trying to get lifeboat off at Eastbourne. Name of vessel unknown"*. As soon as this telegram was received at Hastings Post Office it was sent to Capt. Gambier's clerk, Mr. Dixon, at the Priory Coastguard Station, who sent the following reply, *"Telegraph back immediately if Eastbourne lifeboat has got off. If not shall Hastings boat launch?"* Mr. Dixon waited for the reply which by noon had not arrived. He then sent word to Mr. George Hutchings, the secretary of the Hastings & St. Leonards Branch of the National Lifeboat Institution, to get the lifeboat *Charles Arckoll* ready. The lifeboat crew were mustered and at 1.30pm that afternoon the *Charles Arckoll* was launched in heavy snow. The crew took with them a couple of bottles of spirits donated by Mr. H. Chapman of Hastings House, All Saints Street.

Sometime between 2pm and 3pm that afternoon, with the *Charles Arckoll* well on her way to Eastbourne, a telegram was received in answer to the one sent by Mr. Dixon earlier that morning. The telegram read, *"Vessel broken up and Eastbourne lifeboat damaged; and according to information crew all lost"*. A further telegram was received from Eastbourne at 4.12pm, *"One life saved. Vessel total wreck. Eastbourne lifeboat damaged in launching. Hastings lifeboat no use in sending, and has not been seen off this station"*. Meanwhile the *Charles Arckoll* arrived off Beachy Head at about 4pm, by which time their services were clearly no longer required. Instead of returning immediately back to Hastings the 13 man crew put in at Eastbourne where they spent the night at the Workmen's Hall, Seaside being cared for by the steward, Mr. Powell. The final telegram from Eastbourne to Hastings was sent at 6.28pm and read, *"Hastings lifeboat landed here in safety. No use at wreck"*.

On seeing the perilous state that the mate Toben was in, a local fisherman, Henry Boniface, assisted by coastguardsmen Phillips, Collins and Markwick, rushed into the sea. Luckily Boniface managed to get hold of Toben and pull him safely to the shore taking him to the house of a relative, James Boniface. It was here that Dr. Sherwood attended to Toben for the effects of the cold and exhaustion. Once Toben had recovered sufficiently his first request was for a pipe of tobacco. The Rev. Mr. Ibbotson and one of the sisters from All Saints Convalescent Home also attended the scene, with a stretcher and blankets, having agreed to accept Toben at the Home until he had fully recovered. Henrich Toben was to be the only survivor with Johann Dieu, the master; three seamen Jacob Schmidt, Rudolf Oltof, Herman Burkes and the vessel's boy, Wilhem Goldberg, all being lost.

At 8am on Saturday 22nd January a coastguard from Beachy Head, Charles Reynolds, was patrolling the beach 2 miles/2.1km west of Holywell when he found the body of the seaman Herman Burkes. The body was taken to the Ship Inn, Meads, Eastbourne where, on the following Tuesday, the Inquest was held before Mr. Wynne E. Baxter, the Coroner for the Eastern Division of Sussex. Henrich Toben gave his evidence through an interpreter, Monsieur Lambert of 4, Sussex Gardens, Eastbourne, a professor of French and German. At the end of the Inquest a collection was made among the Jury who collected £1.1s.0d/£1.05p for Toben who was given an additional 10s.6d/52½d by Monsieur Lambert which was his interpreting fee. At 3pm the same day, after the Inquest, his funeral took place at Eastbourne Cemetery.

On Tuesday 8th February at 6.30am the body of another member of the crew, believed to be Jacob Schmidt, was found on the beach at Holywell by Edward Boniface. The body was badly decomposed but at the Inquest, again held at the Ship Inn, a local doctor, Mr. H. Farmer, told the Coroner, Mr. Wynne E. Baxter, that among other things there were the initials 'J.S.' round the last button hole on the deceased's shirt. Police Constable Ranger told the hearing that the body had a ring on the third finger of the right hand marked on the inside 'M.M. 1877'. The Inquest was unable to hear from Henrich Toben because he had by this time returned to Germany.

At 11.15am on Thursday 10th February a local fisherman, William French of 13 Willow Walk, Eastbourne, was on the parade under the pier when he found another body from the *Aphrodite* crew. It was similarly badly decomposed and with Toben already having returned to Germany, the Inquest before the Deputy Coroner for East Sussex, Mr. J.E. Fullagar, on Saturday 12th February at the Devonshire Park Smoking Room, was unable to formally identify the body. Despite the lack of positive evidence of identification the Jury inferred that the body was one of the lost crew, and returned an open verdict.

*Ref: SIBI; EG 19.1.1881 & 16.2.1881; HT 22.1.1881& 29.1.1881; SE 2.1.1881 & 12.2.1881; EC 22.1.1881 & 29.1.1881*

# FAIRFAX

| | |
|---|---|
| **Date:** | 10.2.1881 |
| **Wreck Location:** | Ashore 590yds/539.5m from Crowlink Gap Coastguard Station |
| **Description of Vessel:** | |
| **Gross Tonnage -** | 930 |
| **Length -** | 225ft/68.75m |
| **Beam -** | 29ft/8.78m |
| **Vessel Type -** | British iron collier steamship |
| **Cargo:** | General |
| **Home Port:** | London |
| **Voyage:** | Le Havre to the Tyne |
| **Date Built, Builder:** | c.1865 by London & Glasgow Co. at Glasgow |
| **Owner:** | General Iron Screw Collier Co. Ltd., London |
| **Ship's Master:** | C. F. Butler |
| **Number of Crew:** | 16 |

The three-masted iron steamship *Fairfax* left Le Havre on the night of Wednesday 9th February 1881 and during the course of the night encountered a force 8 north-westerly storm. The vessel fought against the heavy seas and wind but, being a light vessel and with damaged steering gear, soon became unmanageable in these conditions. The *Fairfax* was driven ever closer to Beachy Head until the white chalk cliffs were clearly visible to the crew.

Just before dawn of the following day, the *Fairfax* was finally driven ashore about 590 yards/539.5m from the Crowlink Coastguard Station with such force that the vessel's bowsprit almost touched the cliff face. Fortunately for those on board, the look-out at the coastguard station had seen the plight of the *Fairfax*. The station officer, John Jessey, sent a message to the next coastguard station at Birling Gap requesting the rocket apparatus be brought as soon as possible to the scene. In the meantime John Jessey and four of his men went up onto the cliff edge above the *Fairfax,* with three cliff rope ladders which, when joined together, extended to 40 fathoms/74m. The men set about driving iron stakes into the ground above the vessel and the chain of the three rope ladders was dropped over the cliff edge to the shore below. However, they could not make contact with those on the vessel, so John Jessey left two of his men at the cliff edge and with the other two went back down to Crowlink Gap and on to the beach.

Jessey and his two coastguards made their way along the foot of the cliffs towards the stranded vessel taking with them some surf lines. They eventually reached the foot of their rope ladder. The surf lines were tied to it with the other end of the surf lines being thrown onto the *Fairfax* for the crew to haul in. Each crew member then took it in turn to hold the rope ladder and be pulled ashore by the coastguards but only as far as a fallen rock due to the state of the sea and tide. All crew, having reached this 5ft/1.5m square rock, then spent the next 3½ hours on it while the heavy surf washed around them until the tide receded sufficiently for them to walk to safety along the beach.

The rescued crew were taken to Crowlink Coastguard Station where they were cared for before being returned to London on the night train from Seaford.

At 3pm on Friday 18th February the vessel, as it laid under the cliffs, together with its contents were sold by public auction by Messrs. Easter & Wright on behalf of Messrs. J. & N.C. Bull, the Lloyd's Agents at Newhaven. The vessel was sold as one lot for the sum of £665 to Mr. Cohen of London.

*Ref: SIBI; SE 12.2.1881; EG 16.2.1881; HC 23.2.1881*

# JUNO

| | |
|---|---|
| **Date:** | 3.3.1881 |
| **Wreck Location:** | 4 miles/6.4km south-east of Royal Sovereign Light |
| **Description of Vessel:** | |
| **Length -** | 88ft/26.97m |
| **Beam -** | 22ft/6.65m |
| **Vessel Type -** | British sailing schooner |
| **Cargo:** | China clay, gunpowder |
| **Home Port:** | Fowey, Cornwall |
| **Voyage:** | Fowey to Newcastle-upon-Tyne |
| **Date Built, Builder:** | c.1864, by Slade at Polruan, Cornwall |
| **Owner:** | S. Slade, Polruan, Cornwall |
| **Ship's Master:** | W. Abbott |
| **Number of Crew:** | 5 |

On the evening of Thursday 3rd March 1881, the *Juno* was 4 miles/6.4km south east of the Royal Sovereign Light in a force 5 south-easterly wind. The *Lady Ruthven* of Greenock was under tow in the same vicinity when she ran the *Juno* down causing the latter to sink within five minutes of the collision. Three of the *Juno* crew were saved by the *Lady Ruthven* but the other three were drowned, two of them going down with the vessel. The three rescued men, namely the Master, the Mate and one seaman, were landed at Plymouth on the following Sunday.

*Ref: SIBI; EG 9.3.1881; HN 11.3.1881*

# SERVITOR

| | |
|---|---|
| **Date:** | 20.7.1881 |
| **Wreck Location:** | Off Hope Gap, Cuckmere |
| **Description of Vessel:** | |
| **Gross Tonnage -** | 19 |
| **Length -** | 55ft/16.94m |
| **Beam -** | 13ft/3.83m |
| **Vessel Type -** | British sailing ketch |
| **Cargo:** | Sand |
| **Home Port:** | Newhaven |
| **Voyage:** | Newhaven to Lewes |
| **Date Built, Builder:** | c.1868 at Lewes |
| **Owner:** | Frank Charles Berry, William Bussey & Charles William Hemsley |
| **Number of Crew:** | 4 |

The crew of the *Servitor,* namely Frederick Haffenden, Trayton Trash, Charles Hemsley and a man named Upton, were all from the town of Lewes. They had been tasked by the owners of the vessel, who were building contractors, to recover iron from a wreck (identity unknown) that was lying off Birling Gap. The salvaged iron was for the Lewes and Eastbourne ironfounders, Messrs. E. Morris & Son.

On the night of Wednesday 20th July 1881, the *Servitor* was on the return journey with the salvaged iron in a force 2 south-westerly wind, off Hope Gap, between Cuckmere and Newhaven when the vessel suddenly sank in less than three minutes. Although it was not fully understood why the vessel sank it is believed the bottom of the vessel gave way. Unfortunately, as it did so, Frederick Haffenden went down with the vessel. The remaining three men managed to hang on to floating debris for two hours before they were finally rescued by the local coastguard boat, who had been alerted by a woman who saw the vessel go down.

A couple of weeks later a body was found in the sea off Hastings and after an Inquest was buried as a person unknown. However, as the result of Lewes Police becoming aware that Frederick Haffenden had a particular knife with him they made contact with Supt. Glenister of Hastings Police who forwarded to Lewes Police the knife found on the body. The knife was positively identified by Trayton Trash as his knife, that he had lent to Haffenden. The Police were also later to confirm that tattoo marks on the body were similar to those the survivors had seen on Haffenden.

*Ref: SIBI; SE 23.7.1881 & 26.7.1881; HO 13.8.1881*

# EUGENIE

| | |
|---|---|
| **Date:** | 1.8.1881 |
| **Wreck Location:** | 7 miles/11.27km north-east of Beachy Head |
| **Description of Vessel:** | |
| **Vessel Type -** | French sailing schooner |
| **Cargo:** | Granite |
| **Voyage:** | Boulogne to St. Malo |
| **Date Built, Builder:** | c.1861 |
| **Owner:** | P. Duclos, Granville, France |
| **Ship's Master:** | J. F. Carbon |
| **Number of Crew:** | 3 |
| **Number of Passengers:** | 1 |

On Monday 1st August 1881 the *Eugenie,* while in a force 1 northerly wind, suddenly sprang a leak and sank. There is no reported loss of life and so it is assumed that the crew took to their boats and were picked up by another vessel.

*Ref: SIBI; EC 13.8.1881*

# LITTLE WONDER

**Date:** 1.8.1881

**Wreck Location:** 100yds/91.4m off Beachy Head near the Coastguard Station

**Description of Vessel:**
**Vessel Type -** Small pleasure rowing boat

**Home Port:** Eastbourne

**Voyage:** Eastbourne to Beachy Head and return

**Ship's Master:** Frederick W. Brougham

**Number of Passengers:** 1

---

On Bank Holiday Monday, 1ˢᵗ August 1881, Frederick William Brougham, a cashier at the Army & Navy Stores, Victoria Street, London, left his home address of 21 Newbridge Street, Blackfriars, and travelled to Eastbourne for the day, to see his friend Ellen Bunn. She was a parlourmaid who lived at Homehurst, Blackwater Road, Eastbourne. Brougham had also intended looking for a room as he was going to stay for a fortnight's holiday in Eastbourne the following month.

On his arrival in Eastbourne, Brougham decided to take Bunn out for a trip in a rowing boat. At 3.30pm they both went down to the beach and hired a boat, *Little Wonder,* from Richard Carter of 9, Carlton Road, Pevensey Road, Eastbourne, a licensed waterman. Carter confirmed that Brougham could row such a boat and told them that they should stay within the pier. The reason being that the tide would help them on their return journey in the easterly wind. However, they were not far off when Brougham started rowing in the opposite direction towards Beachy Head. However, they were too far for Carter to call out to them.

The sea was very smooth as Brougham made his way towards Beachy Head and the sea remained like this until they started their return journey at 4.45pm when a large swell started to appear on the sea. An exceptionally large wave was seen by Brougham bearing down on their small rowing boat which prompted him to say to Ellen Bunn '*I don't know how we shall get back, there's a large wave coming that will upset the boat*'. As soon as the wave hit the stern of *Little Wonder* it capsized throwing both of them into the sea. They both managed to hang on to the upturned boat when another large wave crashed right over them breaking their hold on the boat. Fortunately Ellen Bunn managed to regain her grip on the boat. Brougham was not so lucky, as once his grip and been broken he was immediately in difficulties. He called out to Bunn for help but there was little she could do. Suddenly with his arms stretched above him he went down.

Clement Stephen Reed, a gardener of 8, Rose Terrace, Pevensey Road, was walking along the beach under Beachy Head when he heard cries for help coming from off shore. It was then that he saw the upturned *Little Wonder* with Bunn and the body of Brougham in the water. As they were quite close he partly undressed and waded into the heavy surf, but being a poor swimmer he was not able to go too far beyond his depth, however, this was just far enough for Ellen Bunn. Reed managed to get hold of her just as heavy surf struck both of them taking them under the water together. Reed held Bunn's arm very tightly and with great difficulty got her safely on to the beach.

Richard Sanders, a coastguard stationed at Beachy Head, had been made aware of the plight of the *Little Wonder* and when he arrived at the scene he got undressed and went into the surf to try and find Brougham. He had swum for about 200 yards/183m when as the surf rose he saw the body of the deceased. Together with the help of his colleagues the deceased was brought ashore. On examining Frederick Brougham, Richard Sanders found that his watch had stopped at 4.45.

The Inquest was held at 7pm on the following Wednesday evening at the Ship Hotel, Meads, Eastbourne before the Coroner for East Sussex, Mr. Wynne E. Baxter and a Jury. At the end of the evidence the Coroner expressed concern that boats were being hired without any warning being given by watermen of the dangers of the reefs at the Wish Tower and Beachy Head. He also gave Clement Reed 1s.0d/5p as a reward in the rescue of Ellen Bunn, the maximum award he could make. The Jury duly returned a verdict of Death by Drowning and requested that the Coroner draw to the attention of the Royal Humane Society the part Clement Reed played in Ellen Bunn's rescue. As a result the Coroner later presented Reed with a certificate from the Royal Humane Society for saving Ellen Bunn's life.

*Ref: EC 6.8.1881; EG 2.9.1881*

# LOUIS

| | |
|---|---|
| **Date:** | 25.9.1881 |
| **Wreck Location:** | 10 miles/16.1km south-west of Beachy Head |
| **Description of Vessel:** | |
| **Length -** | 106ft/32.37m |
| **Beam -** | 23ft/7.11m |
| **Vessel Type -** | French sailing brig |
| **Home Port:** | St. Malo |
| **Voyage:** | Brest to Riga |
| **Date Built, Builder:** | c.1863 |
| **Owner:** | F. Henry, St Malo |
| **Ship's Master:** | Boutrais |
| **Number of Crew:** | 7 |

The *Louis,* previously named *Result*, sank after being in collision with the barque *Seiriol Wyn* in a force 6 south-westerly gale. All the crew were lost except one.

*Ref: SIBI*

# JOHNNY BOY

**Date:** 1.11.1881

**Wreck Location:** Near Eastbourne

**Description of Vessel:**
**Vessel Type -** British sailing ketch

**Cargo:** Stone

**Home Port:** Southampton

**Voyage:** Swanage to Eastbourne

**Date Built, Builder:** c.1854

**Owner:** J. Bray, Woolston Hampshire

**Ship's Master:** G. T. Barnett

**Number of Crew:** 2

---

The *Johnny Boy* became a loss near Eastbourne on Tuesday 1st November 1881

*Ref: SIBI*

# MICHAEL HENRY

| | |
|---|---|
| **Date:** | 26.11.1881 |
| **Wreck Location:** | Newhaven Harbour |
| **Description of Vessel:** | |
| **Length -** | 37ft/22.32m |
| **Beam -** | 9ft/2.6m |
| **Vessel Type -** | Newhaven self-righting Lifeboat |
| **Home Port:** | Newhaven |
| **Voyage:** | Newhaven to sea rescue and return |
| **Date Built, Builder:** | c.1877, Forrestt, Limehouse, London |
| **Owner:** | Royal National Lifeboat Institution |
| **Ship's Master:** | Richard Lower (Coxswain) |
| **Number of Crew:** | 12 |

The *Michael Henry* replaced the Newhaven Lifeboat *Elizabeth Boys* on 28th August 1877 having been built at a cost of £392.10s.0d./£392.50p. The money having been supplied from a fund to which Jewish school children throughout the United Kingdom had donated to. The fund being the creation of Michael Henry after whom the new lifeboat was named at a ceremony on 3rd September 1877.

At 10am on Saturday 26th November 1881 the 330 ton brigantine *Harriett*, left Newhaven harbour under tow of the tug *Tipper,* bound for Sunderland in ballast. Throughout the previous night a squally stiff breeze had been blowing veering from north west to south west. However, by 10am it had abated slightly, hence the decision was made by Mr. Fieldgate, the master of the *Harriett*, to go to sea. Unfortunately by the time the *Harriett* actually cleared the harbour piers the wind had turned southerly and increased to gale force. With this change in wind strength and direction, it made it almost impossible for her sails to fill and was therefore entirely reliant on the towing tug. One of those watching ashore, Mr. Jenkins the Officer in Charge of the local coastguard station, could see the *Harriett* was starting drift leeward. He was so concerned as to the safety of the vessel that he ordered the lifeboat be got ready.

It was not long before a lifeboat crew for the *Michael Henry* had been mustered, consisting mainly of regular crew members with a number of volunteers making up the deficit. The 12 strong crew, under the command of the coxswain Richard Lower, were Matthew Lower, George Alexander, William Winder, Shadrach Wood, James Balcombe, David Beale, Benjamin Foster, James Frosdyke, James Willsher, George Bryant, Richard Winter, and Jarvis Mitchell. With the crew all ready and wearing their cork jackets, they rowed towards the harbour entrance.

Once clear of the harbour, the lifeboat crew set their sails and made very rapid progress towards the *Harriett,* which by now was off Seaford, about 3 miles/4.8km from Newhaven harbour. The tow line between the tug and the *Harriet* had broken by now but fortuitously the wind had also turned slightly more westerly which allowed the vessel to fill her sails and become manageable.

The lifeboat coxswain had also seen that the brigantine was now under sail and that his services were no longer required and so returned to Newhaven harbour. However, when about 880yds/805m from the harbour entrance, a tremendous wave broke over the lifeboat filling it with water causing it to capsize. As the lifeboat went over two of the crew were trapped underneath but otherwise unharmed. The remainder of the crew managed either to hang onto the lines from the upturned lifeboat or sit astride the keel. Richard Lower, with those crew members on the outside of the lifeboat, tried to right her by all getting to one side, but this was unsuccessful. With the waves constantly breaking over the upturned boat, it slowly drifted for the next 30 minutes, towards the harbour entrance, still with two men trapped underneath.

News of the lifeboat's plight had now brought a large crowd to the harbour and as it drifted nearer, many in the crowd had lines ready for the crew. As the lifeboat neared the entrance the sea threw it twice against the east pier. Striking the pier for the second time caused the lifeboat to right itself throwing the crew on the outside of the upturned boat into the water. The two men that were underneath came up with the lifeboat and with the help of the lines from those on the pier, all 13 men of the lifeboat were brought safely onto the east pier. The men received a medical check-up from Dr. Dalton and all were found to be uninjured.

The steam tug *Tipper* towed the lifeboat into the harbour where it was found to have suffered severe damage with both sides having been stoved in. It was not the sails that prevented the lifeboat from self-righting, because the masts had snapped at the thwarts when it capsized. It was however, the generally held view that this lifeboat was not a good vessel in heavy seas. The Royal National Lifeboat Institution decided to replace the *Michael Henry* with another self-righting lifeboat, with the same name, on 12th December 1881.

One of the numerous people that watched these events from the east pier was the Right Honorable Sir Henry Brand, Speaker of the House of Commons, who gave the coxswain a sovereign to buy a grog\* for each of the crew.

\* Grog is a spirit drink (especially rum) with water.

*Ref: SNLB; SE 29.11.1881; LL 21087 28.11.81*

# GANNET

| | |
|---|---|
| **Date:** | 14.2.1882 |
| **Wreck Location:** | Ashore 880yds/805m west of Seaford Head |
| **Description of Vessel:** | |
| **Gross Tonnage -** | 1824 |
| **Length -** | 300ft/91.92m |
| **Beam -** | 33ft/10.12m |
| **Vessel Type -** | British iron steamship |
| **Cargo:** | Indigo, silk, cotton, jute, tea, coffee, linseed, buck-horns, hides |
| **Home Port:** | Leith |
| **Voyage:** | Calcutta to London |
| **Date Built, Builder:** | c.1879 by Barclay Curle & Co., Glasgow |
| **Owner:** | Seater & J. White, Leith (The Bird Line) |
| **Ship's Master:** | W.C. Smith |
| **Number of Crew:** | 36 |

---

The steamship *Gannet* (see photograph page 24), valued at £50,000, left London on 1st November 1881 for Calcutta and was on her return voyage via the Suez Canal, when disaster struck off Seaford.

On the night of Monday 13th February 1882, the vessel was sailing up the Channel with a cargo valued at £120,000, when she ran into very thick fog accompanied by squally force 6 south-westerly winds. The effect of these conditions was that the vessel had sailed closer to shore than would otherwise be the case. This, together with the officer of the watch mistaking the lights of Newhaven for a place further east, instilled the belief that they had cleared Beachy Head.

The crew of the *Gannet* did not realise their true position until they had got to the east of Newhaven, and immediately the engines were put into reverse. Unfortunately this response was not soon enough and with the heavy sea running at the time the vessel struck the shore broadside on between "*Mr. Crook's house and Pelham Place*" at 2.30am on the morning of Tuesday 14th February. The effect of the heavy sea caused the vessel to drift further east until it came to rest between the Assembly Rooms and the Martello Tower. Immediately the vessel went aground the crew raised the alarm by firing several rockets and sounding the vessel's whistle.

Just prior to the vessel going aground, George Doran, the look-out at the Blatchington Coastguard Station, had noticed the *Gannet* was in difficulties and informed the officer in charge, Mr. Pride. Mr. Pride, together with a number of his men, were soon at the scene with the rocket apparatus and it was not very long before the first rocket had been fired over the vessel and a line secured to the *Gannet*. The crew of the steamship then hauled a rope on board and by this some twenty crew were pulled safely ashore. By daylight the last of these 20 men was ashore but the remaining crew decided to stay on board, together with a coastguardsman from the Blatchington Station, until low tide.

In the meantime, at 6am, the new lifeboat at Newhaven, the *Michael Henry,* was towed out by the steam tug *Tipper* in readiness to offer any assistance required. Eventually the lifeboat services were not required, on this its first active launch since arriving on station on 12th December 1881.

At 7.30am, while waiting for the tide to recede, those on shore, which now included many spectators, were surprised to see one of the crew still on the *Gannet* suddenly jump over the side of the vessel into the sea. A coastguardsman on the beach rushed into the sea and managed to pull him to safety although he was unconscious and remained so for quite some time. It appeared that the seaman had been drinking after an argument with a fellow crew member.

At 11am, when the tide had receded sufficiently, there was much activity by both crew and spectators unloading as much of the *Gannet's* cargo as possible before the returning tide. It was hoped then to be able to re-float the vessel. 120 tons of the cargo had been salvaged by the time the tide returned with squally winds and further thick fog. These conditions meant any hope of re-floating the *Gannet* by tugs was abandoned.

Throughout Tuesday night the conditions were very stormy and the heavy seas continuously knocked the vessel about and by morning the seas were breaking right over the vessel as high as the mast head. Once the tide had receded yet again, more cargo was salvaged and this continued throughout the following days between each tide with the cargo being taken away in carts to Seaford railway station where it was later sent to London. Fortunately, as the salvage operation progressed, the weather calmed which assisted the unloading process .

On the morning of Wednesday 1st March, the return of the bad weather saw heavy seas breaking over the stricken vessel with terrific force. After each wave crashed into the side of the vessel it rolled violently and soon after 8am broke in two with the contents of the saloon and cabins being washed out. This was the beginning of the end of the *Gannet*, as throughout the day, with the constant battering by the sea, the funnel collapsed, the engines were washed out onto the beach and slowly the sea broke the vessel to pieces.

The continuous activity around the *Gannet* had become of great interest with people travelling from as far as Lewes, Eastbourne and Rottingdean, just to watch. In the evenings when the spectators left to go home, an extended train from Seaford was only just long enough to accommodate them all.

As one can imagine, during the salvage operation, a large quantity of items were left on the beach at various times. The police, with the assistance of the coastguard, were employed to ensure than none of these items were stolen. There was, however, one detected theft when a man was arrested for stealing a piece of copper. He was brought before the Magistrates sitting at Seaford Town Hall on Thursday 2nd March and fined.

*Ref: SIBI; EC 18.2.1882; SE 18.2.1882; SWA 21.2.1882 & 7.3.1882*

# LITTLE DICK

| | |
|---|---|
| **Date:** | 2.4.1882 |
| **Wreck Location:** | 1½ miles/2.4km off Seaford |
| **Description of Vessel:** | |
| **Vessel Type -** | British sailing dandy |
| **Cargo:** | Ballast |
| **Home Port:** | Newhaven |
| **Voyage:** | Newhaven and return |
| **Date Built, Builder:** | c.1866 |
| **Owner:** | J. Hagar, Newhaven |
| **Ship's Master:** | Bradford |
| **Number of Crew:** | 2 |

---

On the evening of Sunday 2nd April 1881, a number of Seaford residents were taking their evening stroll along the promenade. The wind at the time was blowing northerly force 7 with gusts. It was in these conditions at 7.30pm that the *Little Dick,* was off Seaford, en route to collect boulders from the beach, under the command of the master, Mr. Bradford, with his crew of Charles Stone and Robert Stevens. Suddenly a strong gust of wind caught the *Little Dick* capsizing the vessel and throwing the three-man crew into the sea. The crew managed to climb onto the keel of the upturned vessel and were fortunately seen by some of the promenade strollers, who raised the alarm.

Mr. George Green, a local fishmonger, wasted no time in getting one of his boats afloat. With the help of others he soon had one of his boats carried from the land side of the sea wall, where it was kept, down to the water's edge. He and his crew of 4 men (J. Walters, James Simmons, Robert Simmons Jr., and Mr. Caulfield) were quickly alongside the upturned vessel and taking on board the crew of the *Little Dick*. Although exhausted from their ordeal they were otherwise uninjured and were later conveyed to Newhaven.

It was believed that this was the thirteenth time that Charles Stone had been rescued from the sea!

*Ref: SIBI; SWA 4.4.1882*

# NOATUM

| | |
|---|---|
| **Date:** | 18.4.1882 |
| **Wreck Location:** | Off Beachy Head |
| **Description of Vessel:** | |
| **Vessel Type -** | Danish sailing brig |
| **Voyage:** | Galveston to Hamburg |
| **Ship's Master:** | Laerke |

At 2am on Tuesday 18th April 1882, when off Beachy Head, the *Noatum* was in collision with the barque *Ida* of Helsingor which was bound for Rio de Janeiro with timber. The collision was so severe that the *Noatum* sunk within three minutes of the impact. The crew were picked up by the *Ida* and landed at Dover, when the *Ida* was towed in there for repairs by the tug *Rescue*. The *Ida* suffered damage to its bowsprit and hull which had been sufficient to cause the vessel to become waterlogged.

*Ref: SIBI; SWA 25.4.1881*

# ALBERT

| | |
|---|---|
| **Date:** | 26.7.1882 |
| **Wreck Location:** | Ashore 500yds/457m west of Newhaven Harbour |
| **Description of Vessel:** | |
| **Vessel Type -** | British sailing dandy |
| **Cargo:** | Boulders |
| **Voyage:** | Newhaven and return |
| **Date Built, Builder:** | c.1855 |
| **Owner:** | W. Redman, Newhaven |
| **Ship's Master:** | J. Frosdick |
| **Number of Crew:** | 1 |

---

The *Albert* was driven ashore just west of Newhaven harbour, while collecting boulders in a south-easterly force 5 wind on Wednesday 26th July 1882

*Ref: SIBI*

# FRISK

| | |
|---|---|
| **Date:** | 24.10.1882 |
| **Wreck Location:** | Crowlink near Cuckmere |
| **Description of Vessel:** | |
| **Gross Tonnage -** | 619 |
| **Vessel Type -** | Norwegian sailing barque |
| **Cargo:** | Timber |
| **Voyage:** | Mirimichi to Grimsby |
| **Date Built, Builder:** | c.1855 |
| **Owner:** | Suhrke & Co, Frederikshald |
| **Ship's Master:** | R. Pedersen |
| **Number of Crew:** | 12 |

On the morning of Tuesday 24th October 1882 a south-easterly force 11 storm blew with torrential rain and hail. The wind was so strong it caused a great deal of structural damage to buildings and property as well as making it very difficult to stand without being blown over.

In these horrendous weather conditions and mountainous seas, the *Frisk* was being driven before the storm off Seaford, having already lost part of the rigging. The vessel was finally driven onto rocks some distance from the shore at Crowlink, between the Cuckmere River and Beachy Head. The coastguards at the Cuckmere Station, who were aware of the plight of the *Frisk*, had already made for the scene with their rocket apparatus, but on arrival it was evident that the *Frisk* was too far off for it to be of any use. Eventually the stranded crew took to their boat and with great difficulty in these terrible conditions made it safely to the shore. The abandoned *Frisk* continued to be battered by the violent seas until it became a complete wreck. However, the anchors, chains, sails, rigging, ropes and blocks were later salvaged and taken to the Railway Quay, at Newhaven.

At 2pm on Monday 6th November 1882, these salvaged items, together with the hull, were sold by auction at Exceat Farm, near Cuckmere by the Eastbourne auctioneers Messrs. Easter & Wright. The sale was on behalf of the local Lloyd's Agents Messrs. J. & N. C. Bull.

*Ref: SIBI; EC 28.10.1882 & 4.11.1882*

# UNKNOWN

**Date:** 13.11.1882

**Wreck Location:** 15 miles/24km south off Beachy
Head

**Description of Vessel:**
**Vessel Type -** Barque rigged steamship

**Number of Passengers:** 70

---

The identity of this steamship which sank after being in collision with the German steamship *Westphalia,* bound for Hamburg from New York with 70 passengers and general cargo, has never been established. The collision between these two vessels occurred at 1.30am Monday 13th November 1882 about 15 miles/24km south of Beachy Head in strong gale force winds with rain and heavy seas.

Immediately after the impact the engines of the *Westphalia* were stopped and it remained near the scene of the impact. The master ordered the lifeboat be lowered to go in search of survivors. It was equipped with oars and sail but no provisions, and manned by the third officer Mr. Brock and six seamen. Mr. Ludwig, the master of the *Westphalia,* gave Brock orders to try and make for the shore whenever they could as he felt he would be unable to get back to them in the conditions prevailing at the time. As soon as they pulled away from the *Westphalia* Mr. Brock could see the other vessel being driven before the storm about 300yds/274m away. He could also see that the vessel was in danger of sinking and that there was a fire onboard, so his crew rowed their lifeboat towards the stricken vessel. However, before getting much closer the vessel went down with all hands.

Mr. Brock and his lifeboat, in terrible conditions for such a craft, stayed in the area for the next six hours looking for survivors but found none. At 7am that morning he and his crew were picked up by a Belgian pilot vessel who tended to their immediate needs, but they were unable to make fast their boat, and so had to return to it and sail towards Seaford, where they arrived on Tuesday night. However, Mr Brock decided not to come ashore because of the conditions and so they remained in their small boat for one more night, before coming in at Newhaven on Wednesday morning. It was then that Mr. Brock reported the details of the collision to the Customs House at Newhaven. Mr. Hall, the local Lloyd's agent, looked after them before putting them on a train to Portsmouth to re-join the *Westphalia*.

While Mr. Brock and his crew were searching for survivors from the other vessel involved in this collision, it was discovered that the *Westphalia* had been badly damaged with a large hole in her bow down to the water-line. The vessel was taking in so much water that the steam pumps were set to work in the three flooded compartments. The master, Mr. Ludwig, decided that he had to make for Portsmouth to save his vessel and those on board, hence abandoning his third officer and the six seaman in the lifeboat. The *Westphalia* docked at Portsmouth that same evening.

Once in dock it was found that the *Westphalia* required extensive repair. As a result, the crew and the seventy passengers on board were sent by train to London to continue their journey on another of the owner's vessels which was lying at the time in St. Katherine Docks.

*Ref: SIBI; EG 15.11.1882; EC 18.11.1882; SWA 21.11.1882*

# CYLLENNE

| | |
|---|---|
| **Date:** | 23.1.1883 |
| **Wreck Location:** | Off Beachy Head |
| **Description of Vessel:** | |
| **Vessel Type -** | Thames sailing barge |
| **Home Port:** | Harwich |
| **Date Built, Builder:** | c.1873 by Parsons & Cann, Harwich |
| **Owner:** | R. S. Barnes, Harwich |
| **Ship's Master:** | Jacob Fance |

This vessel was lost off Beachy Head on Tuesday 23rd January 1883. It is not known how many were on board other than the master, if any at all, but there were no survivors.

*Ref: SIBI*

# THOMAS & JOHN

| | |
|---|---|
| **Date:** | 17.2.1883 |
| **Wreck Location:** | Ashore at east pier, Newhaven harbour |
| **Description of Vessel:** | |
| **Vessel Type -** | British sailing dandy |
| **Cargo:** | Bagged cement |
| **Home Port:** | Fowey |
| **Voyage:** | Northfleet to Plymouth |
| **Date Built, Builder:** | c.1871 |
| **Owner:** | T. Varcoe, Pentewan, Cornwall |
| **Ship's Master:** | A. Mably |
| **Number of Crew:** | 2 |

On the afternoon of Saturday 17th February 1883 the *Thomas and John* sprung a leak whist in the Channel and had to employ the constant use of the pumps to prevent the vessel sinking. The master decided to make a run for Newhaven harbour in the prevailing force 4 south-westerly wind, in an attempt to alleviate his vessel's predicament. Unfortunately, as the vessel approached the harbour, it was low tide resulting in the vessel striking the sand bar at the entrance. The *Thomas and John* then drifted to the back of the east pier and filled with water.

The Newhaven Lifeboat, *Michael Henry* was launched at 2.15pm and managed to come alongside the stricken vessel and rescue the master and his two crew. Shortly after the crew had been taken off, the *Thomas and John* went totally to pieces as a result of the battering from the surf.

*Ref: SIBI; SNLB; SWA 20.2.1883*

# PUNCH

| | |
|---|---|
| **Date:** | 16.3.1883 |
| **Wreck Location:** | Ashore Birling Gap |
| **Description of Vessel:** | |
| **Vessel Type -** | British sailing dandy |
| **Cargo:** | Boulders |
| **Home Port:** | Newhaven |
| **Voyage:** | Newhaven and return |
| **Date Built, Builder:** | c.1871 |
| **Owner:** | W. Gaston, Newhaven |
| **Ship's Master:** | F. Richardson |
| **Number of Crew:** | 2 |

The *Punch* was lost on Friday 16th March 1883 while collecting boulders from the beach at Birling Gap in force 6 west wind.

*Ref: SIBI*

# DIANA

| | |
|---|---|
| **Date:** | 19.6.1883 |
| **Wreck Location:** | Ashore Birling Gap |
| **Description of Vessel:** | |
| **Vessel Type -** | British sailing dandy |
| **Cargo:** | Granite boulders |
| **Voyage:** | Newhaven and return |
| **Owner:** | J. Eager, Newhaven |
| **Ship's Master:** | A. Winder |
| **Number of Crew:** | 2 |

The *Diana* was lost on Tuesday 19th June 1883 while collecting boulders from the beach at Birling Gap in force 2 south-easterly wind.

*Ref: SIBI*

*ACHILLE*

| | |
|---|---|
| **Date:** | 17.7.1883 |
| **Wreck Location:** | Near Horse Rocks, 3 miles/4.8km west off Royal Sovereign Light |
| **Description of Vessel:** | |
| **Vessel Type -** | Italian sailing Barque |
| **Cargo:** | Oil, petrol |
| **Voyage:** | Buenos Aires to Antwerp |
| **Date Built, Builder:** | c.1868 |
| **Owner:** | L. Negretto, Genoa |
| **Ship's Master:** | L. Negretto |
| **Number of Crew:** | 10 |

For an hour after midnight on Tuesday 17th July 1883, the crew of the Royal Sovereign Lightship had noticed a large steamer, the *Glenogle,* bound for China from London, in the vicinity of the Horse Rocks, to the west of the Lightship. At no time while they were watching the steamer did they notice any other vessels in the area. However, unbeknown to them there was another vessel in the vicinity, the *Achille*, which had been run down by the steamer *Glenogle* whilst at anchor in the dark. The *Glenogle,* once aware of the collision, stopped and rescued all those on board the *Achille* except for three of the crew whose bodies they could not find. Obviously at this time nobody locally was either aware of this or of the fact that the majority of the crew had been saved and were on board the *Glenogle*. They where later to be put ashore in Malta.

The first that anything was thought to have occurred was in the afternoon of the following day when the Coastguard at Eastbourne and Mr. Sawdie, the Eastbourne Piermaster, noticed three masts protruding from the sea. It was later hotly debated as to why those ashore at Eastbourne saw the masts of a sunken vessel before those on board the Royal Sovereign Lightship. Having seen the masts, the information was relayed to Mr. Rudd, of the Albion Hotel, Eastbourne, who was the Lloyd's agent in Eastbourne. Mr. Rudd arranged for a boat to take him to the scene to investigate, in the company of a number of local Coastguardsmen.

The sea was very choppy and the distance of the wreck from the shore meant it took Mr. Rudd's boat quite a long time to reach it. When they finally reached the wreck of the *Achille* which was laying in about fifteen fathoms of water, there was no sign of survivors and no means whereby to identify the sunken vessel. This vessel was of great concern to Rudd as it lay directly on the path that all large ships took when travelling up this part of the Channel. On his return to shore he informed Trinity House in London of the location of the wreck and the hazard it would be to shipping. They arranged for divers to go down to the wreck during the following week with the intention of blowing it up to remove the hazard. However, when the divers reached the *Achille* and saw that its cargo was petrol and oil, the idea was abandoned although the three masts were destroyed using gun cotton as an explosive.

It was not until Monday 30th July, when the *Glenogle* put in at Malta, that those at Eastbourne were made aware of the full story surrounding the demise of the *Achille* and the plight of her crew.

*SIBI; EC 21.7.1883; HN 3.8.1883*

# MARIA JOSEPH

**Date:**                                 21.7.1883

**Wreck Location:**               12 miles/19km off Eastbourne near
                                         Royal Sovereign Light

**Description of Vessel:**
**Gross Tonnage -**               53
**Vessel Type -**                   French sailing schooner

**Cargo:**                            Cement

**Home Port:**                      Boulogne

**Voyage:**                           Boulogne to Bordeaux

**Number of Crew:**             3 and 1 boy

---

This vessel is also referred to as the *Francis Joseph*.

The cause of the sinking of the *Maria Joseph* on Saturday 21st July 1883 is not really known but is thought to be due to the vessel not being able to take the strain of her cargo because of its age in the heavy seas. Fortunately for the complement of four, a German schooner, the *Pollux*, was nearby and took the crew off before it actually sank. The schooner later transferred the crew to a pilot boat which landed them at Eastbourne on Monday 23rd July.

That same evening, the local Lloyd's Agent, Mr. Rudd, arranged for the crew to travel by train to Newhaven to be taken care of by Mr. John Bull, the French Consul at the port.

*Ref: EG 25.7.1883; EC 28.7.1883; HT 28.7.1883;*

# MARGUERITE

| | |
|---|---|
| **Date:** | 28.8.1883 |
| **Wreck Location:** | Ashore near the Buckle Inn, Seaford |
| **Description of Vessel:** | |
| **Vessel Type -** | French steam fishing trawler |
| **Home Port:** | Trouville |
| **Voyage:** | From Trouville fishing and return |
| **Date Built, Builder:** | c.1882 |
| **Owner:** | Clement, Trouville, France |
| **Ship's Master:** | Lefort |
| **Number of Crew:** | 7 and a boy |

---

The French steam trawler *Marguerite* was 15 miles/24km south-west of Beachy Head on the evening of Tuesday 28th August 1883 when, at about 9pm, an explosion occurred in the boiler of the vessel causing a fire. The crew soon launched signal rockets to bring attention to their plight, which were seen by Seaford Coastguard Station. In the force 6 south-westerly wind the vessel drifted towards Seaford and a large beacon was built and lit on the beach to indicate to the crew the best place to come ashore. By 11pm the vessel was not far too off the beach but well ablaze, so the crew took to their boat and came safely ashore near the Assembly Rooms at Seaford. They were taken to the New Inn Hotel where the proprietor Mr. Richards and Mr. J. Bull, the French Consul at Newhaven, looked after the men.

Meanwhile the drifting *Marguerite* was finally washed ashore near the Buckle Inn totally destroyed and burnt to the water line.

*Ref: SIBI; SE 1.9.1883; EC 1.9.1883*

# VOLONTE DE DIEU

| | |
|---|---|
| **Date:** | 11.9.1883 |
| **Wreck Location:** | 15 miles/24km south-east off Beachy Head |
| **Description of Vessel:** | |
| **Vessel Type -** | French sailing fishing lugger |
| **Voyage:** | Boulogne fishing and return |
| **Owner:** | R. Germe, Boulogne |
| **Ship's Master:** | R.N. Germe |

---

In a north-easterly force 2 wind the *Volonte de Dieu* sank after colliding with the steamship *Matthew Bedlington* of Whitby on Tuesday 11th September 1883.

*Ref: SIBI*

# NEW BRUNSWICK

| | |
|---|---|
| **Date:** | 25.11.1883 |
| **Wreck Location:** | Ashore east of Birling Gap |
| **Description of Vessel:** | |
| **Gross Tonnage -** | 480 |
| **Vessel Type -** | Norwegian three masted sailing barque |
| **Cargo:** | Timber |
| **Home Port:** | Brevig |
| **Voyage:** | Quebec to West Hartlepool |
| **Ship's Master:** | P. Tobisen |
| **Number of Crew:** | 10 |

On 3rd October 1883 the *New Brunswick* left Quebec for West Hartlepool experiencing little or no difficulties until reaching the Channel, when she was met by a severe south-westerly gale. The vessel was driven before the storm over the next couple of days, during which time the sails were ripped to shreds by the force of the winds as well as her topmasts being carried away. The *New Brunswick* was continually battered by the mountainous waves as the hurricane force winds blew the vessel ever nearer to Beachy Head. As daylight broke on the morning of Sunday 25th November 1883, the crew found themselves about 1 mile/1.6km off the white cliffs and being helplessly driven ever closer to them.

The master, in an attempt to arrest the drift towards the cliffs, dropped two anchors which, for a while, successfully stopped the drifting vessel. However, it was not long in these terrible conditions that the anchors started to drag, with the vessel again slowly drifting towards the rocks, eventually stopping about 1200yds/1km from the shore just east of Birling Gap. The crew hoisted distress signals which were seen by the local Coastguards, and to the crew's great relief a number of people started to gather on the beach, but still had no means of communicating with them. The huge waves continued to wash over the vessel, so the crew lashed themselves to the remains of the rigging to prevent being washed overboard. As the tide started to ebb it revealed huge rocks between their stricken vessel and the safety of the shore.

Meanwhile ashore, news of the plight of the *New Brunswick,* had been conveyed to Eastbourne. The messenger arrived at 10.45am at Vestry Hall just as the Mayor and the Corporation were leaving for the Mayor's Sunday parade. Alderman Rudd, Lloyd's agent, and Councillor Thomas Bennett, Lloyd's sub-agent, immediately left the procession and sent a telegram to Newhaven. It was thought that the Newhaven Lifeboat would be able to get there quicker than the one at Eastbourne which would be heading straight into the south-westerly gale. There were discussions between these two men and Mr. Emary, local secretary of the Lifeboat Institution, and the coxswain Charles 'Bones' Hide as to whether the Eastbourne Lifeboat, *William and Mary* should be sent at all. However, while these discussions and arrangements were being made, the crew of the Eastbourne Lifeboat mustered at their station.

As soon as the telegram was received at Newhaven the muster guns at the lifeboat house were fired. It was not long before the lifeboat crew were gathered together and attempting to leave the harbour. Unfortunately the strength of the wind and the terrific seas made it impossible for the lifeboat to get clear of the harbour. The steam tug *Tipper*, which was usually used to tow the lifeboat out to sea, was not prepared and would have taken too long to get sufficient steam up for the lifeboat to be of any use to the crew of the *New Brunswick.*

With the knowledge that the Newhaven Lifeboat would not be able to get to sea, there was much discussion at Eastbourne between the two Lloyd's Agents, the secretary and coxswain of the lifeboat as to the viability of launching. The issues they had to consider were (i) the time it would take the lifeboat to cover the 4 miles/6.5km to reach the *New Brunswick* heading straight into the gale force winds (ii) when and if it reached the vessel, would they be too late to be of use to the stricken crew (iii) as a result they may well be putting the lives of the lifeboat crew at risk unnecessarily. The four men finally decided to take the lifeboat overland to Birling Gap and launch from there, and so started a monumental effort to rescue the crew of the *New Brunswick.*

The lifeboat *William and Mary* was brought out of the lifeboat house on its carriage and the crew, together with volunteers, making a total of some 200 persons, manually hauled the carriage to South Street. Here the first team of six horses, supplied by Mr. Newman of the Anchor Inn, were attached to the carriage with a further four horses being later supplied by Mr. Mockett of Meads House. There then started the long struggle up to the top of Beachy Head for the 200 people and the team of 10 horses in driving wind and rain. Once on top of the cliffs both men and horses felt the full force of the weather as they made their way across ploughed fields towards Birling Gap, a journey of about 5 miles/8km. As the lifeboat carriage made its way along the path towards the shore, they found that the banks of the path were too narrow for the carriage to proceed. A gang of men were detailed to start digging out the side of the path while others took the lifeboat off its carriage and dragged along the widened path on pieces of wood found nearby, using them as slides. Having eventually got the lifeboat to Birling Gap, they then found that the last 10ft/3m of the path leading down to the beach had been washed away. Further timber was fortunately found and a make-shift ramp was made down which the lifeboat was lowered onto the beach. At 1.15pm the *William and Mary* was finally launched into mountainous seas under the coxswain Charles 'Bones' Hide and the second coxswain, Matthews. The lifeboat crew in their cork jackets started to row (some of the oars had been double-banked) towards the *New Brunswick*, a journey which took them 45 minutes constantly pumping water out as each wave broke over the craft.

With unbelievable effort by the lifeboat crew, they finally got close enough to throw a line onto the *New Brunswick*. The conditions however, did not allow the lifeboat to come alongside the stricken barque. With a line attached to the *New Brunswick* the lifeboat dropped astern of the vessel and one by one the crew dropped into the sea and were safely hauled into the lifeboat. There being only one casualty, when one of the crew crushed two ribs during his rescue. With the crew safely on board, the lifeboat returned to Birling Gap arriving at 4.30pm, where everybody was still waiting for their return. Once safely ashore the injured man was conveyed to the nearby cottages belonging to the coastguardsmen and attended to by Mr. Scanlan, an assistant to Dr. Colgate.

For the lifeboat crew and volunteers their work was not yet over, as the lifeboat had to be hauled back the way it had come and mounted again on its carriage. Once on the carriage it was returned to the Lifeboat House by the same method it had left, arriving back there at 7.30pm. However, not before everybody involved had taken part of the bread, meat and ale that Councillor Thomas Bennett had brought to them from the Devonshire Hotel, Seaside Road.

The next day the Newhaven steam tug *Tipper* managed to re-float the

*New Brunswick* and tow the damaged vessel into the harbour.

As far as the lifeboat crew were concerned there was a particularly sad sequel to what was an heroic rescue by them. The Newhaven Lifeboat had later gone out to the *New Brunswick* and claimed salvage of the vessel which they were duly paid. However, the Eastbourne Lifeboat made a claim for 'life salvage' which was in total contravention of the Lifeboat Institution's rules. This claim was paid by the owners of the Norwegian barque but the Lifeboat Institution with great reluctance had to dismiss the entire Eastbourne Lifeboat crew as a result.

*Ref: SELB; SE 27.11.1883; EG 28.11.1883; EC 1.12.1883; LL 21708 7.11.83; LL 21709 28.11.83*

# STATEMAN

| | |
|---|---|
| **Date:** | 3.2.1884 |
| **Wreck Location:** | 5 miles/8km off Beachy Head |
| **Description of Vessel:** | |
| **Gross Tonnage -** | 150 |
| **Length -** | 90ft/27.55m |
| **Beam -** | 22ft/6.64m |
| **Vessel Type -** | British sailing brig |
| **Cargo:** | Coal |
| **Home Port:** | Faversham |
| **Voyage:** | South Shields to France |
| **Owner:** | G. Baker, Whitstable |
| **Ship's Master:** | G. Baker |
| **Number of Crew:** | 5 |

At 4am on Sunday 3rd February 1884 in a north-easterly force 2 wind the *Stateman* and the full-rigged barque *Theodore H. Rand* of Parrsboro, Nova Scotia from New York, were in collision 5 miles/8km from Beachy Head. All hands on the *Stateman* were drowned except one.

*Ref: SIBI; EG 6.2.1884*

# SANTA MARGUERITE LIGURE

| | |
|---|---|
| **Date:** | 25.9.1884 |
| **Wreck Location:** | 6 miles/9.7km off Beachy Head |
| **Description of Vessel:** | |
| **Vessel Type -** | Italian sailing barque |
| **Cargo:** | Wheat |
| **Voyage:** | Falmouth to Antwerp |
| **Date Built, Builder:** | c.1866 |
| **Owner:** | F. Rainusso, Genoa |
| **Ship's Master:** | Legune |
| **Number of Crew:** | 9 |
| **Number of Passengers:** | 1 (Pilot) |

On Tuesday 23rd September 1884, the *Santa Marguerite Ligure* left Falmouth bound for Antwerp with a cargo of wheat. Just as daylight was breaking, on the Thursday morning, the watch on board the *Santa Marguerite Ligure* saw the 1000 ton steamship *Wiltshire* bearing down on them at full speed. Both vessels were displaying their lights and visibility was clear in the force 5 north-westerly wind. Despite the watch trying to attract the attention of those on board the *Wiltshire*, a collision was unavoidable and the *Wiltshire* struck the Italian barque amidships with terrible force. Although just prior to the impact the *Wiltshire* did reverse her engines, it was far too late to make any impression on her speed.

The damage to the *Santa Marguerite Ligure* was so severe that the vessel filled instantly with water and sank almost immediately. The crew had no time to lower their boat and a number of the crew were sucked down by the vortex created by the vessel sinking. Two of the crew lost their lives but in the circumstances it could have been far worse. It was believed that they were caught in the rigging as the vessel went down.

The remainder of the crew, master, mate and six seamen were picked up by the *Wiltshire* and landed later that afternoon at Dover. The survivors were taken to the National Sailor's Home in Dover, where two of the crew who sustained injuries were tended to by Dr. Tomlins. After treatment, the injured and the other survivors were put on the evening train to London. A pilot was on board the *Santa Marguerite Ligure* at the time of the collision, but it is not known if he survived or was one of the fatalities.

The *Santa Marguerite Ligure* went down in quite shallow water in the shipping lane that vessels take between Dungeness and Beachy Head, with its top mast and mizzen mast protruding above the level of the sea. As it was clearly a hazard to other vessels, officials from both Lloyd's and the Trinity Board visited the site and stationed a Trinity Board vessel at the scene to warn other vessels of the danger until they could blow the vessel up two days later.

*Ref: SIBI; EG 1.10.1884 & 26.10.1887*

# LITTLE WILY

**Date:**  21.2.1885

**Wreck Location:**  ¾ mile/1.2km west of Newhaven

**Description of Vessel:**
**Gross Tonnage -**  9
**Vessel Type -**  British sailing dandy

**Cargo:**  Boulders

**Home Port:**  Newhaven

**Voyage:**  Newhaven and return

**Ship's Master:**  George Winder

**Number of Crew:**  1

---

On Saturday 21st February 1884 the vessel *Little Wily,* with George Winder and Samuel Head on board, was returning to Newhaven harbour with a cargo of boulders collected from the beach. As it approached the entrance, in a force 5 south-easterly wind, the vessel suddenly developed a leak and went down. Fortunately for both men on board, Stephen Roberts happened to be close by in his vessel and came to their aid. It was thought that had he not done so both men would have drowned.

*Ref: SIBI; HI 26.2.1885*

# CHARLES GEORGE

| | |
|---|---|
| **Date:** | 23.4.1885 |
| **Wreck Location:** | 13 miles/21km south-west of Beachy Head |
| **Description of Vessel:** | |
| **Gross Tonnage -** | 194 |
| **Length -** | 95ft/28.98m |
| **Beam -** | 24ft/7.26m |
| **Vessel Type -** | British sailing brig |
| **Cargo:** | Ballast |
| **Home Port:** | Cowes, Isle of Wight |
| **Voyage:** | Cowes to Seaham |
| **Date Built, Builder:** | c.1865 by Liddle of Sunderland |
| **Owner:** | C. Odell, Isle of Wight |
| **Ship's Master:** | William .T. Odell |
| **Number of Crew:** | 7 |

The brig *Charles George* and the Peninsular and Oriental steamship *Cathay* of Glasgow, en route to Calcutta from London, were in collision at 3am on Thursday 23rd April 1885. This resulted in the brig sinking with the loss of five crew. The remaining crew were picked up by the steamship and landed the following day at Bembridge on the Isle of Wight. At the time there was hazy visibility in a force 4 south-westerly wind.

One of those lost was the master, William Odell. His body was found the following Sunday morning on the beach near Piddinghoe, by John Smith, a coastguard at the Portobello Coastguard Station. At the Inquest held the following evening at the Newhaven Coastguard Station before the Coroner for East Sussex, Mr. Wynne E. Baxter, the body was identified as that of the master by a man named McArthur. He told the Inquest he had been present at Cowes when the vessel had started its voyage. He also knew that Odell was the landlord of the Dolphin Inn, Newport on the Isle of Wight. A second witness also identified the body as that of Odell. This second man was retired ship owner, Mr. W.R. Horrocks of Shoreham, who said that the deceased was about 50 years of age. The Inquest Jury returned a verdict of 'Found Drowned'.

*Ref: SIBI; SE 28.4.1885; HI 30.4.1885*

# HANNAH

| | |
|---|---|
| **Date:** | 18.9.1885 |
| **Wreck Location:** | Near Newhaven |
| **Description of Vessel:** | |
| **Vessel Type -** | British sailing smack |
| **Cargo:** | Boulders |
| **Home Port:** | Newhaven |
| **Voyage:** | Newhaven and return |
| **Date Built, Builder:** | c.1850 |
| **Owner:** | H. & C. Lower |
| **Ship's Master:** | R. Saunders |
| **Number of Crew:** | 2 |

---

This vessel became a loss in a force 2 south-easterly wind while collecting boulders from the beach on Friday 18th September 1885.

*Ref: SIBI*

# NEREIDE

| | |
|---|---|
| **Date:** | 15.11.1885 |
| **Wreck Location:** | Near Royal Sovereign Light |
| **Description of Vessel:** | |
| **Gross Tonnage -** | 432 |
| **Length -** | 122ft/37.33m |
| **Beam -** | 28ft/8.47m |
| **Vessel Type -** | British sailing brigantine |
| **Cargo:** | Coal |
| **Home Port:** | London |
| **Voyage:** | Blyth to Colon, Chile |
| **Date Built, Builder:** | c.1858 |
| **Owner:** | J. Huison, Sunderland |
| **Ship's Master:** | J. Lowthian |
| **Number of Crew:** | 9 and 1 boy |

---

In a northerly force 4 wind at 6am on Sunday 15th November 1885, the *Nereide* was in collision with the barque *Southerfield* of Maryport, U.S.A., bound for London from Iquique, Chile, with a cargo of saltpetre. It is a coincidence that one vessel was on voyage from Chile whereas the other was on a voyage to Chile, albeit different ports.

The *Nereide* went down within two minutes of the impact, taking with her the master who at the time was standing on the vessel's rail. It is believed that he was caught in the vessel's rigging. Fortunately for the rest of the crew of nine men and a boy, they were rescued by the jolly boats from the *Southerfield*. However, this was not without mishap as one of the *Southerfield* crew was severely injured when a bolt, securing one of the jolly boats, fell whilst it was being launched, and the bolt entered his head under the chin.

Briscoe, the master of the *Southerfield*, examined his vessel after the collision and found that it was severely damaged with the bowsprit carried away, mizzen topmast gone, bows knocked in, and a large amount of copper sheathing having been ripped off. As a result the vessel was leaking considerably and at a real risk of sinking as well.

Fortunately for the *Southerfield* the London steam tug *Challenge* was soon at hand to tow her towards Newhaven harbour, but because of a 19½ft/6m draught and the state of the tide, was unable to take the vessel inside the harbour. The *Southerfield* had to wait until 2pm when, on the rising tide, the local tug *Tipper* came out to tow the vessel inside the harbour. The crew of the *Nereide* were landed and taken care of by the local Shipwrecked Mariners Society.

*Ref: SIBI; HI 19.11.1885; HN 20.11.1885*

# BESSIE

| | |
|---|---|
| **Date:** | 19.11.1885 |
| **Wreck Location:** | ½ mile/804m south-west of Seaford Cliff |
| **Description of Vessel:**<br>**Vessel Type -** | British sailing fishing vessel |
| **Home Port:** | Rye |
| **Voyage:** | Newhaven fishing and return |
| **Date Built, Builder:** | c.1876 |
| **Owner:** | J. Gallop, Rye |
| **Ship's Master:** | A. Brackpool |
| **Number of Crew:** | 3 |

The *Bessie* sank following a collision with the *Daring,* a snow of Shoreham, on Thursday 19th November 1885, in a force 5 north-easterly wind.

*Ref: SIBI*

# SAPHIR

| | |
|---|---|
| **Date:** | 30.10.1886 |
| **Wreck Location:** | Off Beachy Head |
| **Description of Vessel:** | |
| **Gross Tonnage -** | 250 |
| **Vessel Type -** | Norwegian sailing brig |
| **Cargo:** | Timber |
| **Voyage:** | Kragcroe, Norway to Cardiff |
| **Date Built, Builder:** | c.1877 |
| **Ship's Master:** | Krag |
| **Number of Crew:** | 14 |

---

The *Saphir* was found drifting on its beam ends with bow and stern completely knocked in, on the morning of Sunday 31st October 1886, off Beachy Head. This discovery was made by the Rye fishing smack *Conster* and another smack from Brighton. The vessel was totally empty of any cargo and there was certainly no sign of the crew.

The London steam tug *Cambria* towed the copper-bottomed *Saphir* into Seaford Bay where it was beached near Blatchington. The local Lloyd's agent, Mr. John Bull, then took charge of the vessel. It was not until later that a dispatch was received from Amsterdam explaining the demise of the *Saphir*. It transpired that the vessel was run down by the Dutch mail steamer *Sumatra* the previous day, Saturday 30th October, in a force 2 south-westerly wind, with all the crew being picked up by the mail steamer.

A number of items salvaged from the *Saphir* were sold by auction on Saturday 13th November 1886. The items sold were ropes, rigging, sails, blocks, charts, chronometer and other instruments. However, it is reported they did not fetch very high prices.

*Ref: SIBI; EG 3.11.1886 & 17.11.1886; HI 4.11.1886*

# TALLY HO

| | |
|---|---|
| **Date:** | 26.12.1886 |
| **Wreck Location:** | Ashore east of the Redoubt, Eastbourne |
| **Description of Vessel:** | |
| **Gross Tonnage -** | 189 |
| **Length -** | 103ft/31.39m |
| **Beam -** | 12ft/3.81m |
| **Vessel Type -** | British sailing brig |
| **Cargo:** | 320 tons of coal |
| **Home Port:** | Shoreham |
| **Voyage:** | Sunderland to Littlehampton |
| **Date Built, Builder:** | c.1854 at Kingston, Shoreham |
| **Owner:** | T. Gates & Co., Shoreham |
| **Ship's Master:** | Joseph Gasston |
| **Number of Crew:** | 7 |

The *Tally Ho* (see photograph page 25) left Sunderland at noon on Thursday 23rd December 1886 on its voyage to Littlehampton under the command of the master, Joseph Gasston and his seven man crew; James Scott (mate), Albert Greenyer (cook), and 5 seamen Alfred Brown, William Young, Charles Leggett, David William Rumney and James Mitchell. The master had been with the vessel for the previous sixteen years and during that time the *Tally Ho* had been overhauled at least twice, the last time being three weeks prior to the start of this voyage.

The vessel started to leak soon after leaving Sunderland but not to any great extent, although throughout the voyage the pumps were used to keep the water level down. The weather for most of the voyage was nothing to cause the vessel or its crew too many problems, not that is until 2pm on the afternoon of Boxing Day when off Fairlight Church, near Hastings. The *Tally Ho* tacked off to the south-east for two hours and then turned westward, with the wind still in the south-west. However, the strong winds were increasing all the time and turning more southerly with accompanying rain and mist, making it very difficult for the *Tally Ho,* to make westward progress. Although the crew had been using the pumps from the outset, the leak in the vessel was increasing so much that the pumps were now constantly manned. Despite their efforts the pumps were not capable of stemming the flow of water and by 6pm they had ceased to be effective, although they were kept manned for a further two hours.

With increased level of water in the vessel, the *Tally Ho* was becoming unmanageable in these ever worsening conditions and by 7pm it was south-west of Royal Sovereign Light and about 18 miles/29km from Newhaven. Joseph Gasston at first thought that he would try and make for the port but it soon became apparent that in these conditions this was not going to be possible. One of the crew who had been manning the pumps, William Young, told Joseph Gasston of the lack of effect the pumps were having. Gasston then caught a glimpse of the lights of Eastbourne and decided that he would now make a run for the town and try and beach the *Tally Ho* to save the lives of the crew.

At 10.15pm that evening with the tide a full two hours from high water, one of the distress flare lights of paraffin oil, that had been hauled to the masthead, was seen by the coastguards at Eastbourne who informed the Officer in Charge, Mr. Angus Teeling. On closer inspection Mr. Teeling saw an ordinary white light assuming therefore it was a not a light of distress. The light suddenly went out and it was then that he could see the *Tally Ho* which was now broadside-on in broken water about ½ mile/804m off shore. His initial reaction was to send a messenger to muster his men for the lifeboat but he soon realised the vessel was making for the shore. He stood down the request for the lifeboat and ordered his men to make for the beach with life lines instead.

The *Tally Ho* was being driven before the storm towards the Redoubt in what were now huge waves. The vessel just managed to clear the Pier, with sails still set and travelling at great speed, eventually striking the beach with considerable force at 11pm, 100yds/91m east of the Redoubt with her bow securely pinned in a newly constructed groyne. As soon as it struck the beach the action of the sea turned the vessel broadside-on with the waves sweeping right over the vessel with horrendous force. With each wave that crashed over the vessel it rocked violently from side to side which soon brought the masts down.

Where the vessel had run aground the beach was very steep down to the water, creating a barrier which prevented potential rescuers from getting to the vessel and also preventing the stranded mariners getting to the shore. With each wave that came in over the vessel it created a very strong current in the water between the vessel and the shore. The stranded crew were calling out for the rocket apparatus but the nearest ones were at Belle Tout and Pevensey which were miles away and would take far too long to get there to be of any use. The coastguardsmen and lifeboat crew started to throw life lines onto the *Tally Ho* which was made extremely difficult by the darkness and the weather but eventually one line was successfully got on board.

The first to make use of the life lines was James Scott (mate), who tied the line around himself and using the rigging laying over the side of the vessel, made his way towards the beach assisted by those ashore.

The next crew member to make an attempt to leave the *Tally Ho* was William Young. One of the lines thrown onto the vessel was intended to be used to haul a heavier rope on board to assist with the rescue of all the crew. However, when the lifeline landed on the vessel William Young tied it around his body and jumped into the sea against the advice of the master Joseph Gasston. However, in the darkness those ashore had not expected the line to be used like this, so when the line went taught they assumed it was being hauled onto the vessel. By the time they realised there was weight on the end of the line and hauled it in, it was too late despite the efforts of a Dr. J. Pitcairn-Brookless (a visitor to the town) and Dr. Reid, nothing could be done for William Young. He was later taken to the local coastguard station where he was pronounced dead.

While some were engaged in the actual rescue of the crew, others on the beach searched for fuel to make a fire so as to light the area. Eventually enough wood and other items, including tar, were found to build a fire and after a number of attempts in the strong wind, managed to get the fire alight. This lit up an unreal sight of desperate men on a vessel stranded only a few yards from the shore but being impossible to reach it, with huge waves sweeping right across the vessel.

In the following 30 minutes another 3 members of the crew, including the master, were brought safely ashore by the use of the land lines. However, in the process the master sustained a serious leg injury as he dropped over the deck. Two of the remaining crew were washed off the decks of the *Tally Ho* by the sea, although one was seen to hang onto the rudder for a short while before disappearing beneath the waves. The last mariner on the vessel was clinging to the stern crying out in piercing shrieks *"Save me! save me!"*. It was heart rending to those just a few yards away but unable to do anything. A couple of lines were eventually thrown to within his reach, but he was too exhausted, too cold and too numb to be able make the physical effort to grasp the line. After an hour of hanging onto the stern being constantly washed by the sea, he finally fell into a hatchway and was drowned.

The rescued mariners, Joseph Gasston (master), James Scott (mate), Albert Greenyer (cook) and one of the seamen Alfred Brown, were taken to the local coastguard station and tended to by Doctors Pitcairn-Brookless and Reid. The coastguardsmen provided the rescued men with all the comforts they could including giving up their beds for the night.

The next day, Monday 27th December, was a public holiday and a constant stream of visitors came to inspect the wreck of the *Tally Ho*. A collection was made at the wreck and a small charge 6d/2½p was made of those who wanted to go on board the vessel, which was high and dry at low water. A total of £18.11s.0½d/£18.55p was collected for the families of the four crew members who died.

At 4pm on Tuesday 28th December the Inquests into the deaths of the four mariners was held at the Hartington Hotel before the Coroner Mr. Hillman. The Jury consisted mainly of boatmen and fishermen of whom the foreman was John Henry Wright. Mr. W.H. Burt, a solicitor, represented the owners of the *Tally Ho* at the Inquests. The first one was into the death of 50 year old William Young from West Brighton. The witnesses called were James Scott (mate) and Joseph Gasston (master) who outlined the events as described above. The next witness was Angus Teeling the officer in charge of the local coastguard. During the course of his evidence he said that the light he first saw of the *Tally Ho* was white and not blue. Although the seaworthiness of the vessel was called into question the Coroner said that it was for a Board of Trade Inquiry to determine.

The next Inquest was into the death of 20 year old Charles Leggett from Fishers Gate, Southwick, whose body was found on the morning prior to the Inquest by James Pierce, about 80yds/73m west of Langney Fort at the high water mark. James Scott again gave evidence, as did James Pierce.

The third of the four Inquests was into the death of 22 year old James Mitchell from 30 Queens Street, Brighton, whose body had also been found the previous morning, at 7am 20yds/18.3m from the high water mark at Langney Point by James Timms, a soldier. This was Mitchell's first sea voyage, having joined the vessel at Shoreham.

The fourth and final Inquest was into the death of David William Rumney, 21 years of age from Brighton who was on his third voyage when he died. His body was found in the hold of *Tally Ho* on the morning of the Inquests.

A verdict of Accidental Drowning was returned in each of the four Inquests. However, the Jury added the rider (i) that the Board of Trade be informed that had a rocket apparatus been available at Eastbourne then the lives of the deceased would have been saved and such apparatus should be installed at Eastbourne and (ii) Eastbourne Council should be asked to provide red lights above the high water mark at the fishermen's cottages, as had such lights been installed they would have guided the master of the *Tally Ho*.

On Thursday 30th December the funeral took place of Leggett, Mitchell and Rumney at Eastbourne cemetery, where Rev. F.A.M. Shepherd of St. Mary's church officiated. The coffins were carried to the cemetery by local coastguardsmen and fishermen. The body of William Young was returned to West Brighton for interment.

The following Monday, 3rd January 1887, a public auction was held for the sale of the hull and cargo. The hull was bought by a Brighton man for £22 and 200 tons of the coal was purchased for £125 by the Eastbourne Sanitary Steam Laundry Company.

A Board of Trade inquiry into the *Tally Ho* wreck was held at the Shipwreck Commissioner's Court in London on Tuesday 25th January 1887 before Mr. H.C. Rothery, the Wreck Commissioner, sitting with Admiral Carne and Captain Ward as assessors. The owners of the vessel were represented by Mr. Williams and the Board of Trade was represented by Mr. Davies, a barrister. It was Mr. Davies who outlined the detail of events and disclosed that the master, Joseph Gasston did not have a master's certificate. After hearing evidence from Mr. Gates (the owner), Gasston, Scott and others, the Judgement of the court was that no blame could be attributed to either the owners or the master. They found that the vessel was seaworthy and that it was the severity of the gale on the night that was the cause of the loss of the vessel and crew. The court confirmed that had the vessel not been run ashore by the master then loss of life would have been even greater.

*Ref: SIBI; EG 29.12.1886 & 5.1.1887; EC 8.1.1887; HN 7.1.1887 & 8.1.1887; HI 30.12.1886*

# SJORDRONNINGEN

**Date:** 4.1.1887

**Wreck Location:** Ashore 1 mile/1.6km east of Beachy Head near Belle Tout Light

**Description of Vessel:**
**Gross Tonnage -** 858
**Vessel Type -** Norwegian sailing barque

**Cargo:** Petroleum

**Home Port:** Stavanger

**Voyage:** New York to Hamburg

**Date Built, Builder:** c.1861

**Owner:** Holdland Isaksen

**Ship's Master:** C.M. Aase

**Number of Crew:** 15

---

The *Sjordronningen* left New York for Hamburg on 2ⁿᵈ December 1886 and had only been three days out when it met an horrendous storm with terrific seas washing over the decks. It was during this storm that the vessel lost three of its boats overboard. Throughout the remainder of the Atlantic crossing the *Sjordronningen* was continually battered by heavy gales but finally put into Portland on 30ᵗʰ December and purchased a boat to replace at least one of those lost during the Atlantic crossing. Having purchased their new boat, the vessel set off again up the Channel intending to make for Dungeness. The conditions had not improved much since leaving New York and they were still having to contend with heavy seas and stormy conditions.

At 4am on Tuesday 4ᵗʰ January 1887 the *Sjordronningen* was off Beachy Head to the west in thick fog, driving snow and a south-westerly gale. The master at this time believed that he was 12 miles/19km south of Beachy Head, when the lookout reported being able to see the Belle Tout Light. Unfortunately, the view of the light was constantly being obscured due to the weather and sea conditions. Up to this point, the vessel was under her lower topsails and immediately the master was made aware of their true position he hauled the vessel to wind, but it was too late in these conditions. At 4.30am the *Sjordronningen* ran aground on rocks 1 mile/1.6km east of Beachy Head near an area known locally as the 'Gun Garden'. As soon as the vessel struck, it turned starboard onto the shore with her bow facing the sea. It was soon after that the vessel's back broke and rapidly filled with water. The impact was so severe that it caused the mainmast to collapse and puncture four holes in the hull. In order to preserve themselves in this perilous situation, the crew had to hang onto the vessel all night until help finally arrived.

The coastguards at Birling Gap station and Eastbourne Lifeboat were aware of the plight of the *Sjordronningen* and were making their way with the rocket apparatus. However, when they arrived on the cliff top above the vessel and having fired three rockets which failed to reach the vessel, it soon became apparent that the apparatus was not going to be of any practical use.

The Eastbourne Lifeboat had also been made aware of the vessel's situation when they saw the flare-up lights that had been lit by the stricken crew, at about 5.30am. The crew of the lifeboat *William and Mary* were soon mustered under the new coxswain Jesse Huggett. This was to be his, and the new crew's first service call since being appointed after the dismissal of the previous coxswain and crew by the Royal National Lifeboat Institution over the 'life salvage' claim of the *New Brunswick* crew (see page 349). Jesse Huggett's crew consisted of not only new crew members but one or two of the previous crew including Charles 'Bone' Hide the previously dismissed coxswain.

The *William and Mary* was brought out on its carriage, then, with the help of horses and cattle, was drawn along the snow covered Grand Parade to the Wish Tower where it was launched with the help of the many on-lookers who had now arrived. Once afloat, soon after 8am, it took about 1½ hours hard rowing to bring the *William and Mary* to the bow of the *Sjordronningen* in a wind that had turned more easterly. The crew of the stricken Norwegian barque had lowered a rope from the stem and a line was thrown from the lifeboat to the barque and fastened. With these two in place the crew, one by one, slid down the rope into the waiting arms of the lifeboat crew and to safety. After about 15 minutes, with all 16 crew safely in the lifeboat, they immediately set out on the return journey to Eastbourne in the driving snow, strong winds and heavy seas.

The return journey for the lifeboat took longer as the crew were rowing into a more head-on wind and against the tide. However, at about midday the lifeboat was spotted by those still on the beach at the Wish Tower waiting for its return. They could just make out the craft rising and falling on the waves in the driving snow. As the lifeboat approached the beach the coastguard, under the command of Chief Officer Teeling, and assisted by many volunteers, were ready with lines to pull the craft ashore. As soon as it touched the beach the lines were attached and it was very quickly hauled clear of the surf. The lifeboat crew and the rescued Norwegian crew were then immediately given hot coffee which had been arranged by Alderman Rudd (Lloyd's agent), and Councillor Bennett (Deputy Lloyd's agent) and supplied by Messrs. H. Gardiner, Jesse Hide and Arthur Hide. The rescued crew were then taken in cabs to the dining rooms owned by Mr. Powell in Seaside Road where they were provided with clothing and food. Meanwhile, the crew of the lifeboat had got the lifeboat back on to its carriage and both lifeboat and crew were paraded back to the boat-house in triumph. The following day the lifeboat crew were treated to a hearty lunch with tea and coffee, by Mr. & Mrs. Harry Stevens of the Fishermen's Mutual Association in recognition of their endeavours in rescuing the seamen on board the *Sjordronningen.*

On Thursday 6th January the rescued crew, (with the exception of the master) who had managed to save only their own personal belongings, left Eastbourne on the 2.15pm train for London, where the Norwegian Consul General was to make arrangements for them to return home via Hull.

*Ref: SIBI; EG 5.1.1887; EC 8.1.1887; HN 14.1.1887;*

# BREEZE

| | |
|---|---|
| **Date:** | 17.4.1887 |
| **Wreck Location:** | 8 miles/13km east of Beachy Head |

**Description of Vessel:**

| | |
|---|---|
| Gross Tonnage - | 55 |
| Length - | 54ft/16.61m |
| Beam - | 14ft/4.24m |
| Vessel Type - | British sailing yawl |

| | |
|---|---|
| **Cargo:** | Ballast |
| **Home Port:** | Cowes |
| **Voyage:** | Fowey to Great Yarmouth |
| **Date Built, Builder:** | c.1836 at Gosport |
| **Owner:** | George Freeth, Duporth, St. Austell |
| **Ship's Master:** | Alfred Smith |
| **Number of Crew:** | 3 |
| **Number of Passengers:** | 1 |

On 1st April 1887, the 55 ton yacht the *Breeze* was made a gift to the 'Mission to Deep Sea Fishermen'. It was very common for wealthy philanthropists of the day to donate such vessels to the Mission (now named the Royal National Mission to Deep Sea Fishermen).

The *Breeze* left Fowey on Friday 15th April 1887 for Great Yarmouth under the 32 year old master Alfred Smith. The others on board the vessel were Colporteur* William W. Field acting as mate, and able seamen J. Sheridan and John White. This four man crew having been sent to Fowey by the 'Mission' to bring the vessel round to Great Yarmouth. There was also a passenger on board, Charles H. Pannell, a 25 year old single man who was a senior clerk in the publications department of the 'Mission to Deep Sea Fishermen' who was taking the voyage as part of a holiday.

All was going well until just before midnight on Sunday 17th April when the vessel was 8 miles/13 km east of Beachy Head in force 1 north-easterly wind. The mate, William Field, was at the tiller, and John White had just gone below to put the kettle on to make a drink before waking the master to take his watch. The master, Smith, like the other two men on the vessel, was asleep below. Suddenly the mate saw the German steamship *Australia*, of and from Bremen and bound for Cardiff, loom out of the darkness travelling at full speed straight towards him.

On seeing the *Australia,* Field let out a loud scream which brought White rapidly on deck just in time to see its bows about to crash into the port side of his vessel. However, White did just manage to get a life belt before the impact crushed the *Breeze,* causing it to sink. Within a few seconds the towering hull of the *Australia* was gone into the darkness. The three men asleep below in their berths went down with their vessel, there being no time at all to warn them of the impending danger.

Once White had regained his composure he was aware that he was surrounded in the darkness by the floating wreckage of the *Breeze.* He then heard the voice of the mate William Field calling out, 'Steamer ahoy!'. White immediately started to swim towards the voice coming from the darkness, with the intention that Field could share the life belt with him. As he got nearer he could hear Field praying, 'O Heavenly Father, don't let me be drowned' and then it suddenly went silent.

The *Australia,* being aware that it had run down a vessel, lowered one of its boats which made a search and fortunately found John White. He was taken back to the steamer where it continued on its voyage, putting him, the sole survivor, ashore at the vessel's destination of Cardiff two days later.

The master, Alfred Smith, left a widow but there were no children, William W. Field left a widow and three children and J. Sheridan left a widow and seven children, the eldest being 7 years old. Charles H. Pannell was the sole provider for his elderly parents.

At this time, the Council of the 'Mission to Deep Sea Fishermen' had taken steps to provide a Widow and Orphan Superannuation Fund by assisting with the premiums of Life Assurance cover for their employees who were constantly at sea. This number of men exceeded fifty at any one time.

* A Colporteur is a bookseller especially employed by a society to distribute Bibles.

*Ref: SIBI; TOTD Vol 2, No.18 June 1887; EG 27.4.1887*

# PLANTEUR

| | |
|---|---|
| **Date:** | 18.10.1887 |
| **Wreck Location:** | 4 miles/6.4km off Beachy head |
| **Description of Vessel:** | |
| **Gross Tonnage -** | 340 |
| **Vessel Type -** | German sailing barque |
| **Cargo:** | Ballast |
| **Home Port:** | Strasland |
| **Voyage:** | London to Buenos Aires |
| **Date Built, Builder:** | c.1877 |
| **Owner:** | Drews & Co |
| **Ship's Master:** | Peter C. Drews |
| **Number of Crew:** | 6 and 2 boys, and Pilot |
| **Number of Passengers:** | 3 |

When the *Planteur* left London bound for Buenos Aires via Cardiff, on board the vessel, apart from the master and 8 crew, were the master's wife, Matilda, and their daughter from the North Prussian town of Sweimunde. The third passenger on the vessel was Matilda's brother. The crew consisted of the mate (Richard Hall), carpenter, cook, two boys and three seamen. There was also a pilot on board the vessel under whose charge the vessel was when it became a loss.

On 12th October 1887 the City of Cork Steam Packet Company's steamship *Upupa,* under the master O'Toole, left Cork bound for London. At about 3am on Tuesday 18th October both the *Upupa* and the *Planteur* were approaching each other about 4 miles/6.4km off Beachy Head. It appears that as the vessels neared each other the *Upupa* experienced some difficulty in starboarding the helm which resulted in it running into the *Planteur* cutting the wooden vessel down to the water line. Immediately upon impact the *Upupa* reversed its engines and the master got the pinnace* lowered to search for survivors. One of those who crewed the pinnace was passenger Dr. Thomas Hartie.

At the time of impact most of those on board the *Planteur* were sleeping in their bunks, including the two survivors, the mate Richard Hall and one of the seamen named Buff. They were the only two survivors from a total of thirteen persons who were on board the *Planteur* when she went down. Immediately the vessels collided those below ran on deck to find themselves sinking rapidly with no time to get their own boat afloat. Like the others, Hall found himself in the water but successfully managed to swim to the *Upupa*.

With the pinnace from the *Upupa* afloat they proceeded to look for survivors from the sinking barque but only found the seaman Buff. After about an hour of searching they made back to the *Upupa* and en route found the 37 year old master of the *Planteur,* Peter Drews. He was a heavily built man and the pinnace crew had great difficulty in getting him on board. However, when they did so Dr. Hartie found him in a critical condition and, despite his efforts, failed to revive him.

On Friday 21st October the Inquest into the death of the master Peter Drews was held at the White Hart Inn, Greenfield Street, Whitechapel before the Coroner for the Eastern Division of Middlesex, Mr. Wynne E. Baxter. After hearing the evidence, which mainly came from Dr. Hartie of 1, St. Patrick's Crescent, Cork, the Jury returned a verdict of 'Found Drowned'.

The badly decomposed body of Matilda Drews was later found at Ramsgate and on 5th November the Inquest into her death was held in that town before the Coroner, Mr. Martin. The mate, Richard Hall, gave evidence but was unable to say how the collision between the two vessels occurred as he was asleep at the time, but stated that the vessel went down within a minute. He also identified Matilda from a diamond ring engraved 'M.D.' and from some bits of clothing with the same initials found near the body.

* Pinnace is a small boat used as a tender.

*Ref: SIBI; EC 22.10.1887; SE 25.10.1887; BC 29.10.1887; EG 9.11.1887*

# CLIFF

| | |
|---|---|
| **Date:** | 12.12.1887 |
| **Wreck Location:** | Ashore at Newhaven |
| **Description of Vessel:** | |
| **Vessel Type -** | British Thames sailing barge |
| **Cargo:** | Shingle |
| **Voyage:** | Newhaven to Lewes |
| **Owner:** | C. Winter, Newhaven |
| **Ship's Master:** | C. Winter |
| **Number of Crew:** | 3 |

This vessel was driven ashore near Newhaven in a force 4 southerly wind and became a total loss.

*Ref: SIBI*

# DELVETI DUBROVACKI

| | |
|---|---|
| **Date:** | 25.12.1887 |
| **Wreck Location:** | 6 miles/97.km off Beachy Head |
| **Description of Vessel:** | |
| **Gross Tonnage -** | 640 |
| **Vessel Type -** | Austrian sailing barque |
| **Cargo:** | Coal |
| **Voyage:** | Leith to Demarara |
| **Date Built, Builder:** | c.1872 |
| **Owner:** | A. Brailla, Ragusa, Austria |
| **Ship's Master:** | A. Brailla |
| **Number of Crew:** | 12 |
| **Number of Passengers:** | 1 |

The *Delveti Dubrovacki* sank after a collision with the steamship *Pathan* of Rochester, in a force 5 north-westerly wind. Two of the crew were lost in the collision.

*Ref: SIBI*

# PILOT BOAT NO. 8

| | |
|---|---|
| **Date:** | 5.5.1888 |
| **Wreck Location:** | 4 miles/6.4km off Beachy Head |
| **Description of Vessel:** | |
| **Gross Tonnage -** | 90 |
| **Length -** | 59ft/17.98m |
| **Beam -** | 18ft/5.48m |
| **Vessel Type -** | Belgian iron sailing sloop |
| **Home Port:** | Antwerp |
| **Voyage:** | Flushing to Seeking |
| **Owner:** | Belgian Government |
| **Ship's Master:** | C.L. Timmerman |
| **Number of Crew:** | 6 |

At about 4am on Saturday 5th May 188 there was thick fog in the Channel off Eastbourne with a slight force 1 south-westerly wind blowing. It was in these conditions, when about 4 miles/6.4km off Beachy Head, that *Pilot Boat No. 8* collided with the steamship *Amethyst* of Glasgow bound for Penzance from Rotterdam. Damage to the port bow of the *Pilot Boat No. 8* caused it to sink within twenty minutes but due to the quick thinking of the master they managed to get their small boat off before their vessel went down. All Pilots and crew managed to get into the small boat and row towards the shore.

They came ashore between the Pier and the Redoubt at Eastbourne where they were cared for by Mr. J.R. Crispin, the local agent of the Shipwrecked Mariners Society, who took them to Mr. Powell's Dining Rooms in Seaside. After having had their breakfast the Pilots and crew left Eastbourne by train for Dover en route home.

*Ref: SIBI; EG 9.5.1888; EC 12.5.1888; BC 12.5.1888*

# ACTIVE

| | |
|---|---|
| **Date:** | 00.6.1888 |
| **Wreck Location:** | Off Beachy Head |
| **Description of Vessel:** | |
| **Vessel Type -** | British sailing Thames barge |
| **Cargo:** | Government stores |
| **Home Port:** | Harwich |
| **Voyage:** | Deptford to Plymouth |
| **Date Built, Builder:** | c.1877 by Vaux at Harwich |
| **Owner:** | R. Lewis, Harwich |
| **Ship's Master:** | Rudrum Meachen |

The *Active* sank during June of 1888 after being in collision with an unknown vessel. The crew of the stricken vessel were picked up and later landed at Brixham.

*Ref: SIBI*

# PIONEER

| | |
|---|---|
| **Date:** | 20.6.1888 |
| **Wreck Location:** | Ashore below the Coastguard Station at Beachy Head |
| **Description of Vessel:** | |
| **Gross Tonnage -** | 270 |
| **Length -** | 119ft/36.3m |
| **Beam -** | 26ft/8.05m |
| **Vessel Type -** | British sailing brig |
| **Cargo:** | 460 ton of coal |
| **Home Port:** | Shoreham |
| **Voyage:** | Newcastle to Shoreham |
| **Date Built, Builder:** | c.1863 by Bailey at Shoreham |
| **Owner:** | T. Gates, Shoreham and three others |
| **Ship's Master:** | G. Ball |
| **Number of Crew:** | 7 |

The *Pioneer* left Newcastle on Sunday 17th June 1888 bound for Shoreham with 460 tons of coal. At 5am on Wednesday 20th June the master went to get some sleep leaving the vessel in charge of the mate. Two hours later the vessel was off Beachy Head in reasonably fine weather and either due to careless helmsman-ship or the look-out failing in his duty, the vessel ran aground at low tide on rocks beneath the coastguard station at Beachy Head.

The crew all managed to get ashore safely with their belongings and were looked after by Mr. Crispin, the local agent of the Shipwrecked Mariners Society, who arranged their transport home.

On Wednesday 27th June the vessel and its cargo were sold at auction by Messrs. Easter & Wright of Eastbourne for £7.7s.0d/£7.35p to a Mr. Guy. Although the vessel was completely covered by each high tide much of the cargo of coal was later removed by barges and discharged at Newhaven.

*Ref: SIBI; EC 23.6.1888; EG 27.6.1888 & 4.7.1888*

# EMMA

| | |
|---|---|
| **Date:** | 25.10.1888 |
| **Wreck Location:** | 6 miles/9.7km off Royal Sovereign Light |
| **Description of Vessel:** | |
| **Vessel Type -** | British sailing schooner |
| **Cargo:** | Boulders |
| **Home Port:** | Liverpool |
| **Voyage:** | Portland to London |
| **Date Built, Builder:** | c.1857 |
| **Owner:** | Williamson Alexander, Dunfermline |
| **Ship's Master:** | Williamson Alexander |
| **Number of Crew:** | 3 |
| **Number of Passengers:** | 1 |

At 8.10pm on the evening of Thursday 25th October 1888 the *Emma* was travelling up the Channel bound for London with its cargo of stone. Travelling down the Channel from Hamburg for New York was the full rigged American barque *E.W. Trickett*. When about 6 miles/9.7km off the Royal Sovereign Light in a force 6 south-westerly wind and in rough seas, the American barque ran into the *Emma* amidships causing considerable damage. Williamson Alexander, master of the *Emma* later maintained that his vessel was showing lights whereas the American barque could not have been, otherwise he would have seen them and taken evasive action.

The master of the *Emma*, who also had his wife on board, together with Arthur Henry Shave the mate, and two seamen, took to their small jolly boat as their vessel was in imminent danger of sinking. The men rowed towards the *E.W. Trickett* as it had hauled-to close by. However, their reception on board the American vessel was not a warm one and it is said that the stranded crew were even refused a drink of water. It was clear that the stranded crew were not welcome and so they took to their boat again and started to row towards the shore in a rough sea. Unfortunately their small boat started to leak and fill with water but, by chance, at 2.30am the following morning, the Hastings fishing lugger *RX 33* under the command of Charles Simmonds came upon the hapless crew. They were taken on board and later landed at Hastings where they were taken to the Royal Standard public house and provided with breakfast.

Mr. George Hutchings, the local honorary agent for the Shipwrecked Mariners Society, arranged for clothing for the crew and their journey to the society's headquarters at Dock Street, East London. It was there that news reached them that the *Emma* had been towed into Dover on the morning of Saturday 27th October. So the master and his crew made for that port instead of making their way to their homes in Dundee, Dunfermline, Sunderland and Newcastle, as had been intended.

The master/owner had insured the *Emma* for £200.

*Ref: SIBI; HT 27.10.1888; HO 27.10.1888; SWA 31.10.1888*

# PALATINE

| | |
|---|---|
| **Date:** | 20.11.1888 |
| **Wreck Location:** | 1 mile/1.6km off shore between Beachy Head and the Parade, Eastbourne |
| **Description of Vessel:** | |
| **Length -** | 17ft/5.2m |
| **Beam -** | 5ft/1.5m |
| **Vessel Type -** | British sailing fishing lugger |
| **Home Port:** | Eastbourne |
| **Voyage:** | Eastbourne fishing and return |
| **Date Built, Builder:** | c.1884 |
| **Owner:** | James Francis |
| **Ship's Master:** | James Francis |
| **Number of Crew:** | 1 |

---

The two men on this ill-fated vessel were James Francis and Richard Wood, who were both licensed boatmen from Eastbourne. They had left home at about 9am on Tuesday 20th November 1888 to go hook fishing in the *Palatine* which was a small open boat. The two men set off from the beach about an hour later and at this time there was a strong north-westerly wind blowing and because it was off-shore, the sea for about ½ mile/ 804m out was reasonably calm and nothing to cause concern among the two men. However, further out to sea it was exceptionally rough.

The *Palatine* was not the only vessel to put off from Eastbourne at about 10am on this morning as several others had also set off including the *Elaine,* with Joseph Jones and William French on board, and the *Genesta* with the brothers F. & J. Heard on board. The *Palatine* dropped its anchor about 1 mile/804m from the shore and about ¾ mile/1.2km inside the *Genesta.* At about noon James Francis and Richard Wood decided to return to shore because of the ever increasing heavy seas and large waves, which were starting to cause difficulties for the *Palatine.* They had stowed their fishing tackle and put two reefs in the foresail, one in the mizzen, and set out for Eastbourne. They had not gone far when they were suddenly hit by a particularly violent squall which capsized the vessel throwing both men into the sea - they drowned instantly.

James Francis who lived in Longstone Road left a wife of 12 months and two children by a former marriage. Richard Wood, brother of the Town Crier, lived at 38, Tideswell Road also left a wife but they did not have any children.

Those on board the *Elaine* were suddenly aware that they could no longer see the *Palatine,* and fearing that the vessel was in distress made back to Eastbourne as quickly as was possible. Jones and French contemplated going in search of the *Palatine* but the conditions were getting so bad, with the sea washing over the *Elaine,* that they would themselves have been swamped had they tried a search.

At 12.25pm the *Elaine* arrived on the beach and the crew spoke to T. Swain, A. Sayers and Richard Hide Jun., three local fishermen. On hearing their story these three men put off in the yacht *Lord Randolph* and went in search of the *Palatine* and its crew. The local lifeboat had also been aware of the missing vessel but there was, for some unknown reason, a two hour delay between being told about the *Palatine* and the actual launching of the lifeboat *William and Mary.* However, a crew was mustered of the following men, Jessie Hugget (coxswain), Tom Boniface (second coxswain), R. Heard, Erridge, J. Heard, Charles 'Bones' Hide, Fred Hide, R. Wood, R. Swain, Tom Sayers, Cummings, R. Boniface, Carter and Standbridge. Charles 'Bones' Hide and Erridge had only just come ashore themselves, having also been out in this sea in their own boat, *Frederick.* Having come ashore they saw the lifeboat being got ready to go in search of the *Palatine* so they both immediately volunteered to join the crew.

Despite the search by both the *Lord Randolph* and the lifeboat *William and Mary* nothing was ever found of either the vessel or the crew from the *Palatine.* The only information the lifeboat managed to obtain during the search was when they came upon a steam-tug which reported having earlier seen an upturned small boat off Beachy Head.

That same evening the crew of the lifeboat *William and Mary* were treated to a meal at the Anchor Hotel as a sign of appreciation of the crew's efforts earlier in the day. Two days later, on the evening of Thursday 22nd November, the three man crew of the *Lord Randolph,* together with the crew of the *Elaine,* were likewise treated to a meal as a token of appreciation of their endeavours the previous Tuesday. The meal at the Marine Inn, Seaside, was at the invitation of the *Lord Randolph's* owner William Moore of 29 Royal Parade, Eastbourne.

On the morning of Thursday 20th December the body of Richard Wood was found near the Kewhurst Coastguard Station, 2 miles/3.2km west of Bexhill. The Inquest into his death was held at noon the following day at the Wheatsheaf Inn, Bexhill before Mr. C. Sheppard, the Coroner for the district of Battle. The Jury returned a verdict of 'Death by accidental drowning'. The body was returned to Eastbourne on the Friday afternoon following the Inquest, in readiness for the funeral the next day at 2.30pm at the Ocklynge cemetery. The funeral cortege consisted of seven carriages, and left Richard Wood's home in Tideswell Road at 2pm.

*Ref: SIBI; EG 21.11.1888 & 26.12.1888; EC 24.11.1888; HI 27.12.1888*

# MARY DAVIES

| | |
|---|---|
| **Date:** | 24.12.1888 |
| **Wreck Location:** | Ashore at Seaford between Seaford Head and Martello Tower |
| **Description of Vessel:** | |
| **Gross Tonnage -** | 59 |
| **Length -** | 56ft/17.19m |
| **Beam -** | 17ft/5.24m |
| **Vessel Type -** | British sailing schooner |
| **Cargo:** | Stone |
| **Home Port:** | Aberystwyth |
| **Voyage:** | Portland to London |
| **Date Built, Builder:** | c.1853 at Newquay |
| **Owner:** | W. Williams, Cardiganshire |
| **Ship's Master:** | Richard Davies |
| **Number of Crew:** | 1 and a boy |

---

Problems for the *Mary Davies* started at 10pm on Sunday 23rd December 1888 when the vessel developed quite a serious leak that required the three man crew, consisting of Richard Davies, Thomas Francis and a boy, to man the pumps throughout the night. During the early hours of the following morning, Christmas Eve, a force 6 south-westerly gale blew up, so the master decided that he would make for Newhaven harbour.

As the *Mary Davies* approached the harbour she failed to answer the helm due to the ever increasing amount of water the vessel was shipping through the leak. This lack of control left the vessel to drift before the very strong winds past the harbour entrance and through the turbulent surf as it approached the shore between the Martello Tower at Seaford and

Seaford Head.

By the time the *Mary Davies* struck the beach, word had gone round the town that the vessel was in distress. This resulted in a large number of spectators gathering on the sea wall to watch the drama. This was fortunate because once on the beach, the crew tied ropes around their bodies and with the help of many of the spectators were all hauled ashore safely before the coastguards from Blatchington Station arrived.

Although when the coastguard arrived under the command of Lieutenant Pride they were not required, it only took them 20 minutes from the time they were informed to cover the 1½ miles/2.4km to the *Mary Davies* with the rocket apparatus. However, they did take charge of the stricken crew, taking them to the Inn Hotel to recover from their ordeal.

The heavy seas and surf continued to sweep over the *Mary Davies* and by 1am the masts had gone. Shortly after this, following the next high tide, the vessel was smashed to pieces. The vessel was insured however, with the Cambrian Mutual Marine Insurance Company Limited.

*Ref: SIBI; EC 29.12.1888*

# PILOT BOAT NO. 5

| | |
|---|---|
| **Date:** | 27.1.1889 |
| **Wreck Location:** | 3 miles/4.8km south-west of Royal Sovereign Light |
| **Description of Vessel:** | |
| **Vessel Type -** | Belgian sailing Pilot schooner |
| **Home Port:** | Antwerp |
| **Voyage:** | From unknown port patrolling English Channel |
| **Date Built, Builder:** | c.1879 |
| **Owner:** | Belgian Government |
| **Ship's Master:** | Beniesz |
| **Number of Crew:** | 6 |
| **Number of Passengers:** | 7 (Pilots) |

The *Pilot Boat No. 5* left Antwerp on Saturday 26th January 1889 with seven pilots on board, under the command of the master Beniesz and his six man crew. Their task was to cruise the Channel to supply pilots for Belgian and Dutch vessels. At about 5.30am the following morning the vessel was south-west of the Royal Sovereign Light when the duty watch reported that a steamship was approaching them. Those on board *Pilot Boat No. 5* believed it was a vessel requiring a pilot, which in fact was the case. The conditions were almost perfect, with good visibility, a smooth sea, and a slight easterly wind.

The steamship approaching the pilot vessel was the *Ardanach* of 1100 tons, under the command of its master Mr. Glover, en route from the Mediterranean to Amsterdam with a cargo of currants. The nearer the steamship got the more concerned those on the pilot vessel became as it was on course straight for them. When the steamship got near enough those on the deck of the pilot vessel called to warn the steamship, but it was to no avail and the *Ardanach* struck *Pilot Boat No. 5* amidships on the port side.

The force of the impact was such that the port side of the pilot vessel nearly went right under the water and the bow of the steamship came to rest halfway across it. It was extremely fortunate that there were no injuries or fatalities as most of those on board the pilot vessel were in their berths asleep at the time. However, as soon as the vessels collided those on the pilot vessel gathered on deck to find their vessel had a huge hole in the side and taking in water rapidly. Some of those from the pilot vessel then climbed onto the steamship before it pulled away, while the others managed to launch the pilot vessel's two boats and pull clear just before the vessel went down.

The *Ardanach* safely picked up all fourteen men on board the pilot vessel safely and put them off at Dover 1pm that Sunday afternoon. They were cared for by the Mayor of the town, Mr. W.H. Crundall, who also happened to be the Belgian Vice-Consul. They left Dover later the same day for Ostend on a mail packet vessel

This was the second such unfortunate collision to befall *Pilot Boat No. 5*. It was run down a couple years earlier in the Channel and had to be taken into Dover for repairs.

*Ref: SIBI; SWA 28.1.1889; HT 2.2.1889*

# GLENCOE

| | |
|---|---|
| **Date:** | 4.2.1889 |
| **Wreck Location:** | Off Beachy Head |
| **Description of Vessel:** | |
| Gross Tonnage - | 2613 |
| Length - | 386ft/118.08m |
| Beam - | 38ft/11.64m |
| Vessel Type - | British iron steamship |
| **Cargo:** | Ballast |
| **Home Port:** | Glasgow |
| **Voyage:** | Liverpool to London |
| **Date Built, Builder:** | c.1878 by London & Glasgow Co., Glasgow |
| **Owner:** | McGregor Gow & Co. (The Glen Line) |
| **Ship's Master:** | D.O. Mackinlay |
| **Number of Crew:** | 50 |
| **Number of Passengers:** | 1 (Pilot) |

The weather off Beachy Head on the night of Monday 4th February 1889 was particularly unpleasant with heavy snow, extremely poor visibility and a force 6 north-easterly wind blowing with very heavy seas. It was in these conditions that the *Glencoe,* with its 51 crew and the Channel Pilot, were making their way up the Channel en route to London from Liverpool. Although the vessel was a passenger vessel it did not have any passengers on board at the time, other than the Pilot. Also in the vicinity was the *Largo Bay* (see page 393) sailing down the Channel en route for Auckland,

New Zealand from London under her master, J. Smith and his 20 man crew. Unfortunately, unknown to the master of either vessel, their respective courses were taking them on a collision with each other.

The first that either was aware of the other was when those on the sailing barque, *Largo Bay*, suddenly saw the approaching steamship *Glencoe* loom out of the snow. Within minutes, the *Glencoe* struck the bows of the *Largo Bay*. The force of the impact was so severe that the bowsprit, jibboom, main topgallant, and the mizzen topmast head, together with the associated rigging, were all carried away. The foremast broke close to the deck and collapsed onto the deck of the *Largo Bay* killing a young apprentice boy who was to be the only casualty on the sailing barque. Below deck a large hole had been made in the vessel and the fore compartment was starting to fill with water. The crew set about manning the pumps and removing the carnage on the decks and had little time to worry about the fate of the *Glencoe,* which was even more tragic.

The *Glencoe* started to sink immediately after the impact and within eight minutes the vessel had complete disappeared below the sea with the loss of all hands. They just did not have enough time to get the boats off. Those who lost their lives were: the master D.O. Mackinlay; J.H. Davis (first officer), A.T. Moon (second officer), J.C. Williams (third officer, who lived at Providence House, Ore, Hastings), Peter Keith (fourth officer), D. Davis (boatswain), J. McLeod (carpenter), C. Godfrey (lamp trimmer), Robert Sadler (first engineer), A. McKenzie (second engineer), W. Burns (third engineer), A. Lindsay (fourth engineer), J. Middleton (storekeeper), G. Perry (first steward), G. Britton (second steward), T. Sinclair (pantryman), A. Colecorn (mess room steward), T.G. Williams (Channel Pilot), Lund (deck hand), three Chinese cooks, ten seamen whose names are not known, and twenty Chinese firemen.

The considerably damaged *Largo Bay* started to drift down the Channel displaying distress signals. However, these signals were not answered until the vessel was 60 miles/96.5km south-east off St. Catherines Point, Isle of Wight. The steamship *Urpeth* under the command of the master Davies, bound for Shields from Le Havre, answered the distress signals and took the *Largo Bay* in tow to the Cowes Roads where the barque was finally anchored. However, the tow was only on the understanding that £1000 would be paid in salvage by the *Largo Bay* owners.

At a subsequent inquiry it was found that the *Glencoe* was to blame for this disaster, by porting its helm. No blame was attached to the *Largo Bay*.

*Ref: SIBI; HT 9.2.1889; BC 9.2.1889; EC 9.2.1889; EG 27.3.1889*

# LARGO BAY

**Date:**                                                4.2.1889

**Wreck Location:**                     Off Beachy Head

**Description of Vessel:**
**Gross Tonnage -**                    1255
**Length -**                                222ft/67.64m
**Beam -**                                 36ft/10.91m
**Vessel Type -**                      British sailing iron barque

**Cargo:**                            General

**Home Port:**                       Glasgow

**Voyage:**                        London to Auckland, New Zealand

**Date Built, Builder:**         c.1878 by J. Key & Sons (Cameron & Co), Kinghorn

**Owner:**                         J.S. Hatfield, Cameron & Co., Glasgow

**Ship's Master:**                  J. Smith

**Number of Crew:**               20

---

See *Glencoe* (page 391).

# CARRIE DINGLE

| | |
|---|---|
| **Date:** | 6.4.1889 |
| **Wreck Location:** | 7 miles/11.3km south of Royal Sovereign Light |

**Description of Vessel:**

| | |
|---|---|
| **Gross Tonnage -** | 183 |
| **Length -** | 105ft/32.18m |
| **Beam -** | 24ft/7.46m |
| **Vessel Type -** | British sailing brigantine |

| | |
|---|---|
| **Cargo:** | Slates |
| **Home Port:** | Liverpool |
| **Voyage:** | Port Madoc to Hamburg |
| **Date Built, Builder:** | c.1873 by Williams, Plymouth |
| **Owner:** | E. Roberts, Bangor |
| **Ship's Master:** | Charles Roberts |
| **Number of Crew:** | 4 |

At 8.30pm on Saturday 6th April 1889 the *Carrie Dingle* was 7 miles/ 11.3km south of the Royal Sovereign Light in very clear weather and a slight breeze when the crew saw, about 4 miles/6.4km away, the Red Star steamship liner *Nordenland*. The *Nordenland,* under the command of its master Nickeers, was bound for New York from Antwerp and heading towards the *Carrie Dingle* on a collision course. Charles Roberts got all his crew on deck and they shouted at the liner to attract the attention of those on the steamship, throughout the time it was steaming towards them, but to no avail.

The steamship kept its course, colliding with the *Carrie Dingle's* starboard bow completely smashing the fore part of the vessel. The

*Nordenland* was travelling so fast that it took a further mile/1.6km for it to stop and return to the stricken vessel an hour later. Fortunately the *Carrie Dingle* stayed afloat until the steamship returned to lower its boats to pick up the stricken crew. It was not long after the crew were safely on the *Nordenland* that their vessel sank. Once on the deck of the *Nordenland* they were surprised to find that there were 300 emigrants on board the vessel hoping to start a new life in America.

The *Nordenland* later transferred Charles Roberts and his crew onto a Belgian tug which landed them at Dover the following morning, while the *Nordenland* put into Southampton for repairs to the damage it had sustained 3ft/1m above the water line. The *Carrie Dingle* crew, having been put ashore at Dover, were looked after by the Dover National Sailor's Home who arranged for the crew to return that evening to their homes in Wales.

*Ref: SIBI; BC 3.4.1889; SWA 8.4.1889; SE 9.4.1889; EC 13.4.1889*

# CHATEAUX MARGAUX

| | |
|---|---|
| **Date:** | 28.4.1889 |
| **Wreck Location:** | 8 miles/12.9km east of Royal Sovereign Light |
| **Description of Vessel:** | |
| **Gross Tonnage -** | 4035 |
| **Length -** | 385ft/117.8m |
| **Beam -** | 41ft/12.49m |
| **Vessel Type -** | French iron steamship |
| **Cargo:** | General |
| **Home Port:** | Bordeaux |
| **Voyage:** | Le Havre to Antwerp |
| **Date Built, Builder:** | c.1883 by Chantiers & A. de la Giro, Bordeaux |
| **Owner:** | Compagnie Bordelaise de Navigation |
| **Ship's Master:** | A. Sensine |
| **Number of Crew:** | 90 |
| **Number of Passengers:** | 1 |

On Sunday 28th April 1889 the *Chateau Margaux* was 8 miles/12.9km east off the Royal Sovereign Light in a force 3 south-westerly wind when it was in collision with the steamship *Manora* of Glasgow, and sank.

*Ref: SIBI*

# UNKNOWN

| | |
|---|---|
| **Date:** | 5.6.1889 |
| **Wreck Location:** | 1 mile/1.6km off Seaford |
| **Description of Vessel:** | |
| **Length -** | 14ft/4.3m |
| **Beam -** | 5ft/1.5m |
| **Vessel Type -** | Sailing boat |
| **Home Port:** | Newhaven |
| **Voyage:** | Newhaven and return |
| **Owner:** | Cantell |
| **Ship's Master:** | Charles Stevens |
| **Number of Crew:** | 0 |
| **Number of Passengers:** | 5 adults, 1 child |

On the morning of Wednesday 5th June 1889 a Newhaven boatman, Charles Stevens, took a small group out for a sail. The group comprised of Mr. Bishop (who had recently been conducting mission services at the Primitive Methodist Chapel, Newhaven), Mrs. Scadden, two sisters called Fenner, Miss Chilton and 12 year old Rosie Worsley (daughter of Samuel Worsley a builder of Edward Street, Brighton). The wind at the time was from the north-east but with occasional strong gusts.

At 12 noon the craft was 1 mile/1.6km off Seaford and all was going well, when Charles Stevens went to go about, to return back to Newhaven. It was at this exact moment that a sudden and strong gust of wind blew catching the sails and capsizing the craft. With all the occupants in the water, Charles Stevens tried to right the craft but was unable to do so.

Fortunately, being a pleasant day there were a number of vessels out on the water, including Mr. J. Paris who was out in his rowing boat taking a party of visitors out for a trip. He was very quickly on the spot of the capsized craft, as were a number of others, and managed to rescuc all the exhausted adults who were found clinging to the upturned craft. However the young girl, Rosie Worsley, who was staying in Newhaven with Mrs. Fenner her aunt, to recover from a recent illness, was seen to drift away by the others and sink below the water never to be seen again.

With all the adults safely rescued they were returned to the beach where they were taken to the Assembly Rooms and the New Inn Hotel to recover from their ordeal. They were also attended to by Dr. Morgan for their exhaustion.

The capsized craft was later taken in tow by a Pilot boat and taken into Newhaven harbour.

*Ref: EC 8.6.1889*

# HAROLD

| | |
|---|---|
| **Date:** | 11.6.1889 |
| **Wreck Location:** | 5 miles/8km west of Royal Sovereign Light |
| **Description of Vessel:** | |
| **Gross Tonnage -** | 1107 |
| **Length -** | 225ft/68.73m |
| **Beam -** | 31ft/9.32m |
| **Vessel Type -** | British iron steamship |
| **Cargo:** | Iron ore |
| **Home Port:** | Newcastle |
| **Voyage:** | Bilbao to the Tyne |
| **Date Built, Builder:** | c.1872 by A. Leslie & Co., Newcastle-upon-Tyne |
| **Owner:** | W.C. Charlton, Newcastle-upon-Tyne |
| **Ship's Master:** | W. Bedlington |
| **Number of Crew:** | 16 |

---

At 11pm on Tuesday 11th June 1889, while in thick fog 5 miles/8km west of the Royal Sovereign Light, the *Harold* came into collision with the Clyde Shipping Company's *Toward*. The collision between these two steamships resulted in severe bow damage to the *Toward* while the *Harold* sank very soon after the impact. However, 16 of the crew were rescued by the *Toward* with one crew member being lost.

The *Toward* got to Southampton the following day where, after repair to the bow damage, it was able to continue its voyage from London to Glasgow.

*Ref: SIBI; HI 13.6.1889*

# GODILD

| | |
|---|---|
| **Date:** | 20.7.1889 |
| **Wreck Location:** | Birling Gap |
| **Description of Vessel:** | |
| **Vessel Type -** | British sailing dandy |
| **Cargo:** | Granite boulders |
| **Voyage:** | Newhaven to Birling Gap |
| **Owner:** | D. Beal, Newhaven |
| **Ship's Master:** | D. Beal |
| **Number of Crew:** | 4 |

This vessel became a loss on Saturday 27th July 1889 in a force 5 westerly wind while gathering boulders from beach at Birling Gap.

*Ref: SIBI*

# RUTH

| | |
|---|---|
| **Date:** | 13.9.1889 |
| **Wreck Location:** | Ashore at Eastbourne |
| **Description of Vessel:** | |
| **Vessel Type -** | British sailing fishing lugger |
| **Voyage:** | Eastbourne fishing and return |
| **Date Built, Builder:** | c.1884 |
| **Owner:** | J. Read, Eastbourne |
| **Ship's Master:** | J. Read |
| **Number of Crew:** | 2 |

In a force 5 south-easterly wind the *Ruth* was driven ashore at Eastbourne on Wednesday 13th September 1889. The vessel became a total wreck when smashed to pieces by the heavy seas

*Ref: SIBI*

# EHREN

**Date:**                                   24.12.1889

**Wreck Location:**                         Ashore at Seaford between Seaford
                                            Head and Martello Tower

**Description of Vessel:**
**Vessel Type -**                           British sailing schooner

---

The *Ehren* became a wreck exactly 12 months after the *Mary Davies* (see page 387) under very similar circumstances, in that the *Ehren* was trying to make for Newhaven harbour but was driven ashore between Seaford Head and the Martello Tower by the weather.

*Ref: DS*

# SAGITTA

| | |
|---|---|
| **Date:** | 14.1.1890 |
| **Wreck Location:** | 10 miles/16km south-west of Beachy Head |

**Description of Vessel:**

| | |
|---|---|
| **Gross Tonnage -** | 230 |
| **Length -** | 135ft/41.35m |
| **Beam -** | 26ft/7.87m |
| **Vessel Type -** | British sailing barquentine |
| **Cargo:** | Ballast |
| **Home Port:** | Guernsey |
| **Voyage:** | London to Guernsey |
| **Date Built, Builder:** | c.1856 at Guernsey |
| **Owner:** | T.G. Robins, Guernsey |
| **Ship's Master:** | E. Loveridge |
| **Number of Crew:** | 7 |

---

The reason as to why the *Sagitta* and the steamship *County of Salop* collided in the early hours of Tuesday 14th January 1890, is not known. The conditions at the time would appear not to have been a contributory factor as the sea was calm and there was a slight north-westerly wind blowing.

At the time of the collision the 1400 ton *County of Salop* of Liverpool was making for Cardiff in ballast and the *Sagitta* was making for Guernsey, also in ballast having discharged its cargo in London. For whatever reason, at about daybreak both vessels collided with such force that the *Sagitta* was almost cut clean in two and sank within a couple of hours. The *County of Salop* was virtually undamaged. Thankfully there was plenty of time for the crew of the *Sagitta* to launch their boats before the vessel went down. The crew were rescued by the *County of Salop* who later put them ashore at Cardiff where the Shipwreck Mariners Society took care of them.

*Ref: SIBI; HN 17.1.1890*

# POLYNESIA

| | |
|---|---|
| **Date:** | 24.4.1890 |
| **Wreck Location:** | Ashore 300 yards/274m east of Birling Gap |
| **Description of Vessel:** | |
| **Gross Tonnage -** | 1010 |
| **Length -** | 194ft/59.43m |
| **Beam -** | 33ft/10.05m |
| **Vessel Type -** | German sailing clipper |
| **Cargo:** | Nitrate of soda |
| **Home Port:** | Hamburg |
| **Voyage:** | Iquique to Hamburg |
| **Date Built, Builder:** | c.1874 by Reihrs. Shipyard Co., Hamburg |
| **Owner:** | F. Laeisz, Hamburg |
| **Ship's Master:** | A. Reitman |
| **Number of Crew:** | 15 |

During the early hours of Thursday 24th April 1890 there was a very thick fog off the East Sussex coast. One of the vessels making its way up the Channel was the *Polynesia* bound for Hamburg, with a cargo of nitrate of soda worth £30,000. At 6.15am in this dense fog the vessel's master was unaware that he was too close to the shore and ran aground on rocks just east of Birling Gap causing considerable damage to the hull. So severe was the damage that the hull started to fill with water quite quickly and the pumps were manned to keep the water level down.

News of the *Polynesia* did not reach Newhaven until about four hours later but at 10.40am, as soon as it was known, the Newhaven Lifeboat

*Michael Henry* was launched making its way towards the vessel. The local Lloyd's agent, Mr. J. Bull, also made for the scene on the local steam tug *Tipper.* When they arrived they found the *Polynesia* broadside on and being driven further onto the rocks in what was now a strong south-westerly wind with accompanying heavy seas. The lifeboat stood by the vessel until 4.30pm when the master decided that the crew could do no more that day. They were then transferred to the lifeboat which took them back to Newhaven.

The *Tipper* and the *Michael Henry* were not the only craft to visit the unfortunate *Polynesia* that day. The pleasure steamer *Nelson* also visited the scene from Eastbourne with about 100 spectators.

By 4.55pm the following day, Friday, the weather had subsided so the *Tipper* and the *Nelson* returned to the scene towing a number of lighters. The hope was of not only salvaging the cargo but that once some of it had been removed there was the hope of pulling the vessel off the rocks. A number of the crew were put back on the vessel to man the pumps to reduce the 6ft/1.8m of water in her. Over the following few days the pumps were constantly manned while the nitrate of soda was removed and taken back to Newhaven in the lighters. The tugs were paid 15s.0d/75p per day to tow the lighters to Newhaven, where the cargo was stored with the local railway company.

On Sunday 4th May, with sufficient cargo removed and with pumps being manned on board, an attempt was made by the Dover tug *Lady Vita,* to pull the *Polynesia* off the rocks. The attempt was partly successful in that the vessel was pulled clear of the rocks and towed towards Newhaven but only as far as Cuckmere where it was allowed to be beached on the sand because of the amount of water that was getting into the hull. The vessel came to rest on her starboard side such that the deck was facing the sea.

On Tuesday 6th May the *Commerce* left Newhaven bound for Hamburg with 434 tons of the salvaged cargo together with the salvaged sails. The remainder of the cargo had since dissolved once the sea got into it. With the departure of the *Commerce,* the local Lloyd's agent no longer had any interest in the vessel, leaving the *Polynesia* to the elements and the action of the sea to break the vessel up. It was finally destroyed after a very strong gale and heavy seas on Tuesday 20th May.

The stores and other equipment that had been salvaged from the vessel and which had not been returned to Hamburg on the *Commerce,* were sold at auction on 24th May and realised £2,671.17s.0d/£2,671.85p.

*Ref: SIBI; SNLB; CNMM; EC 26.4.1890; EG 30.4.1890*

# EUREKA

| | |
|---|---|
| **Date:** | 8.7.1890 |
| **Wreck Location:** | Ashore at Crumbles, Eastbourne |
| **Description of Vessel:** | |
| **Gross Tonnage -** | 120 |
| **Vessel Type -** | British sailing barge |
| **Cargo:** | 150 quarters* of oats, 245 bags of linseed oil cake |
| **Home Port:** | Rochester |
| **Voyage:** | London to Poole |
| **Owner:** | James Harrington, Rochester |
| **Ship's Master:** | Richard Lunchford |
| **Number of Crew:** | 2 |
| **Number of Passengers:** | 1 (Master's wife) |

For this time of the year, the night of Monday 7th/Tuesday 8th July 1890 saw an exceptionally stormy night with heavy rain. There were a number of vessels caught in this storm with its accompanying rough seas, including the *Eureka*, which like the others, sought refuge from the south-westerly storm by anchoring about 1 mile/1.6km off the Redoubt at Eastbourne, in the shelter of Beachy Head. By its very construction as a barge, the *Eureka* was low in the water, so as the storm intensified the waves started to sweep over the vessel. This, coupled with damaged rudder gear and the vessel starting to drag its anchor in the face of the storm, made it apparent to the master Richard Lunchford, that the vessel was now in serious difficulty.

At 3am on the Tuesday morning, Lunchford raised the distress signals which were fortunately seen by some fishermen on the beach at Eastbourne, who raised the alarm with the lifeboat crew. At about 5am the lifeboat *William and Mary* was launched from its carriage near the Wish Tower, under the command of the coxswain Jessie Huggett, and was soon battling through the raging surf out towards the stricken vessel.

On reaching the *Eureka,* the lifeboat came alongside the vessel and first took the master's wife off followed by the crew, who were returned to the beach by 5.30am. They were taken to the Sea Beach Hotel, Sea Beach Road, where they were looked after by the owner, Mr. A. Matthews.

It was at about the time that the crew were arriving on the beach, that the *Eureka* broke from its anchor cable under the strain of the weather, and started to drift eastwards. The vessel was eventually driven ashore on the Crumble's beach, about 2 miles/3.2km east of Eastbourne town. With the vessel now broadside on to the beach, every wave on the incoming tide crashed against it with such incredible force that it was feared the vessel would be broken to pieces before anything could be salvaged from it. As a result the deputy local Lloyd's agent, Councillor T. Bennett, arranged for a number of horses and wagons to assist in removing as much as possible from the vessel. However, getting the horses and wagons to the scene was not without its own difficulties as they had to come along the beach. There being no roadway between Eastbourne and where the vessel lay at Crumble's beach.

The first things that came off the vessel were cabin furniture, beds, books and the vessel's provisions. There then came some rabbits and a dog which had managed to survive the ordeal, followed by a large proportion of the £500 cargo. This salvage work continued until midday when the combined action of sea and wind started to force the vessel further eastward which by 4pm had drifted a further 2 miles/3.2km to Langney Point.

The following day, Wednesday 9th July, the *Eureka* was got off the beach by a tug and towed into Newhaven, where surprisingly, it was found that the vessel had not suffered too much damage.

The *Eureka* had formerly been used in the Harwich River Service although had often been used for sea-going trade purposes as on this occasion.

* A quarter is 28lbs/12.7kgs

*Ref: SELB; SWA 9.7.1890; BC 12.7.1890; SE 12.7.1890; EC 12.7.1890; LL 16493 8.7.90*

# MIRELLA

| | |
|---|---|
| **Date:** | 8.7.1890 |
| **Wreck Location:** | Entrance to Newhaven Harbour |
| **Description of Vessel:** | |
| **Gross Tonnage -** | 60 |
| **Length -** | 63ft/19.3m |
| **Beam -** | 5ft/1.37m |
| **Vessel Type -** | British sailing schooner |
| **Cargo:** | Ballast |
| **Home Port:** | Southampton |
| **Voyage:** | Le Havre to Newhaven |
| **Date Built, Builder:** | c.1867 by Inman |
| **Owner:** | Alfred Ede, Southampton |
| **Ship's Master:** | William Martin |
| **Number of Crew:** | 5 |
| **Number of Passengers:** | 2 |

At 6am on Tuesday 8th July 1890 the *Mirella* and the Dieppe to Newhaven passenger steamship *Rouen,* were both approaching the entrance to Newhaven harbour in a force 6 south-westerly wind. The *Mirella* from the Royal Southern & Southampton Yacht Club, was under the command of the master, William Martin, who had been the master for the past five years. Apart from the five man crew, also on board was the owner, Alfred Ede and a gentleman friend.

As the *Rouen* entered the harbour under the command of William Breach, it was overtaken by the *Mirella* which struck the port side of the steamship and started to sink almost immediately. As soon as the vessels collided William Martin got all those still below in their berths, up on deck and into the rigging as the vessel went down. William Martin went down with the vessel but fortunately managed to get back to the surface and grasp one of the ropes hanging from the vessel. At the time of this accident a number of the harbour employees were working on the breakwater and within 15 minutes had the harbour boats on the scene. A boat was also put off from the slightly damaged *Rouen* to assist in the rescue.

By now the vessel had settled down on the bottom with only the tops of the masts showing above the water level, to which crew and passengers were hanging on, except for the master who was still in the water clinging to the rope. The harbour boats were first on the scene and safely brought all those on board the *Mirella* ashore.

The Newhaven harbour master, Capt. White, was now tasked with getting the *Mirella* removed from the mouth of the harbour which was successfully achieved on Thursday 10th July and the vessel was then towed into the harbour.

Alfred Ede, the owner of the *Mirella,* later brought an action against the South Coast Railway Company, owners of the *Rouen*, in the Admiralty Court, London. The action was to recover damages for the loss of his yacht. Sir James Hannen presided at the hearing, where Alfred Ede the plaintiff was represented by Sir W. Philimore QC and Mr. J. Aspinal, and the defendants were represented by Mr. G. Barnes QC and Dr. Raikes. The defence put forward by the South Coast Railway Company was that the *Mirella* had not kept a good look-out, was carrying too much sail for the conditions, and although having altered course, brought about the collision. Sir James Hannen's judgement at the end of the hearing was that the master of the steamship *Rouen*, after having run into the yacht, failed to stop his engines and lower boats immediately. He said the conduct of the steamship could not be defended in leaving the rescue of the yacht's crew to the chance that other boats would do it. The hearing's decision was that the *Rouen* alone was to blame for the collision and judgement was accordingly entered for the plaintiff with costs.

*Ref: SIBI; EC 12.7.1890; SE 12.7.1890; BC 13.12.1890*

# THYRA

| | |
|---|---|
| **Date:** | 13.10.1890 |
| **Wreck Location:** | Off Beachy Head |

**Description of Vessel:**

| | |
|---|---|
| **Gross Tonnage -** | 1035 |
| **Length -** | 212ft/64.68m |
| **Beam -** | 29ft/9.01m |
| **Vessel Type -** | German iron steamship |
| **Cargo:** | General |
| **Home Port:** | Flensburg |
| **Voyage:** | St. Ubes to Hamburg |
| **Date Built, Builder:** | c.1881 |
| **Owner:** | F.M. Bruhn |
| **Ship's Master:** | E.A. Jacobson |
| **Number of Crew:** | 17 |

This vessel sank in calm conditions after colliding with the steamship *Ursula* of Scarborough, on Monday 13th October 1890.

*Ref: SIBI*

# GARRON TOWER

**Date:**                           19.12.1890

**Wreck Location:**                 Near Beachy Head

**Description of Vessel:**
**Gross Tonnage -**                 650
**Length -**                        179ft/54.86m
**Beam -**                          28ft/8.59m
**Vessel Type -**                   British steel steamship

**Cargo:**                          Coal

**Home Port:**                      Sunderland

**Voyage:**                         From unknown port to Santander

**Date Built, Builder:**            c.1876 by E. Withy & Co, West
                                    Hartlepool

**Owner:**                          Marquis of Londonderry

**Ship's Master:**                  D. Horlock

**Number of Crew:**                 13

---

On the night of Friday 19th December 1890, the steamship *Garron Tower* was run down, when off Beachy Head, by an unknown barque. The force of the collision was such that it caused both masts, the bridge and the vessel's funnel to be carried away. As one of the masts fell four of the crew who were on deck were severely injured by it. The barque failed to stop and assist the crew of the *Garron Tower* despite their calls for help. The identity of the barque is not known despite its figurehead and jibboom falling onto the *Garron Tower* at the time of impact.

Fortunately for the crew the steamship *Bessemer* of Middlesborough was close at hand and picked the men up, putting them ashore on Sunday afternoon at Seaham, that is all except one, named Maynard. It was believed he jumped onto the barque at the time of the collision.

Although unrelated to this event what happened off Newhaven the following Monday 22nd December, illustrates the hardships suffered by mariners of this era. The Newhaven port health officer, Doctor Cunningham, had received information that laying ¾ mile/1.2km off Newhaven was the 155 ton *The Ward* of Guernsey under the command of its master P.H. Wright and his crew of 6 seamen. The information Dr. Cunningham had was that the crew were suffering a severe illness and had just buried one of their number. Dr. Cunningham went out to *The Ward* to be told that the vessel had left Guernsey the previous Thursday and encountered terrible weather which carried away the main boom. As the main boom was torn from the vessel it killed one man and broke the arm of another. When Dr. Cunningham treated the man's broken arm he found that all his fingers were totally frost bitten. For this to have happened the weather they experienced must have been extreme, which supported their claim that they had been unable to sail the vessel properly due to the sails and the ropes being frozen.

*Ref: SIBI; HI 25.12.1890; EC 27.12.1890*

# WELCOME HOME

| | |
|---|---|
| **Date:** | 9.3.1891 |
| **Wreck Location:** | Ashore 2 miles/3.2km west of Beachy Head |
| **Description of Vessel:** | |
| **Vessel Type -** | British sailing fishing lugger |
| **Home Port:** | Folkestone |
| **Voyage:** | Folkestone and return |
| **Date Built, Builder:** | c.1884 |
| **Owner:** | H. May, Folkestone |
| **Ship's Master:** | W. Burt |
| **Number of Crew:** | 4 |

On Monday 9th March 1891 there was a terrific snow storm along the East Sussex coast, with gale force winds. In Seaford the snow drifts were several feet deep, the trains had stop running, telegraph wires had fallen down and the mail could not get through. In fact Seaford was completely cut off from the rest of the county for several hours.

It was in these terrible conditions that the Folkestone fishing vessel *Welcome Home* was off Beachy Head. The conditions eventually overcame the vessel and it ran ashore 2 miles/3.2km west of Beachy Head at 11.30pm. Fortunately, the crew managed to scramble ashore but did not know where they were or in which direction to walk. In the end they walked for most of the night arriving in Seaford at about daybreak, where a Mr. J. Martin of Church Road took the men in suffering from exposure.

*Ref: SIBI; CNMM; SWA 16.3.1891*

# OWL

| | |
|---|---|
| **Date:** | 26.8.1891 |
| **Wreck Location:** | Ashore at Birling Gap |
| **Description of Vessel:** | |
| **Vessel Type -** | British sailing fishing lugger |
| **Voyage:** | Folkestone and return |
| **Owner:** | J. Goldsmith, Eastbourne |
| **Ship's Master:** | J. Goldsmith |
| **Number of Crew:** | 0 |

This vessel was blown ashore on Wednesday 26th August 1891 in a force 7 south-westerly wind and became a total loss. The owner and master J. Goldsmith was the only person on board the *Owl*.

*Ref: SIBI*

# ALBERTINE

| | |
|---|---|
| **Date:** | 2.11.1891 |
| **Wreck Location:** | 1½ miles/2.4km off Birling Gap |
| **Description of Vessel:** | |
| **Vessel Type -** | British sailing dandy |
| **Cargo:** | Ballast |
| **Home Port:** | Rye |
| **Voyage:** | Newhaven to unknown destination |
| **Date Built, Builder:** | c.1865 |
| **Owner:** | J. Martin, Newhaven |
| **Ship's Master:** | J. Eager |
| **Number of Crew:** | 2 |

On Monday 2nd November 1891 the *Albertine* sank while en route to collect boulders from the shore, in a squally north-easterly wind.

This vessel is possibly the first of two vessels with the name *Albertine,* that were built at Hastings.

*Ref: SIBI*

# FRIENDS

| | |
|---|---|
| **Date:** | 25.11.1891 |
| **Wreck Location:** | Ashore at Birling Gap |
| **Description of Vessel:** | |
| **Gross Tonnage -** | 7 |
| **Vessel Type -** | British sailing ketch |
| **Cargo:** | Boulders |
| **Home Port:** | Newhaven |
| **Voyage:** | Newhaven and return |
| **Owner:** | Henry Lower, Newhaven |
| **Ship's Master:** | F. Richardson |
| **Number of Crew:** | 3 |

The *Friends* and the *Alice and Beatrice* (see next page) were both off Birling Gap at anchor sitting out a south-westerly force 4 wind when the anchor cable of both vessels broke and were driven ashore and smashed to pieces.

Both vessels had a four man crew and those on board the *Alice and Beatrice* were William Roberts, Henry Richardson, L. Winder and George Richardson. Their boat and gear was valued at about £100 whereas the *Friends* was valued at about £30. The *Alice and Beatrice* crew, having got safely ashore, made for Birling Gap Coastguard Station where they were looked after for the night.

*Ref: SIBI; SWA 30.11.1891; HI 3.12.1891*

# ALICE & BEATRICE

| | |
|---|---|
| **Date:** | 25.11.1891 |
| **Wreck Location:** | Ashore at Birling Gap |
| **Description of Vessel:** | |
| **Gross Tonnage -** | 12 |
| **Vessel Type -** | British sailing ketch |
| **Cargo:** | Boulders |
| **Home Port:** | Newhaven |
| **Voyage:** | Newhaven and return |
| **Owner:** | W.D. Redmond, Newhaven |
| **Ship's Master:** | William Roberts |
| **Number of Crew:** | 3 |

See *Friends* (previous page).

*Ref: SIBI*

# ACHILLE

| | |
|---|---|
| **Date:** | 11.3.1892 |
| **Wreck Location:** | 1 mile/1.6km south of Royal Sovereign Light |
| **Description of Vessel:** | |
| **Vessel Type -** | French sailing brig |
| **Cargo:** | Zinc, ore |
| **Voyage:** | Requejada, Spain to Dunkirk |
| **Date Built, Builder:** | c.1870 |
| **Owner:** | A. Delrue, Dunkirk |
| **Ship's Master:** | Benard |
| **Number of Crew:** | 7 |

This vessel was in collision with the steamship *Rameh*, of Liverpool, on Friday 11ᵗʰ March 1892, in a force 5 north-westerly wind when 1 mile/ 1.6km south of the Royal Sovereign Light. Five members of the eight-man crew of the *Achille* lost their lives.

*Ref: SIBI*

# ERIN

| | |
|---|---|
| **Date:** | 16.3.1892 |
| **Wreck Location:** | Seaford Bay |
| **Description of Vessel:** | |
| **Gross Tonnage -** | 260 |
| **Vessel Type -** | Norwegian sailing brig |
| **Cargo:** | Ballast |
| **Home Port:** | Grinstatd |
| **Voyage:** | Cowes, I.o.W., to Grinstatd |
| **Date Built, Builder:** | c.1849 |
| **Owner:** | F.H. Holst, Grinstatd |
| **Ship's Master:** | F.H. Holst |
| **Number of Crew:** | 7 |

---

The *Erin* left Cowes on the Isle of Wight in ballast, at 5.30am on Tuesday 15th March 1892, having discharged a cargo of timber. During the afternoon the vessel encountered a force 9 severe gale when off the East Sussex coast. By 6pm that same afternoon the *Erin* was in great difficulty in these conditions and was being driven before the gale and heavy seas, with all sails closely reefed. Despite the master's best efforts the vessel was being driven ever closer to the shore at Seaford. Once amongst the low tide surf his cause was lost as he was unable to manoeuvre the vessel out of it, so he immediately flew his distress signal. It was not long after this that the vessel went aground opposite the Martello Tower about 50 yards/45m from the beach.

Those ashore had earlier seen that the vessel was in great difficulty and the coastguards at Blatchington had been made aware of the *Erin's* plight The officer in charge at Blatchington, Mr. Night, was already on his way with his men and the rocket apparatus, arriving opposite the vessel at 7pm. The coastguard fired a rocket over the vessel which went between the two masts and it was not long before the line had been made fast and the crew were being pulled safely ashore. Once ashore they were taken to the New Inn to recover and were later taken care of by Capt. White who was the acting Norwegian and Swedish Consul. He arranged for the crew to travel to London on the 4.05pm train the following day.

Not only did the coastguards attend this wreck but the Newhaven Lifeboat *Michael Henry* was also in attendance. The lifeboat coxswain, Mr. Lower, had received details of the *Erin* at about 6.45pm and within 15 minutes of firing the signal gun, the lifeboat was afloat and making for the *Erin*. The crew struggled with the terrible conditions, eventually arriving at 8pm just as the last man was being hauled ashore by the Blatchington coastguardsmen. With their services not required, the lifeboat made back towards Newhaven arriving an hour later.

The *Erin* was left to the following tides which soon broke up the ageing vessel albeit the remains of the vessel were subsequently sold for £14. With the loss of his vessel the master and owner had lost everything, and it was said that he would now have to take up fishing to make a living although the *Erin* was allegedly insured for £360.

*Ref: SIBI; HN 18.3.1892; EC 19.3.1892; HC 23.3.1892*

# LADY OF THE LAKE

| | |
|---|---|
| **Date:** | 9.12.1892 |
| **Wreck Location:** | Ashore at Eastbourne |
| **Description of Vessel:** | |
| **Vessel Type -** | British sailing fishing lugger |
| **Home Port:** | Brighton |
| **Voyage:** | Newhaven to Eastbourne |
| **Date Built, Builder:** | c.1880 |
| **Owner:** | J.H. Howell, Brighton |
| **Ship's Master:** | George Bishop |
| **Number of Crew:** | 3 |

On the night of Thursday 8th/Friday 9th December 1892 there was a south-westerly force 8 gale in the Channel. During the early hours of Friday morning many fishing vessels off Eastbourne ran for shore and were safely beached. However, one of the vessels out that night, the *Lady of the Lake,* with George Bishop and his crew of three on board, was not quite so fortunate.

The *Lady of the Lake* was 2 miles/3.2km off Eastbourne and George Bishop was trying to keep the vessel head in to wind but the wind and heavy sea conditions prevented him from achieving this and the vessel was driven towards the shore. As soon as it made the shore the three crew members jumped and got on to the beach. Before George Bishop could get off, a huge wave took it back towards the open sea. Fortunately, another large wave pushed it back towards the shore enabling George Bishop to get ashore safely. No sooner was he on the beach, when yet another wave took the vessel away again and it was never seen again.

After recovering, the crew returned to Brighton later in the day.

*Ref: SIBI; 14.12.1892*

# GANNETT

| | |
|---|---|
| **Date:** | 30.12.1892 |
| **Wreck Location:** | Near Newhaven |
| **Description of Vessel:** | |
| **Vessel Type -** | British sailing lugger |
| **Cargo:** | Boulders |
| **Home Port:** | Newhaven |
| **Voyage:** | Newhaven and return |
| **Date Built, Builder:** | c.1881 |
| **Owner:** | T. Brown, Newhaven |
| **Ship's Master:** | T. Brown |
| **Number of Crew:** | 1 |

This vessel became a loss while collecting boulders from the beach on Friday 30th December 1892 when blown ashore in a force 5 south-easterly wind.

*Ref: SIBI*

# PETER DE GROSSE

| | |
|---|---|
| **Date:** | 13.3.1893 |
| **Wreck Location:** | Off Beachy Head |
| **Description of Vessel:** | |
| **Gross Tonnage -** | 846 |
| **Length -** | 198ft/60.65m |
| **Beam -** | 28ft/8.65m |
| **Vessel Type -** | Russian iron steamship |
| **Home Port:** | St. Petersburg |
| **Voyage:** | Hamburg to Greenock |
| **Date Built, Builder:** | c.1872 by Nordd. Schffsb. Act, Kiel |
| **Owner:** | St. Petersburg Damp'schff. Ges |
| **Ship's Master:** | Schrock |

---

Also referred to as *Peter Der Grosse.*

On 10th March 1893 the *Peter De Grosse* left Hamburg for Greencok but during the night of 13th/14th March, when off Beachy Head, was run down by the German steamship *Preussen*, and sank. All those on board were rescued by the *Preussen,* which was en route from China to Bremen, and put ashore at Antwerp on 14th March.

*Ref: SIBI; EG 22.3.1893; LL 17329 15.3.93*

# MARINER

**Date:**      9.3.1893

**Wreck Location:**   5 miles/8km east of Royal Sovereign
         Light

**Description of Vessel:**
**Gross Tonnage -**   298
**Length -**      119ft/36.36m
**Beam -**      27ft/8.1m
**Vessel Type -**    British sailing brigantine

**Cargo:**      Ballast

**Home Port:**    Newhaven

**Voyage:**     Newhaven to Shields

**Date Built, Builder:**  c.1871 at Kingston-by-sea,
         Shoreham

**Owner:**      J.H. Bull & 11 others, Newhaven

**Ship's Master:**   C. Care

**Number of Crew:**  7

---

The *Mariner* left Newhaven during Wednesday 8th March 1893 with her crew of eight. The vessel had not got far before the weather, although calm, became very foggy indeed. At about 3am the next morning the *Mariner* was 5 miles/8km east of the Royal Sovereign Light in thick fog, when the master heard the horn of a vessel nearby. The *Mariner* replied to alert the nearby vessel of its presence. The horn of the other vessel was heard continuously for about ten minutes when suddenly out of the fog appeared the 2,000 Dutch steamship *Hispania*. The steamship struck the *Mariner* on the port side smashing the foremast and causing so much other damage that it was clear it would sink very quickly as a result. The master and crew managed to climb aboard the *Hispania* (which was bound for Spain from London) without having enough time to rescue any of their belongings. They had not been on board the *Hispania* long before the *Mariner* sank in very deep water, with little hope of salvage.

The *Hispania* carried on its voyage down the English Channel until it was about 12 miles/19km off Brighton when they came across a fishing smack. The *Mariner* crew were then transferred to the fishing smack and taken back to Newhaven.

*Ref: SIBI; BC 17.3.1893*

# GEORGE B. BALFOUR

**Date:** 3.5.1893

**Wreck Location:** 5 miles/8km south-west x ¾ mile/ 1.2km west of Beachy Head

**Description of Vessel:**
**Gross Tonnage -** 169
**Vessel Type -** British iron sailing schooner

**Cargo:** Cement

**Home Port:** Barrow-in-Furness

**Voyage:** Northfleet to Barrow-in-Furness

**Date Built, Builder:** c.1886

**Owner:** J. Fisher, Barrow-in-Furness

**Ship's Master:** Evans

**Number of Crew:** 5

---

At 9pm on Wednesday 3rd May 1893 the *George B. Balfour* was in collision with the steamship *City of Khios* of Glasgow when off Beachy Head. As a result of the impact the *George B. Balfour* went down with the loss of all 6 hands and the steamship was severely damaged below the water line which flooded its fore-hold. However, the *City of Khios* made it safely to Dover where the collision was reported the next day.

*Ref: SIBI; HN 5.5.1893*

# ALBERT & ALFRED

| | |
|---|---|
| **Date:** | 5.6.1893 |
| **Wreck Location:** | 1 mile/1.6km south-south-east of Belle Tout Light |
| **Description of Vessel:** | |
| **Vessel Type -** | British sailing fishing lugger |
| **Voyage:** | Eastbourne and return |
| **Date Built, Builder:** | c.1869 |
| **Owner:** | George Hide, Eastbourne |
| **Ship's Master:** | Harry Cummings |
| **Number of Crew:** | 4 |

At 1.30pm on Monday 5th June 1893 the *Little Stranger,* under the command of Charles Boniface, and the *Albert and Alfred* left Eastbourne together to go mackerel fishing near Newhaven. It had only been the previous day that the *Albert and Alfred* had landed a catch of 900 mackerel, so the crew were keen to return to the same fishing grounds. Those on board the *Albert and Alfred* (locally known as *The Gruff*) were the master Harry Cummings, William Novis, Percy Catt, Alfred Tulliford and William Marchant.

One and a half hours later both vessels were about 1 mile/1.6km south-south-east of the Belle Tout Light in clear bright weather with a moderate breeze, when the crew of the *Albert and Alfred* saw the steamship *Ogmore,* of Dundee bound for Falmouth, approaching them. Although the steamship was heading directly for them it was assumed it would veer away in plenty of time to avoid the fishing vessel. This assumption was totally unfounded as the steamship took no measures to avoid the vessel and ran straight into it smashing it to pieces and sinking almost immediately.

William Novis, who was a strong swimmer, jumped into the sea just as they were run down while the other three crew members hung onto a chain from the steamer's bow, until thrown a rope by the steamer's crew.

Harry Cummings, the master, was too exhausted to take hold of this rope and was drowned. The *Little Stranger* was soon on the scene and picked Novis up from the sea and then went alongside the steamer and took off the other three crew members, returning to Eastbourne at about 5pm.

The owner of the *Albert and Alfred,* George Hide, estimated the uninsured loss of both vessel and gear at £400. The nets were, however, later recovered.

Harry Cummings, a widower, who was aged about 50 years left a grown up son.

*Ref: SIBI; EG 7.6.1893; EC 10.6.1893*

# MARY OWENS

| | |
|---|---|
| **Date:** | 31.7.1893 |
| **Wreck Location:** | 5 miles/8km south-west x west of Beachy Head |
| **Description of Vessel:** | |
| **Gross Tonnage -** | 137 |
| **Length -** | 87ft/26.67m |
| **Beam -** | 23ft/6.91m |
| **Vessel Type -** | British sailing schooner |
| **Cargo:** | Oats |
| **Home Port:** | Carnarvon |
| **Voyage:** | Holmstad, Sweden to Penarth |
| **Date Built, Builder:** | c.1874 by Pritchard of Pwllheli |
| **Owner:** | J. Owens, Llanengan, Carnarvon |
| **Ship's Master:** | R. Griffith |
| **Number of Crew:** | 5 |

---

The *Mary Owens* sank after being in collision with the steamship *Presto* of Newcastle-upon-Tyne, at 4pm on Monday 31st July 1893, when off Beachy Head. The crew were all rescued by the *Presto* and landed the following day at Gravesend.

*Ref: SIBI*

# FLORA

| | |
|---|---|
| **Date:** | 19.11.1893 |
| **Wreck Location:** | 5 miles/8km east-south-east of Beachy Head |

**Description of Vessel:**

| | |
|---|---|
| Gross Tonnage - | 73 |
| Length - | 76ft/23.19m |
| Beam - | 20ft/6.12m |
| Vessel Type - | British sailing schooner |

| | |
|---|---|
| **Cargo:** | General |
| **Home Port:** | Truro |
| **Voyage:** | London to Truro |
| **Date Built, Builder:** | c.1877 by Scoble of Malpass, Cornwall |
| **Owner:** | T.F. Hitchins, London |
| **Ship's Master:** | T.H. Sara |
| **Number of Crew:** | 3 |

During the night of Saturday 18th/Sunday 19th November 1893 a north-easterly force 12 hurricane strength wind struck the East Sussex coast. Caught at sea in these horrendous conditions was the *Flora,* bound for Truro. The vessel was managing to cope until 4am on Sunday morning, when it struck some floating wreckage which damaged the hull causing it to fill with water. The crew had to abandon the *Flora* and take to their small boat.

Unbelievably their boat survived the onslaught of wind and sea for the next four hours, until they were picked up by the steamship *Toronto* of Liverpool. The four man crew were put ashore on Monday 10th at Weymouth.

*Ref: SIBI; HN 24.11.1893*

# THISTLE

| | |
|---|---|
| **Date:** | 19.11.1893 |
| **Wreck Location:** | 28 miles/45km off Beachy Head |
| **Description of Vessel:** | |
| **Length -** | 22ft/6.73m |
| **Vessel Type -** | British fishing sailing lugger |
| **Home Port:** | Eastbourne |
| **Voyage:** | Eastbourne fishing and return |
| **Date Built, Builder:** | c.1879 |
| **Owner:** | Joseph Mockett, Seaside, Eastbourne |
| **Ship's Master:** | Charles Hurd |
| **Number of Crew:** | 2 |
| **Number of Passengers:** | 1 |

The fishing lugger *Thistle* put off from Eastbourne at 3pm on Saturday 18th November 1893 with it's master, Charles Hurd, of 22 Tower Street, Eastbourne, and his crew Harry Novis, and 'Curley' Gibbs. Also in the vessel was Tom Simmons who went along as a passenger and not part of the crew. When the vessel set out to fish in Pevensey Bay, there was a northerly wind and there was no indication of what was to come.

At 5pm the crew cast their sixty nets, each about 30 yards/27m long, and started to recover them two hours later. It took until 9pm to recover all the nets and their catch of 40 herrings, but throughout this time the wind was constantly freshening. Charles Hurd then set three reefs in the foresail and moved in to about ½ mile/804m east of Beachy Head. At 10.15pm the foresail broke so the anchor was thrown over but unfortunately the anchor failed to take hold so it was brought up and dropped again by the crew, with the same result. It was decided that the best thing to do was to bring the anchor back on board the *Thistle* and reef the remaining sails and sit the bad weather out until daybreak. The wind now at 11pm was force 9 and the seas were becoming very rough.

As Charles Hurd and his crew had not anticipated staying out this long the only rations on board were two loaves of bread, 1 lb./453gms of cheese and cold fresh water to drink. As the seas increased the waves came over the vessel and the crew had to take turns at manning the pump to keep the water level down. The crew were becoming very wet and cold and although there was a brazier on board they could not get it alight because all the wood was wet.

Throughout the night the *Thistle* was blown about by this terrific northerly gale when at 5.15am the next morning, the Bolougne fishing trawler the *Avenir* (No. 1939), under its master, M. Papin, came across the *Thistle* about 6 miles/9.7km off Beachy Head. As the French trawler came alongside, Harry Novis jumped on board it and Charles Hurd was pulled on by the trawler's crew. No sooner were these two onboard the *Avenir* than the two vessels drifted apart leaving Gibbs and Simmons still on the *Thistle* which in no time at all was out of sight of those on the trawler. M. Papin said that he would do all he could to save the other two men and spent the next six hours trying to find the drifting *Thistle*.

At about 11am and 20 miles/32km off Beachy Head, the *Avenir* came across a Dover trawler with all the sails blown away. For the next 2 hours those on the *Avenir* tried to get it under tow, but the warps kept breaking under the strain. While trying to get the Dover vessel under tow the main sheet on the French trawler broke and the crew spent the next 1½ hours repairing it, during which time they lost contact with the Dover trawler.

Having repaired the main sheet they continued their search for the *Thistle* and at about 4.30pm they suddenly saw it. They were now about 28 miles/45km off Beachy Head. When the *Avenir* came alongside the *Thistle* they found Gibbs and Simmons were so cold and exhausted that they could not get themselves onto the French trawler and had to be hauled onboard. Four of Gibbs' fingers were suffering from frost bite.

Two ropes were put on the *Thistle* and it was towed towards Newhaven. Unfortunately, after three hours one of the ropes broke and the remaining rope pulled the vessel over on its side and it filled with water and sank. The vessel was valued at about £60, with the nets and gear being worth about £70. The *Avenir* continued for Newhaven where it arrived with the rescued crew at 11.20am on Monday 20th November.

The *Avenir* was bound for Newhaven when it came upon the *Thistle*. The master, M. Papin, refused to accept any payment for the time and effort he had used to save the crew, despite the great danger to the lives of his own crew. However, he said that he thought Eastbourne was nice town and if they wanted to make him a gift he would accept it. It was at a Council meeting on Monday 24th November that a copy of the following Mayor's resolution was presented to M. Papin. The resolution read: *'We the Mayor, Aldermen, and Burgesses of the Borough of Eastbourne, in the county of Sussex, acting by the Council of the said Borough, do place on record our great appreciation of the gallant conduct displayed by Captain Papin and the crew of the French vessel Avenir, who, after having rescued two Eastbourne fishermen from the small fishing boat Thistle off Beachy Head during a heavy gale on the night of the 18th November 1893, stood by in very tempestuous weather for nearly twelve hours until, they succeeded in rescuing the other two members of the crew of that vessel, delaying their voyage to Boulogne by nearly two days in order to show kindness to those who were foreigners to them'*. The Mayor, Alderman Keay together with Aldermen Morrison and Strange, Councillors Bennett, Job and Wenham and Mr. Norman Evenden, also started a subscription for the crew of the *Avenir*.

*Ref: SIBI; EG 22.11.1893 & 6.12.1893; HI 30.11.1893; LL 17543 21.11.93*

# SAMSON

| | |
|---|---|
| **Date:** | 20.11.1893 |
| **Wreck Location:** | 20 miles/32km south-west of Beachy Head |
| **Description of Vessel:** | |
| **Length -** | 24ft/7.34m |
| **Vessel Type -** | British fishing sailing lugger |
| **Home Port:** | Hastings |
| **Voyage:** | Hastings and return |
| **Date Built, Builder:** | c.1873 |
| **Owner:** | S. Sutton, Hastings |
| **Ship's Master:** | James Mann |
| **Number of Crew:** | 3 and 1 boy |

The crew of the *Samson,* under the master, James Mann, consisted of John Durrant, Frank Morfee, Alfred Haste and a boy named George Ridder. They left Hastings at 3pm on Saturday 18th November 1893 and although the weather at the time was very severe, they believed that it would subside, whereas the opposite was to be the case.

As Saturday passed so the wind and seas increased and during that night the gale carried away the vessel's mizzen sail, but it managed to sit out the vengeful conditions. The crew's hope of Sunday bringing respite were to be dashed as the weather inflicted further damage to the *Samson* when the rudder was broken leaving the craft unmanageable. By now the wind was force 10 from the north-east and the crew feared for their safety as the sea and wind continued to lash the drifting vessel. Throughout, the crew manned the pumps to keep the water level down as the waves continually broke over the open craft.

The *Samson* continued to be driven before the gale, still with its nets down, towards the French coast throughout Sunday night. On Monday morning they were fortunately found by the General Steamboat Navigation Company's steamship *Merlin* bound for London from Le Havre. The master of this steamship, Michael Richards, managed with great difficulty in the strong winds and high seas, to get the crew of the *Samson* on board; an operation which took two hours to complete because of the conditions. Once safely on board, the rescued crew were taken to Newhaven where they were put ashore.

*Ref: SIBI; BC 24.11.1893; HO 25.11.1893*

# DUKE OF NORFOLK

| | |
|---|---|
| **Date:** | 23.11.1893 |
| **Wreck Location:** | ½ mile/804m off between Belle Tout Light and Beachy head |

**Description of Vessel:**

| | |
|---|---|
| Gross Tonnage - | 2½ |
| Length - | 19ft/5.70m |
| Vessel Type - | British fishing sailing lugger |
| **Home Port:** | Eastbourne |
| **Voyage:** | Eastbourne and return |
| **Date Built, Builder:** | c.1881 |
| **Owner:** | James Huggett, Eastbourne |
| **Ship's Master:** | James Huggett |
| **Number of Crew:** | 1 |

---

The *Duke of Norfolk,* with the brothers James and Charles Huggett on board, left Eastbourne on the afternoon of Thursday 23rd November 1893 and made its way towards Newhaven intending to fish off the town, throughout the night. There were a number of other vessels that left Eastbourne that afternoon bound for the same fishing grounds, including the *Little Stranger.*

At 2.45pm the *Duke of Norfolk* was between Beachy Head and the Belle Tout Light and ½ mile/804m off shore, when a sudden northerly squall caught the sails of the vessel. Unfortunately, most of the weight in the vessel was on the leeward side so when this sudden gust caught the sails it capsized the vessel throwing both men and contents into the sea. As the vessel capsized the nets and their cork floats were initially trapped under the upturned vessel, which kept it afloat. James and Charles, still wearing their heavy boots and clothing, managed to hang onto the upturned craft for about five minutes when the nets started to drift out from under the craft. This had the effect of removing the buoyancy that was keeping the vessel afloat and within a very minutes the *Duke of Norfolk* sank.

25 year old James and his brother managed then to climb onto the floating nets in what was fortunately a very calm sea. The brothers had been in the water about 30 minutes when the Rye schooner *Forester* came alongside them, the master Richard Johns, having seen the vessel capsize. Johns lowered his boat with his crew, so that they could pick up the two drifting fishermen.

A number of other vessels including the *Little Stranger*, although not witnessing the capsize, made for the scene as well. The *Little Stranger* then took the Huggett brothers from the *Forester* boat and landed the men back at Eastbourne. The *Duke of Norfolk*, valued at £40, was lost, but the nets were saved.

*Ref: EG 29.11.1893; EC 2.12.1893*

# MARIE STAHL

| | |
|---|---|
| **Date:** | 20.6.1894 |
| **Wreck Location:** | 18 miles/29km off Beachy Head |
| **Description of Vessel:** | |
| **Length -** | 114ft/34.96m |
| **Beam -** | 26ft/8.07m |
| **Vessel Type -** | German sailing Brigantine |
| **Cargo:** | Coal |
| **Home Port:** | Rostock |
| **Date Built, Builder:** | c.1877 by E. Burchard & Co., Rostock |
| **Owner:** | F.W. Fischer |
| **Ship's Master:** | H. Oldenburg |

---

This vessel was in collision with a barquentine on the night of Wednesday 20th June 1894 when in very thick fog. The *Marie Stahl* sank within 5 minutes of impact with the loss of four of the crew.

*Ref: SIBI; HO 23.6.1894*

# EMMA PARKER

| | |
|---|---|
| **Date:** | 11.8.1894 |
| **Wreck Location:** | 10 miles/16km west off Beachy Head |
| **Description of Vessel:** | |
| **Gross Tonnage -** | 513 |
| **Length -** | 140ft/42.95m |
| **Beam -** | 29ft/8.96m |
| **Vessel Type -** | Norwegian sailing Barque |
| **Cargo:** | Timber |
| **Home Port:** | Arendal |
| **Voyage:** | Manzanilla to Bremen |
| **Date Built, Builder:** | c.1869 by D. Ross, Tusket, Nova Scotia |
| **Owner:** | Sch. P. Messel, Norway |
| **Ship's Master:** | C.A. Larsen |
| **Number of Crew:** | 10 |

The *Emma Parker* was in collision with the steamship *Plato* of Hull on Saturday 11th August 1894 when off Beachy Head in a north-easterly force 5 wind. The *Plato* suffered considerable damage to the port side which resulted in it being towed into Dover for repairs.

As to what then happened to the *Emma Parker* is not clear, as there are two stories. The first being that the vessel sank, and the second being that it was also later towed into Dover, full of water.

*Ref: SIBI; EC 18.8.1894*

# MARGHARITA

**Date:**                          20.9.1894

**Wreck Location:**            Ashore Marine Parade, Seaford

**Description of Vessel:**
**Vessel Type -**               French steam trawler

**Cargo:**                    Ballast

---

This French steam trawler was seen by an English Revenue Cutter fishing off Beachy Head within the 3 mile limit on Thursday 20th September 1894. The Cutter was giving chase to the *Margharita* when a lamp on board was knocked over setting the vessel on fire. The crew on board managed to get their boat off and rowed towards the shore opposite the Esplanade Hotel in Seaford.

The burning *Margharita* finally came ashore between the Buckle Inn and the Tide Mill, where it burnt itself out.

*Ref: SIBI; SS; SMLH*

# EVA

| | |
|---|---|
| **Date:** | 19.10.1894 |
| **Wreck Location:** | Off Newhaven |
| **Description of Vessel:** | |
| **Vessel Type -** | German sailing ketch |
| **Cargo:** | Pipe clay |
| **Voyage:** | Poole to Farge (Bremen) |
| **Date Built, Builder:** | c.1870 |
| **Owner:** | J.B. Egbers |
| **Ship's Master:** | J.B. Egbers |

The *Eva* sank off Newhaven on Friday 19th October 1894, in such a position that it was a danger to other shipping as the tops of the vessel's masts were clearly visible at low tide.

*Ref: SIBI; SE 27.10.1894*

# WARNER

| | |
|---|---|
| **Date:** | 21.10.1894 |
| **Wreck Location:** | Ashore at Seaford |
| **Description of Vessel:** | |
| **Vessel Type -** | British Lightship |
| **Voyage:** | Isle of Wight to London |
| **Owner:** | Trinity House |
| **Ship's Master:** | H. Skeats |
| **Number of Crew:** | 2 |
| **Number of Passengers:** | 7 |

---

During the night of Saturday 20th/Sunday 21st October 1894 there was a terrific storm off the Sussex coast, with heavy rain and hail. In Seaford Bay, sitting out this storm, was the Trinity tug *Irene* which had in tow the *Warner,* a lightship also known as *Light Vessel No 22.* Both lightship and tug had their individual anchors down to sit this storm out, as well as the towing hawser between them. The lightship, one of the floating lights that mark the channel of the Solent at Spithead was being taken to London for repairs & while away another lightship took its place.

At 4.30am on Sunday 21st October 1894, at the height of the gale, the towing hawser snapped and the lightship started to drag its anchor. This put too much strain on the anchor cable which in turn broke leaving the lightship drifting very rapidly towards the shore. In the very rough seas, the crew from the *Irene* launched their boat in an attempt to get another line on the lightship. Unfortunately, because of the conditions they got into difficulties and so another small boat, this time from the lightship, was got off to try and help them. This in turn became a victim of the conditions and was itself soon in great difficulties. Both small boats then tried to return to their respective vessels but again this was not successful as they were both driven ever closer to the shore and the boiling white surf that awaited them. Meanwhile, the crew still on the drifting lightship could not raise any distress signals because all their equipment had been put on board the lightship that had taken their place on station in the Solent.

The Blatchington Coastguard Station had, however, seen that the lightship was dragging its anchor and were soon on the beach at Seaford as the two small boats approached. The first boat to reach the surf contained three men, one of whom was named Fuggle. As their boat entered the surf it capsized and was instantly smashed to pieces. Two coastguardsmen, McLonney and Grose, together with Sergeant Instructor Davis of 'C' Company Seaford Engineers, dashed into the surf, but only managed to rescue the man Fuggle who was being thrown about in the surf. He was brought ashore on the verge of drowning and it took Sergeant Instructor Davis 20 minutes of the Sylvester resuscitation method to revive him. Once revived he was taken to Clapham House, Seaford, the home of Mr. & Mrs. C. W. Banks. The other two men were drowned.

Mr. Night, the Officer in Charge of the Blatchington Coastguard Station, arrived soon after at the scene with the rocket apparatus, by which time the lightship had run aground at Seaford. The rocket apparatus was fired but first shot shots failed to reach the lightship because of the wind. However, the third was successful and those still on board were safely got off. The *Warner* was later sold and broken up.

The second small boat with three men on board, then appeared entering the surf but were washed overboard, just as it capsized. One of the men managed to safely reach the shore but the other two drowned. The names of three of the four men in these two small boats who lost their lives were Gardner, William Stone and Webb. The fourth man's name is not known.

The next day, Monday 22nd October, the valuable lighting equipment was removed from the lightship. Also on this day, the body of William Stone, aged about 28 years, was found near Cuckmere and an Inquest was held at Cuckmere before Mr. E. Bedford the Deputy Coroner for East Sussex. The deceased was identified by Benjamin John Taylor who said that he lived with him at 1, Adelaide Road, East Cowes, Isle of Wight and that he was one of the crew on board the lightship. After relating the events of the previous day the Jury returned a verdict of 'accidentally drowned'.

Sergeant Instructor Davis, at a later presentation in the Albert Hall, East Street, Seaford, was presented with a gold watch by 'C' Company, together with a letter from his Commander-in-Chief, in recognition of his endeavours in saving the live of the man Fuggle.

*Ref: SIBI; SMLH; EG 24.10.1894; HI 25.10.1894; SE 10.11.1894*

# ALICE LITTLE

| | |
|---|---|
| **Date:** | 21.10.1894 |
| **Wreck Location:** | Ashore ½ mile/804m east of Newhaven Pier |
| **Description of Vessel:** | |
| **Vessel Type -** | British sailing Thames barge |
| **Cargo:** | Barrels of oil & petroleum |
| **Home Port:** | Rochester |
| **Voyage:** | London to Southampton |
| **Date Built, Builder:** | c.1859 |
| **Owner:** | J. Little, Kent |
| **Ship's Master:** | Tomas H. Gurr |
| **Number of Crew:** | 2 |

This vessel was caught in the same storm that caused the *Warner* (see page 443) to become a wreck on the morning of Sunday 21st October 1894.

At about 6.30am on the Sunday morning the *Alice Little,* having been caught in this horrendous storm, was trying to make for the safety of Newhaven harbour but in the process lost some of her sails. The master immediately let go the anchor when east of the harbour, with the intention of riding the storm out. It was then that Mr. Woolley, Officer in charge of the Newhaven Coastguard Station, was made aware that the vessel was in some difficulties just off the mouth of the harbour. His boat's crew were soon mustered and they set off. However, as soon as they reached the harbour mouth they quickly realised that their boat was no match for the turbulent heavy sea and surf. They therefore put ashore to the east side of the harbour and went on foot along the beach carrying the rocket life saving apparatus and surf lines in readiness for any rescue attempt.

At 7.15am the *Alice Little* parted from the anchor cable and was driven ashore ½ mile/804m to the east of the harbour. The moment the vessel struck the shore the waves swept right along the full length of the craft putting all three men on board in great danger. The coastguardsmen on the beach could see that the master, Thomas Gurr, was struggling in the water, either from being washed overboard or from being struck by part of the rigging. Timothy McCarthy, one of the coastguardsmen on the beach, quickly had a life-belt and surf line on and ran into the boiling surf and rescued him.

Having got Thomas Gurr safely ashore Timothy McCarthy went back into the sea together with a colleague, Mr. W. Honey, and swam out to the stricken craft. With the help of their surf lines they soon had the other two crew members safely ashore as well.

The continual buffeting the *Alice Little* took from the sea over the following hours dislodged many of the barrels from the deck so gangs of men were set to work in recovering as many barrels as possible as they were washed ashore. By noon that day the vessel had started to break up which resulted in the barrels in the hold escaping and being washed onto the beach. Although a number of the barrels were smashed open by the sea a large proportion of the cargo was saved intact. It did not take long after that for the vessel to be totally smashed to pieces by the action of the sea.

*Ref: SIBI; SWA 22.10.1894; HI 25.10.1894*

# CHEERFUL

| | |
|---|---|
| **Date:** | 22.10.1894 |
| **Wreck Location:** | 12 miles/19km south-west of Beachy Head |
| **Description of Vessel:** | |
| **Vessel Type -** | British sailing cutter |
| **Cargo:** | Ballast |
| **Home Port:** | Ramsgate |
| **Voyage:** | Brighton and return |
| **Date Built, Builder:** | c.1867 |
| **Owner:** | R.F. Williams, Kent |
| **Ship's Master:** | A. Williams |
| **Number of Crew:** | 2 |

This vessel sank on Sunday 22nd October 1894 in a force 5 north-easterly wind when 12 miles/19km south west of Beachy Head.

*Ref: SIBI*

# BERNADETTE DE LOURDES

| | |
|---|---|
| **Date:** | 8.11.1894 |
| **Wreck Location:** | 1 mile/1.6km south-east of Eastbourne |
| **Description of Vessel:** | |
| **Vessel Type -** | French sailing schooner |
| **Voyage:** | Bordeaux to London |
| **Date Built, Builder:** | c.1872 |
| **Ship's Master:** | Lebel |
| **Number of Crew:** | 5 |

This French schooner sank while on a voyage from Bordeaux to London on Thursday 8th November 1894.

*Ref: SIBI*

# IRENE

| | |
|---|---|
| **Date:** | 20.11.1894 |
| **Wreck Location:** | Off Eastbourne |
| **Description of Vessel:** | |
| **Gross Tonnage -** | 6 |
| **Vessel Type -** | British sailing dandy |
| **Cargo:** | Ballast |
| **Home Port:** | Newhaven |
| **Voyage:** | Newhaven to Eastbourne |
| **Owner:** | W.I. Toogood |
| **Ship's Master:** | William Thomas Powell |

On the evening of Monday 19th November 1894, the *Irene* left Newhaven making for Eastbourne under the master, William Thomas Powell, together with what are described as a 'couple of crew'. When the vessel was 1½ miles/2.4km off Eastbourne Pier the anchor was dropped and for reasons unknown, the entire crew left the vessel and went ashore.

Early the next morning with a force 3-4 south-westerly wind blowing, Powell returned to the *Irene* to find that in his absence the vessel had drifted eastward dragging its anchor. He was left with no option but try to sail the vessel out towards the open sea. However, adding to his problems, there was a very strong tide running which made this all but impossible for him.

Throughout the day the Powell fought to get the *Irene* out towards the open sea until 4pm when the vessel started to break up beneath him. Powell then lowered and secured all the rigging and other portable parts of the vessel and floated them ashore. The reasons as to why the vessel started to break up is not known but it soon became a total loss.

*Ref: SIBI; SE 24.11.1894*

# MACKEREL

| | |
|---|---|
| **Date:** | 29.12.1894 |
| **Wreck Location:** | Ashore east of Newhaven |
| **Description of Vessel:** | |
| **Vessel Type -** | British sailing fishing schooner |
| **Cargo:** | Ballast |
| **Home Port:** | Brighton |
| **Voyage:** | Shoreham-by-sea and return |
| **Date Built, Builder:** | c.1882 |
| **Owner:** | Smith, Gunn & Carden, Brighton |
| **Ship's Master:** | W.R. Grinyer |
| **Number of Crew:** | 2 |

At 12.30am on the morning of Saturday 29th December 1894, Chief Officer Woolley of the Newhaven Coastguard Station noticed 5 miles/8km east of Newhaven harbour, a vessel dragging its anchor with distress signals burning. The vessel, which was found to be the *Mackerel*, was drifting towards Seaford Bay in very rough seas before a force 10 south-westerly gale. Woolley telephoned the Blatchington Coastguard Station to alert them of the vessel's obvious distress, and then mustered his own men who were soon carrying surf lines along the ashore to the east in readiness should they be required.

Chief Officer Woolley had also sent a messenger to the Lifeboat coxswain with the request that he put to sea as soon as possible. At 1.15am that morning the Newhaven Lifeboat *Michael Henry* was launched and made towards the *Mackerel* whose distress signals were still burning making a mark for the lifeboat. On reaching the casualty at about 2am, it took the lifeboat three attempts in terrible conditions to take the crew safely off the *Mackerel*. The rescued crew being the master W. Grinyer (or Greenyer), Reuben Aldridge and a man named Brooks, all of whom were safely put ashore back at Newhaven. It was soon after the crew were rescued from the *Mackerel* that the vessel was driven ashore east of Newhaven to become a total wreck.

*Ref: SIBI; CNMM; SWA 2.1.1895*

# GUISEPPE

| | |
|---|---|
| **Date:** | 23.3.1895 |
| **Wreck Location:** | 11 miles/17km south-east of Royal Sovereign Light |

**Description of Vessel:**

| | |
|---|---|
| **Gross Tonnage -** | 1010 |
| **Length -** | 180ft/55m |
| **Beam -** | 33ft/10m |
| **Vessel Type -** | Italian sailing barque |
| **Cargo:** | Resin |
| **Home Port:** | Palermo |
| **Voyage:** | Savannah to Hamburg |
| **Date Built, Builder:** | c1886, M.A. Paturzo at Cassano, Italy |
| **Owner:** | C. Mazzarino, Palermo |
| **Ship's Master:** | A. Lauro |
| **Number of Crew:** | 13 |

On Saturday 23rd March 1895, when about 11 miles/17km south-east of the Royal Sovereign Light in a force 5 south-westerly wind, the *Guiseppe* was run down by the steamship *Storm King*, of London.

*Ref: SIBI*

# SEAFORD

| | |
|---|---|
| **Date:** | 21.8.1895 |
| **Wreck Location:** | 25 miles/40km off Newhaven |
| **Description of Vessel:** | |
| **Gross Tonnage -** | 997 |
| **Length -** | 263ft/80.1m |
| **Beam -** | 34ft/10.39m |
| **Vessel Type -** | British iron passenger steamship |
| **Cargo:** | General |
| **Home Port:** | Newhaven |
| **Voyage:** | Newhaven to Dieppe |
| **Date Built, Builder:** | c.1894 by W. Denny & Brothers Ltd., Dumbarton |
| **Owner:** | London, Brighton & South Coast Railway Co. |
| **Ship's Master:** | Richard Sharp |
| **Number of Crew:** | 41 |
| **Number of Passengers:** | 255 |

The *Seaford* was the first passenger screw steamship to ply between the ports of Newhaven and Dieppe and cost £57,500 to build. The *Seaford* was launched on 19th April 1894 at the builder's shipyard on the Clyde, by Mrs. Billington the wife of the Locomotive Superintendent for the owners, London, Brighton & South Coast Railway Company. At the naming ceremony Mrs. Billington was presented with an opal and diamond bracelet of behalf of the builders.

The *Seaford,* which was licensed to carry 775 passengers, arrived at

Newhaven from the Clyde on 19th July. In the same month Richard Sharp was appointed the vessel's master with a wage of £4.10.0d/£4.50p per week and was still the master on the fateful day of 21st August 1895. Richard Sharp was 36 years of age and was the London, Brighton & South Coast railway Company's most senior ship's master, having been with the company since 1881

Once in service the *Seaford* had, by the end of September 1894, completed 23 voyages from Newhaven to Dieppe, consuming 29 tons of coal per trip with each trip taking an average of 3 hours 21 minutes. The Chinese Government were so taken with the speed and seaworthiness of the *Seaford* that on the outbreak of war with Japan, they offered a large sum of money, far in excess of the vessel's value, for it to be transported to the Far East for them to use. The offer was declined by the owners.

The *Seaford* left Dieppe harbour at 1.25pm on Wednesday 21st August 1895 in brilliant sunshine and smooth sea. The master, Richard Sharp, steered the usual course for Newhaven that he had done many times before. The crossing of the English Channel for the first part was uneventful, but when 25 miles/40km off Newhaven the vessel suddenly ran into a totally unexpected bank of very dense fog. Richard Sharp took charge of the vessel and the engine was immediately telegraphed to reduce speed. The speed was reduced still further as the already very dense fog worsened. The fog siren was constantly sounded but initially nothing was heard in response. After about 30 minutes there came a distant response to the *Seaford's* fog siren. As the minutes passed with each sounding of the *Seaford's* fog siren, the other vessel's response grew louder. Suddenly out of the fog on the port side loomed the steamship *Lyons,* less than a half a ship's length away.

The *Lyons* was a cargo steamer, owned by the same company as the *Seaford,* having left Newhaven for Dieppe at 2pm that afternoon. When it encountered the thick fog, the master, M. Gauvin, was aware that the *Seaford* should be in the area as he knew it would be on its return voyage from Dieppe to Newhaven.

Richard Sharp immediately gave the order to the engine room to reverse the engines and the helm to go hard to starboard. The master of the *Lyons,* M. Gauvin, was doing likewise but alas the efforts of both masters did not prevent the inevitable collision, with the *Lyons* striking the *Seaford* amidships. Although both vessels were travelling at slow speeds the damage to the *Seaford* was considerable. The timber decking had been ripped up nearly to the cabins with other timber and glass littering the deck. The dining saloon below the deck was in total chaos as it took the full impact of the collision, just as many of the passengers were enjoying their lunch. Below the water line things were worse and the *Seaford* was taking in water rapidly from a large gash between the engine room and the second class cabins. It was obvious from the outset that the vessel could not be saved. The collision had also severely damaged the *Lyons* at the bow and the pumps had to be constantly worked to keep the vessel afloat.

With the knowledge that the *Seaford* was doomed, Richard Sharp turned all his attention to saving the passengers on board who were all quickly issued with life belts, and he also ordered that the vessel's boats be lowered. The crew acted efficiently and remained calm throughout. Richard Sharp then gave orders that the passengers should be transferred to the *Lyons* which had remained close by and not use the boats. Meanwhile, below decks, the men in the engine room, under the Chief Engineer Moneypenny, had raked out the boiler fires to prevent an explosion taking place on the vessel.

Although the vessels were now some 4ft to 5ft/1.2m to 1.5m apart, most of the passengers managed to scramble across this divide without mishap. Unfortunately Mrs. Pearslow of 24, Wesley Road, Southend, slipped and fell into the water between the two vessels and was in real danger of being crushed by the hulls. She was, however, kept afloat by the life belt she had been issued with. The Second Officer on board the *Seaford*, F. Moore (who held a French Government gold medal for life saving), on seeing Mrs. Pearslow fall, was lowered down by rope and with the help of the crew managed to get her pulled back on to the deck of the *Lyons*. She was found to have broken her ankle. There were some other casualties among the passengers; Charles Pickard of Viraflay near Versailles broke his leg when he was knocked over by the impact of the collision and Mrs. Brown and Miss Flynn also sustained injuries. All the passengers, once on board the *Lyons*, were mustered at the stern of the vessel to keep as much weight as possible away from the damaged bow, although the vessel was fitted with water-tight bulkheads.

The evacuation of the passengers went very smoothly and quickly but the speed with which the vessel was sinking is shown by the fact that the sea was above the portholes before the all passengers had left the *Seaford*.

When Richard Sharp was satisfied that all 255 passengers were safely on board the *Lyons*, the crew got into the *Seaford's* boats, which had already been lowered by the crew. In true tradition, Sharp was the last to leave the sinking passenger steamship and joined his crew in the vessel's boats. They pulled away from the *Seaford* in order not to be sucked down in the vortex that would be created as the vessel sank in 150ft/46m of water. The

*Seaford* finally went down stern first 25 minutes after the original impact with the *Lyons*. The master and the crew stayed around the spot for some little while to make sure that nobody had been left behind. The *Lyons* then took the boats containing the *Seaford's* crew, in tow back to Newhaven arriving at 8pm.

On arrival at Newhaven the injured passengers were taken to the London and Paris Hotel to recover from their ordeal. However, Charles Pickard, who sustained a broken leg, returned to Dieppe that same evening on the night sailing. The remainder of the passengers were looked after by Captain Lambert R.N.R., Marine Superintendent at Newhaven, and Mr. Reeves the Railway Superintendent. Mr. Reeves had arranged for extra trains to be laid on to take those who wanted to leave immediately. However, the majority were happy to spend the night at the London and Paris Hotel. The passengers were so impressed with the way Richard Sharp and his crew had dealt with the incident they made a collection amongst themselves raising £32 to help compensate for the loss of their possessions.

The following Sunday there were services of thanksgiving at all the churches in Newhaven including Christ Church, where a large congregation at the evening service included Captain Lambert R.N.R., the Rev. Brown (husband of one of the injured women on the *Seaford*) and 35 members of the *Seaford's* crew.

A formal fund was established at the Lewes Old Bank, for the crew under a committee of which Mr. V. Luck was the secretary. It was he who arranged various fund raising events including a concert at Lewes. One donation to the fund of £5 came from Captain Pechel, of Bellagio, Italy, who had read about the sinking of the *Seaford* in an English newspaper in Italy. The newspaper article made particular reference to the stokers in the engine room who made sure that there was no likelihood of an explosion before leaving the sinking vessel. Captain Pechel was so impressed by this that not only had he sent the donation but it was he who first suggested (outside the passengers on the vessel) that such a fund be organised.

On 2nd December 1895 at the Newhaven Drill Hall, the Mayor and Mayoress made presentation to the crews of both the *Seaford* and the *Lyons* in recognition of their endeavours on the 21st August that year. The two masters each received a silver smoker's companion, Chief Officer White of the *Seaford* received a large marble clock as did his opposite number on the *Lyons*, M. Silas de Meresman. Other crew members from the *Seaford* who received gifts were Second Officer Moore (gold watch), the carpenter Mr. Percy (a gun), Mr. Eddis and Mr. Bourke (clocks). Those on the *Lyons* who were similarly given gifts were M. Cardon (gold chain), and M. Simon (clock). All the gifts were engraved '*Souvenir of Public Esteem SEAFORD & LYONS 20th August 1895*'. Other crew members, 42 in total, received various gifts of money depending upon their pay.

Although there was never any blame laid at either master for the sinking of the *Seaford*, the Board of Trade could not carry out a formal enquiry as the Foreign Office were unable to secure the crew of the *Lyons* to attend due to he vessel being manned by a French crew.

*Ref: SIBI; CNMM; BC 23.8.1895 & 30.8.1895; SE 24.8.1895, 31.8.1895, 7.9.1895 & 26.10.1895.*

# CONDOR

| | |
|---|---|
| **Date:** | 21.12.1895 |
| **Wreck Location:** | Off Beachy Head |
| **Description of Vessel:** | |
| **Gross Tonnage -** | 398 |
| **Length -** | 131ft/40.2m |
| **Beam -** | 29ft/8.93m |
| **Vessel Type -** | Norwegian sailing barque |
| **Cargo:** | Timber |
| **Home Port:** | Stavanger |
| **Voyage:** | Belize to Goole |
| **Date Built, Builder:** | c.1876 by Jorgensen & Knudsen, |
| Drammen | |
| **Owner:** | T.S. Falck, Norway |
| **Ship's Master:** | H. Rasmussen |
| **Number of Crew:** | 10 |

On Saturday 21st December 1895, the *Condor* was off Beachy Head in a north-easterly force 2 wind, when it was run down by the steamship *Barrister* of Liverpool.

*Ref: SIBI*

# QUEEN OF MISTLEY

| | |
|---|---|
| **Date:** | 12.3.1896 |
| **Wreck Location:** | 10 miles/16.1km south-west of Beachy Head |
| **Description of Vessel:** | |
| **Gross Tonnage -** | 182 |
| **Vessel Type -** | British sailing schooner |
| **Cargo:** | Clay |
| **Home Port:** | Poole |
| **Voyage:** | Poole to London |
| **Date Built, Builder:** | c.1872 |
| **Owner:** | John Mann, Poole |
| **Ship's Master:** | John Mann |
| **Number of Crew:** | 5 |

---

At 5am on Thursday 12th March 1896 the *Queen of Mistley* was 10 miles/ 16.1km south- west of Beachy Head heading up the English Channel bound for London. Travelling in the opposite direction was the steamship *Sayn* (also referred to as the *Sohm*) of Rotterdam bound for Bilboa in ballast.

There was no suggestion of bad weather or poor visibility, so it is not known why the *Sayn* just ran straight into the *Queen of Mistley* cutting the vessel down to the water line. The mate named Knight (some reports say his name was F.W. Wilson from Whitstable) was at the time of the impact below deck when he heard John Mann, the master, say '*My God she is coming straight for us*'. Knight looked round and saw the hull of the steamship bearing down on them and only 40 yards/36.6m away. As a result of the collision Knight was thrown into the water as was John Mann, who had managed to put on a life belt. Suddenly Mann went under the water as the steamer passed and only the torn shreds of his life belt came back to the surface. It is assumed that the screw of the steamship struck him.

Within four minutes of the impact the schooner *Queen of Mistley* went down with only the mate Knight and one other crew member, Laurence McArdle from Liverpool, surviving. They were rescued from the sea by a boat from the steamship and later transferred to a fishing smack who put the rescued men ashore at 12.30pm at Newhaven that same day. At Newhaven Mr. W. Stone, the local agent of the Shipwrecked Fishermen and Mariners Society, looked after them.

*Ref: SIBI; EC 14.3.1896*

# JANE

| | |
|---|---|
| **Date:** | 19.4.1896 |
| **Wreck Location:** | 1 miles/1.6km west x south of Royal Sovereign Light |
| **Description of Vessel:** | |
| **Gross Tonnage -** | 255 |
| **Length -** | 112ft/34.32m |
| **Beam -** | 26ft/7.8m |
| **Vessel Type -** | British sailing barquentine |
| **Cargo:** | Coal |
| **Home Port:** | Whitby |
| **Voyage:** | Sunderland to Portsmouth |
| **Date Built, Builder:** | c.1848 at Littlehampton |
| **Owner:** | Mrs. S. Sharper |
| **Ship's Master:** | E. Wilyman |
| **Number of Crew:** | 8 |

---

On Sunday 19th April 1896 the *Jane* sank after colliding with the French steamship *Fredric Franck* which rescued all the crew, landing them at Antwerp.

The *Jane* had sunk in water that was less than 10 fathoms/60ft/18m deep which meant that the tops of the vessel's masts were protruding out of the sea. The Trinity House steamer *The Warden* found the wreck and removed the fore and mizzen topmasts before marking the wreck with a buoy and putting a light on the main topmast. Having completed this work *The Warden* returned to Ramsgate to await further orders but for some reason was not able to return to the wreck.

Trinity House sent the *Triton* in *The Warden's* place to the wreck of the *Jane* arriving off Eastbourne on the night of Friday 24th April where it anchored. The following morning the divers on board the *Triton* set about removing the wreck's protruding masts with explosives. The divers, wearing their gear weighing 169½ lbs./77kg, went down and laid the explosive charges in the required spot. Each charge consisted of 20lb/9kg of gun cotton (at a cost of £3.10s.0d/£3.50p per charge) which was then electrically detonated.

*Ref: SIBI; EG 29.4.1896*

# HYTHE YACHT

| | |
|---|---|
| **Date:** | 21.9.1896 |
| **Wreck Location:** | Langney near Eastbourne |
| **Description of Vessel:** | |
| **Vessel Type -** | British fishing sailing ketch |
| **Voyage:** | Rye and return |
| **Owner:** | W.M. Breeds |
| **Ship's Master:** | J.W. Tillman |
| **Number of Crew:** | Nil |

On Monday 21st September 1896, this vessel was lost in a force 7 south-westerly wind.

*Ref: SIBI*

# ROECLIFF

**Date:**                                    4.6.1897

**Wreck Location:**                    Near Royal Sovereign Light

**Description of Vessel:**
**Gross Tonnage -**                    3263
**Length -**                                351ft/107.19m
**Beam -**                                  45ft/13.74m
**Vessel Type -**                        British steel steamship

**Cargo:**                                  Grain

**Home Port:**                          Sunderland

**Voyage:**                                Odessa to Hamburg

**Date Built, Builder:**            c.1894 by Short Brothers,
                                                Sunderland

**Owner:**                                J. Westoll, Sunderalnd

**Ship's Master:**                     W. Cook

**Number of Crew:**                27

---

On Friday 4th June 1897 the *Roecliff* sank after being in collision with the steamship *Port Victor* of London.

*Ref: SIBI*

# PETER VARKEVISSER

**Date:**                     8.8.1897

**Wreck Location:**        4 miles/6.4km east of Royal
Sovereign Light

**Description of Vessel:**
**Gross Tonnage -**       69
**Length -**               72ft/22m
**Beam -**                19ft/5.8m
**Vessel Type -**          British sailing ketch

**Cargo:**              Cement

**Home Port:**          Caenarfon

**Voyage:**              Northfleet to Barry

**Date Built, Builder:**    c.1875, W.T. McCann,
Kingston-upon-Hull

**Owner:**              H. Hones, Portmadoc

**Ship's Master:**       J. Evans

**Number of Crew:**    3

---

On Sunday 8th August 1897 the *Peter Varkevisser* sank 4 miles/6.4km east of the Royal Sovereign Light, after being in collision with the steamship *Boileau* of Cardiff.

*Ref: SIBI*

# SIVAH

| | |
|---|---|
| **Date:** | 24.11.1897 |
| **Wreck Location:** | Off Beachy Head |
| **Description of Vessel:** | |
| **Gross Tonnage -** | 305 |
| **Length -** | 124ft/37.83m |
| **Beam -** | 29ft/8.83m |
| **Vessel Type -** | Norwegian sailing schooner |
| **Home Port:** | Arendal |
| **Voyage:** | Newhaven to Arendal |
| **Date Built, Builder:** | c.1878 at Arendal |
| **Owner:** | J.E. Hanssen |
| **Ship's Master:** | B. Jakobsen |

---

The *Sivah* sank after being in collision with the steamship *Vulcan* of Newcastle-upon-Tyne, on Wednesday 24th November 1897.

*Ref: SIBI*

# NOEL

| | |
|---|---|
| **Date:** | 28.11.1897 |
| **Wreck Location:** | Near Royal Sovereign Light |
| **Description of Vessel:** | |
| **Gross Tonnage -** | 1721 |
| **Length -** | 300ft/91.89m |
| **Beam -** | 32ft/9.88m |
| **Vessel Type -** | French iron steamship |
| **Cargo:** | Grain |
| **Home Port:** | Dunkirk |
| **Voyage:** | St. Nazaire to Dunkirk |
| **Date Built, Builder:** | c.1878 by Barrow Shipbuilding Co. Ltd., Barrow-in-Furness |
| **Owner:** | N. Dubuisson, Dunkirk |
| **Ship's Master:** | J. Benoit |
| **Number of Crew:** | 21 |
| **Number of Passengers:** | 1 |

During the early hours of Sunday 28th November 1897, the steamship *Noel,* when just off the Royal Sovereign Light in a terrific gale, was to be involved in not one, but two collisions; the second having terrible consequences.

At 4am the *Noel* was fighting the terrific winds and seas when it firstly struck a three masted sailing vessel, but what became of this vessel is unknown. The second collision happened shortly after when the *Noel* struck another vessel amidships, the four masted steamship *Esparto* (see page 469), almost cutting this vessel in two. The *Esparto* went down very quickly soon after. The master of the *Noel*, M. Benoit, lowered one of his vessel's boats with two men, despite the horrendous conditions, in case they could assist any survivors from the *Esparto*. Sadly these two men were not to be seen again.

M. Benoit believed that as the *Esparto* had gone down quickly from the extensive collision damage, it was highly unlikely that anyone on board managed to survive. However, unbeknown to him the master, mate, carpenter and the steward of the *Esparto* were picked up the steamer *Castlemore* and ten other crew members were rescued by the steamer *Albatross* bound for Bordeaux. The remaining five crew were lost.

The damage to the *Noel* from these two collision was severe with the bows having been completely torn away exposing the fore of the vessel. It was fortunate for those on board the *Noel,* which included the master's wife, that the tug *Gladiator* was in the vicinity and was able to take the *Noel* under tow. Throughout Sunday the *Gladiator* made its way up the Channel until Sunday night when off Littlestone, east of Dungeness, the *Noel* ran aground on a sand bar about ¼ mile/402m off shore.

The *Noel* was firmly stuck on this sand bar with the horrendous seas constantly sweeping right over the vessel and its crew who were still on board. The stranded vessel and crew remained throughout the Monday on the sand bar as conditions prevented any possible attempt at rescue. At times the combined effect of the near hurricane force winds and the heavy seas almost capsized the *Noel.*

Despite the conditions, Dungeness Lifeboat No. 1 did launch intending to try and rescue those on board, but the conditions prevented it from getting close enough to make any rescue attempt. However, one man did manage to get on board the *Noel* when the weather had abated slightly, soon after it first ran aground on Sunday night. He was Mr. Anderson, the local Lloyd's agent, but no sooner was he on board than the weather picked up again and he became stranded on the vessel along with the crew. The storm did not subside sufficiently until late Monday afternoon when all those on board were safely rescued.

The action of the sea had caused the bow of the vessel to slowly submerge into the sand, and the stern to rise out of the sea. It was not long before the vessel became a total wreck.

*Ref: SIBI; EG 1.12.1897; HN 3.12.1897*

# ESPARTO

| | |
|---|---|
| **Date:** | 28.11.1897 |
| **Wreck Location:** | Off Royal Sovereign Light |
| **Description of Vessel:** | |
| **Gross Tonnage -** | 1245 |
| **Length -** | 240ft/73.51m |
| **Beam -** | 33ft/10.08m |
| **Vessel Type -** | British iron steamship |
| **Cargo:** | Coal |
| **Home Port:** | Leith |
| **Voyage:** | Bonell to Barcelona |
| **Date Built, Builder:** | c.1880 by S & H Morton & Co., Leith |
| **Owner:** | London & Edinburgh Shipping Co. |
| **Ship's Master:** | T. Parrott |
| **Number of Crew:** | 18 |

See the *Noel* page 467.

*Ref: SIBI; EG 1.12.1897; HN 3.12.1897*

# DUKE OF YORK

| | |
|---|---|
| **Date:** | 11.5.1898 |
| **Wreck Location:** | Hope Gap near Cuckmere Coastguard Station |
| **Description of Vessel:** | |
| **Vessel Type -** | British sailing dandy |
| **Cargo:** | Boulders |
| **Voyage:** | Newhaven to Cuckmere |
| **Owner:** | G. Cook, Newhaven |
| **Ship's Master:** | G. Winder |
| **Number of Crew:** | 3 |

---

On the evening of Tuesday 10th May 1898 the sailing dandy *The Duke of York* with its crew of four, put into Hope Gap near the Cuckmere Coastguard Station to load boulders. As the evening progressed the wind got ever stronger as the tide rose and prevented the crew from getting the vessel back out to sea and at the same time pushed it further up the beach. At 1am, after a number of hours trying to get the craft back out to sea, the crew abandoned *The Duke of York* which rapidly went to pieces soon after.

*Ref: SIBI; HC 18.5.1898*

# FITZJAMES

| | |
|---|---|
| **Date:** | 23.11.1898 |
| **Wreck Location:** | Off Beachy Head |
| **Description of Vessel:**<br>**Vessel Type -** | British sailing vessel |
| **Cargo:** | General |
| **Voyage:** | London to Swansea |
| **Owner:** | Messrs. Matthew & Luff,<br>Leadenhall Street, London |
| **Ship's Master:** | Charles Pawson |
| **Number of Crew:** | 11 |

---

The *Fitzjames* left Rotherhithe, London on Tuesday 22nd November 1898 bound for Swansea, under the command of the master Charles Pawson, two mates and nine crew. As the vessel made its way down the Channel on Wednesday evening, a terrific gale sprang up with very heavy seas. At 8pm that evening the *Fitzjames* was off Beachy Head when the crew battened down the hatches with three tarpaulins. However, two hours later with the wind having increased, the cover to number two hatch was ripped off by the strength of the wind and before the crew could do anything about replacing it, the sea swept over the vessel from both sides filling the hold.

It was realised that the vessel would soon go down in these conditions so the master gave the order to launch a lifeboat. However, just as the order was given the lifeboat was smashed to pieces by the sea and the cook/steward was washed overboard and drowned. Orders were then given to get out the starboard lifeboat but before this could be done the vessel began to sink. Seven of the crew, including a man named Antonio, left the starboard lifeboat and got into a smaller boat at the stern of the *Fitzjames* and launched that. Unfortunately, the *Fitzjames* went down before they had pulled clear of the vessel and so it took this small boat and its occupants down with it. The master, a fireman and one of the crew, Christopher Kootoa, a Greek seaman, remained on the *Fitzjames* until it went down. Christopher Kootoa on coming to the surface, swam around for a short while and in the darkness found one of the damaged lifeboats from the *Fitzjames*. He managed to climb into it and was still on board when he was rescued by the steamship *Olive* on Thursday morning.

The steamship *Olive,* belonging to Messrs. Burnett Bros., and under the command of James Cornelius Holmes, had also been caught up this terrific storm but had heave-to for the night to sit it out just off Beachy Head. It was not until 11am Thursday morning that the vessel's look-out first saw any wreckage from the *Fitzjames*. The look-out could see half of a small boat with two men hanging onto it. The *Olive* made towards them but the sea was far too rough to launch a small boat to pick the men up, but the *Olive* got as close as possible in the conditions and threw a rope to the men. However, they were too exhausted from their ordeal to be able to get hold of it. Richard Green a seaman on the *Olive* tied a rope around his body, jumped into the sea and swam towards the two exhausted men and pulled their part-boat towards the *Olive*. These two men, who were the only survivors, were found to be Christopher Kootoa and a man named John Pitsack. With these two safely on board the look-out soon saw another small boat, this time upturned with a man on the keel. Richard Green again jumped into the sea and rescued the unconscious man, a 40 year old Austrian seaman named Antonio, suffering severe injuries. He was never to regain consciousness. The remaining crew of the *Fitzjames* all drowned.

At 6pm on Friday 25th November, one of the boats from the *Fitzjames* was washed ashore near St. Leonards pier. Inside the slightly damaged boat were two pairs of oars still lashed to its side, a sea anchor and six air tight boxes. Another boat from the vessel was also washed ashore near Bo Peep, St. Leonards, but was smashed to pieces. From this boat a further five or six air tight boxes were recovered and put in the custody of the local coastguards.

It was also on Friday 25th November, that the receding tide at Dymchurch, Kent revealed the bodies of four seamen from the *Fitzjames*, all wearing life belts. The body of a fifth seaman was washed ashore at Lydd, Kent. Papers found on the seamen indicated that one of them was Edward Hart a fireman on the vessel, and another was W.H. Penman, an engineer. The Inquest was opened the next day but adjourned until Monday 28th November, to enable identification to be made. The master's wife of 107 Fernhead Road, St. Peters, London, had visited both Lydd and

Dymchurch and seen the recovered bodies but none were her husband, Charles Pawson. At the end of the Inquest at Dymchurch the Coroner read out the verdict as death from drowning by the sinking of the *Fitzjames*. However, the Jury foreman was not happy with this as he said that they could not say that was correct. There had been an inference during the course of the evidence that one of the boats may have been run down by the *Olive*. The Coroner reminded the Jury that they had not heard evidence to that effect and the verdict as previously read was accepted.

On Saturday 26th November Mr. E.N. Wood, the deputy Coroner for Rotherhithe, held the Inquest into the death of the seaman Antonio who had died from exposure. Those attending the Inquest included Mr. T.S. Mills a solicitor representing the owners of the *Fitzjames*, an official from the Austrian Consulate, and the nephew of vessel's master on behalf the master, Charles Pawson.

*Ref: SIBI; SE 29.11.1898; HN 2.12.1898; EC 3.12.1898; HO 3.12.1898*

# PERUVIAN

| | |
|---|---|
| **Date:** | 8.2.1899 |
| **Wreck Location:** | Ashore at Seaford |
| **Description of Vessel:** | |
| **Gross Tonnage -** | 639 |
| **Length -** | 163ft/49.77m |
| **Beam -** | 28ft/8.44m |
| **Vessel Type -** | Danish steel hulled sailing barque |
| **Cargo:** | Palm seeds (ivory nuts), timber |
| **Home Port:** | Drdbyfano |
| **Voyage:** | Esmeraldas (Ecuador) to Hamburg |
| **Date Built, Builder:** | c.1875 by D & W Henderson, Glasgow |
| **Owner:** | J. Hansen, Fano, Denmark |
| **Ship's Master:** | O.J. Norholm |
| **Number of Crew:** | 12 |

On Wednesday 8th February 1899 the *Peruvian* (see photograph page 25) was on the last lap of its voyage to Hamburg, being 145 days out from Esmeraldas in Ecuador, when at 3.10am it was driven aground opposite the Esplanade Hotel, Seaford in a force 6 southerly wind. It was just 10 minutes earlier that those ashore where first aware that the vessel was in difficulty. A patrolling coastguardsman noticed that the vessel, then just off Seaford, was displaying distress signals and quickly reported it to Chief Boatman Farrell at the Blatchington Coastguard Station. Farrell, who was deputising for the Chief Officer of the station who was away, answered the vessel's distress signals and then telephoned Chief Officer Woolley at Newhaven requesting that the lifeboat *Michael Henry* make for the scene.

Meanwhile Farrell had gathered together his men with the life saving rocket apparatus and then made towards where the vessel had now gone aground.

On arrival, Farrell and his men were joined by other coastguardsmen from the Cuckmere station under the command of Chief Boatman Lundberg. The rocket apparatus was soon ready but it was not until the fourth rocket had been fired that a line was got on the vessel. For some unaccountable reason those on board the *Peruvian* did not make fast the hawser upon which the 'breeches buoy', is hauled along. While these attempts were being made to get the line onto the vessel, the lifeboat was making for the vessel under the command of coxswain George Winter and was soon alongside the *Peruvian*. The master and nine of the crew from the *Peruvian* were soon taken on the lifeboat and, at the time, the master assumed that all his crew were on board The lifeboat then signalled to the coastguardsmen on shore that all the crew had now been safely taken off the *Peruvian* and was about to return to Newhaven when the master of the *Peruvian* suddenly realised that his first and second mate were missing.

Norholm, the master of the *Peruvian,* called out several times to the two missing crew men to leave the vessel and get on board the lifeboat, but there was no response. It was clear that the two men were not on deck but were below getting their possessions together. They could be seen through one of the port holes. The lifeboat crew called out to the two men again and again but there was still no response. The lifeboat waited for a further 15 minutes and still there was no reply from the two men. Coxswain Winter then decided that for everybody's safety he would have to return to Newhaven with those he had rescued. Once ashore at Newhaven the rescued crew were looked after by Mr. John Bull, the local Lloyd's agent.

Having received the signal from the lifeboat that all the crew had been rescued, Chief Boatman Farrell and his men started to haul in their hawser. However, the endless line, known as the 'whip', which is part of the rescue equipment that runs through a block for the 'breeches buoy', was still on the *Peruvian* which had now been forced by the heavy seas and wind to less than 100 yards/91 metres from the shore.

At 5am, the coastguardsmen were still going about recovering their equipment when they heard cries of help coming from the *Peruvian*. Although it was far too dark to see anybody on the vessel, they realised that not all the crew had been rescued by the lifeboat. The coastguardsmen heard a voice say in broken English *"Pull away"*. Farrell and his men started to pull on the 'whip' and as they did so they could see a man with a lifebuoy round him coming through the surf. He was very quickly pulled safely on to the beach and taken to the nearby Wellington Hotel, where the proprietors Mr. & Mrs. Hadlow, looked after the seaman whom it transpired was the second mate on the *Peruvian*. He later denied hearing the shouts from the master of the stricken vessel or of even knowing the lifeboat had come alongside the *Peruvian*.

A short while after this rescue a further cry for help was heard coming from the *Peruvian*. So again Farrell and his men were quickly pulling on the 'whip' to find a second seaman holding on to the line, struggling as he was pulled through the surf. It was Neilson, the first mate of the *Peruvian*, who had refused to wear a lifebuoy despite the second mate's insistence. Unfortunately, because he was not wearing a lifebuoy when he let go of the whip and started to wade ashore and was suddenly struck by a large wave he disappeared under the water. Coastguardsmen French and Burnard, together with Mr. C. Simmons, a waterman, rushed into the violent surf up to their waists and managed to get hold of Neilson, but sadly he was already dead.

During the remainder of Wednesday and Thursday Mr. Bull, the local Lloyds agent, arranged for the sails and spars to be removed from the *Peruvian*. At midday on the Thursday it was intended to remove part or all of the cargo to lighten the vessel with the aim of getting the *Peruvian* afloat again but on closer inspection it was found that the vessel was full of water. Although from original inspections it was thought to be water tight, a huge rent had in fact been torn in the starboard bow below the water line. This discovery thwarted any possibility of re-floating the vessel again and with every tide the vessel was moving and settling further down in the beach. On Friday the vessel was just 40 yards/36.5 metres from the seawall at Seaford. The cargo of palm seed was also being washed out with every tide and the locals were being offered 2s.0d./10p for every cwt./51kg they recovered from the beach. The vessel finally went to pieces on the morning of Saturday 12th February from the effects of a severe south-westerly gale that sprang up over night.

On Friday 17th February the sale of the wrecked *Peruvian* was sold. The remains of the hull, anchors, chains, and a mass of other wreckage were sold as one lot for £192. The salvaged sails and spars were sold separately.

*Ref: SIBI; CNMM; SMLH; HC 15.2.1899 & 22.2.1899*

# HEATHPOOL

| | |
|---|---|
| **Date:** | 31.3.1899 |
| **Wreck Location:** | Near Royal Sovereign Light |
| **Description of Vessel:** | |
| **Gross Tonnage -** | 975 |
| **Length -** | 209ft/64m |
| **Beam -** | 32ft/9.84m |
| **Vessel Type -** | British iron steamship |
| **Cargo:** | 1200 tons of coal |
| **Home Port:** | Sunderland |
| **Voyage:** | Sunderland to St. Nazaire |
| **Date Built, Builder:** | c.1885 at Sunderland |
| **Owner:** | Lambton Collieries Ltd., Sunderland |
| **Ship's Master:** | J. Todd |
| **Number of Crew:** | 15 |

The *Heathpool* left Sunderland on Thursday 30th March 1899 for St. Nazaire with its cargo of coal. At 9.30pm the following evening, when the vessel was near the Royal Sovereign Light, it ran into very thick fog. Suddenly, without any warning, the 2,500 ton steamship *Ethel Hilda* of Whitby bound for London from the River Plate, came out of the fog and struck the *Heathpool* on the starboard side near the bridge.

The damage was so severe that the *Heathpool* started to sink immediately. The ship's master called out to the *Ethel Hilda* to go slow ahead in the hope that the *Heathpool* would stay afloat long enough for his crew to be rescued. However, the *Ethel Hilda* the bigger of the two vessels, reversed away from the *Heathpool* and swung round resulting in the *Heathpool* sinking very quickly.

A fireman on the *Heathpool* named Thomas Coulson, took hold of a piece of timber and jumped into the sea hoping to be rescued by the *Ethel Hilda*. Although he could hear the fog horn of the *Ethel Hilda* he could not see or find the vessel in the thick fog. After some considerable time swimming about in the fog he came across one of the lifeboats that had been knocked off the *Heathpool*. He managed to get into it and drifted alone for several hours before he was finally rescued by the Cardiff tug *William Thomas Lewis*.

Unbeknown to Coulson seven of the crew from the *Heathpool* had been picked up by the *Ethel Hilda* and were put ashore at Dover later that same afternoon. They were the second mate C. Johnson, firemen C. Smith and D. Small, able seamen F. Johnson, R. Curtis, and G. Stewart and the second engineer R. Brod. The master and seven of his crew were never found.

*Ref: SIBI; SE 4.4.1899; EG 5.4.1899; HN 7.4.1899; BO 8.4.1899*

# PONTOS

| | |
|---|---|
| **Date:** | 31.3.1899 |
| **Wreck Location:** | East of Royal Sovereign Light |
| **Description of Vessel:** | |
| **Gross Tonnage -** | 2710 |
| **Length -** | 300ft/91m |
| **Beam -** | 42ft/12.8m |
| **Vessel Type -** | German steel steamship |
| **Cargo:** | 164 head of cattle, 970 head of sheep |
| **Home Port:** | Hamburg |
| **Voyage:** | Buenos Aires to Deptford, London |
| **Date Built, Builder:** | c.1885, Richardson Duck & Co., Stockton-on-Tees |
| **Owner:** | A.C. de Freitas & Co., Hamburg |
| **Ship's Master:** | Julius Terchan |
| **Number of Crew:** | 38 |
| **Number of Passengers:** | 5 |

---

The *Pontos* left Buenos Aires 29 days prior to this collision with a cargo of live animals and two passengers. She steamed up to Rio Grande where a further three passengers were taken on board, before setting out for London.

During the early hours of Friday 31st March 1899, the *Pontos* encountered thick fog while coming up the English Channel so reduced its speed considerably due to the very poor visibility and was constantly sounding the fog horn. As the vessel approached the Royal Sovereign Light another fog horn could be heard in the distance, but the volume increased quite quickly, indicating that the approaching vessel was travelling at a fast speed. Suddenly, at 9.15pm, the *Star of New Zealand*, of Belfast bound for New Zealand from London, loomed out of the fog on the port side. Julius Terchan, the master of the *Pontos*, ordered "Full steam ahead" but this was to no avail as the *Star of New Zealand* struck the *Pontos* amidships in front of the bridge with such force that it nearly sliced the vessel in half. The *Star of New Zealand* went astern with the result that the 20ft/6m wide gaping hole that she had inflicted, rapidly filled with water causing the *Pontos* to sink 20 minutes later.

A voice called out from the *Star of New Zealand*, "*Shall I send you boats*", to which Terchan replied "*I am sinking*". The Master of the *Star of New Zealand* immediately got off three boats for the stricken crew and passengers and rescued 12 of them in one of the boats. Many of the animals on board the *Pontos* were already dead and drifting on the surface, while others were trying to swim. One bullock had been completely cut in two by the impact.

The crew and passengers that were in the other two boats not picked up by the *Star of New Zealand,* were left to drift in the thick fog, which was not without its own dangers. While drifting, they could hear the fog horns of other ships around them. This only served to heightened their anxiety and concern for their safety. Suddenly two large steamships appeared out of the fog, side by side. Had it not been for Terchan's swift response to give orders to manoeuvre their boats they would definitely have been swamped or run down. Fortunately, they all survived but were left tossing and bobbing about on the wakes of the two steamers who were completely oblivious to them.

At about 2am, nearly five hours after the original collision, a Hastings fishing boat, the *Ellen,* under the command of Benjamin Gallop, could hear people shouting for help and blowing whistles. He pulled up his trawl and tried to find where these voices were coming from. He eventually found one of the drifting boats containing 20 people, which included the master, Second Officer Henrick, Chief Engineer F. Husadel, three cattlemen, and three passengers Miss Eplaie, Miss Hostheide and Mr. O.M. Fleischer. It was reported that "Neither of the ladies were wearing hats" !

Those rescued by the *Ellen* were taken to Hastings where Mr. W.H. Gallop, the local agent of the Shipwrecked Mariners Society, took them to the Shaftesbury Restaurant where the proprietor, Mr. Carter, tended to them.

The other boat containing 12 other members of the *Pontos* crew were later found by the *Snowdrop* of Aberdeen and taken to Dover suffering from exposure.

Those rescued from the *Pontos* by the *Star of New Zealand* were taken to Tilbury, where the *Star of New Zealand* was later to receive repairs. However, before arriving at Tilbury the *Star of New Zealand* anchored at Holehaven to discharge part of her cargo of dynamite!

*Ref: SIBI; LL No. 19208.1.4.1899; LR 1899-1900.542(P); HO 3.4.1899; EG 5.4.1899; HN 7.4.1899*

# WILD ROSE

| | |
|---|---|
| **Date:** | 13.4.1899 |
| **Wreck Location:** | 8 miles/13km south-east of Beachy Head |
| **Description of Vessel:** | |
| **Vessel Type -** | British sailing fishing sloop |
| **Cargo:** | Ballast |
| **Home Port:** | Lowestoft |
| **Voyage:** | Swansea fishing and return |
| **Date Built, Builder:** | c.1894 |
| **Owner:** | W.J. Head, Lowestoft |
| **Ship's Master:** | W.J. Head |
| **Number of Crew:** | 4 |

On Thursday 13th April 1899 the *Wild Rose* sank after being in collision with the brigantine *Greenwich* in a force 4 south-easterly wind.

*Ref: SIBI*

# VENUS

| | |
|---|---|
| **Date:** | 17.6.1899 |
| **Wreck Location:** | 8 miles/13 km north-east of Royal Sovereign Light |
| **Description of Vessel:** | |
| **Gross Tonnage -** | 2940 |
| **Length -** | 313ft/95.7m |
| **Beam -** | 40ft/12.34m |
| **Vessel Type -** | British steel steamship |
| **Cargo:** | Grain |
| **Home Port:** | Aberystwyth |
| **Voyage:** | Odessa to Rotterdam |
| **Date Built, Builder:** | c.1891 by Ropner & Sons, Stockton-on-Tees |
| **Owner:** | Glan Steamship Co. Ltd., Aberystwyth |
| **Ship's Master:** | D. Jones |
| **Number of Crew:** | 24 |

On Saturday 17th June 1899, the *Venus* was in collision with the Greek steamship *Amphitrite* in calm conditions, when 8 miles/13km north-east of the Royal Sovereign Light. However, the vessel drifted until it came ashore near Dungeness where it was to become a complete wreck.

*Ref: SIBI*

# TURTLE

| | |
|---|---|
| **Date:** | 21.7.1899 |
| **Wreck Location:** | 8 miles/13km west of Beachy Head |
| **Description of Vessel:** | |
| **Vessel Type -** | British barge |
| **Voyage:** | Dover to Plymouth |
| **Owner:** | Sir J. Jackson, Devonport |

---

This vessel became a complete loss on Friday 21st July 1899 when 8 miles/ 13km west of Beachy Head.

*Ref: SIBI*

# GEORGE I

| | |
|---|---|
| **Date:** | 15.9.1899 |
| **Wreck Location:** | Ashore at Newhaven |
| **Description of Vessel:** | |
| **Vessel Type -** | British sailing lugger |
| **Cargo:** | Shingle |
| **Voyage:** | Newhaven to destination unknown |
| **Owner:** | A. Adkins, Sussex. |
| **Ship's Master:** | A. Adkins |
| **Number of Crew:** | 1 |

This vessel became a wreck while loading a cargo of shingle from the beach near Newhaven on Friday 15th September 1899 in a force 7 south-westerly wind.

*Ref: SIBI*

# INTERNATIONAL

| | |
|---|---|
| **Date:** | 30.9.1899 |
| **Wreck Location:** | Ashore at Birling Gap Coastguard Station |
| **Description of Vessel:** | |
| **Gross Tonnage -** | 1381 |
| **Length -** | 239ft/73.15m |
| **Beam -** | 30ft/9.16m |
| **Vessel Type -** | British iron cable steamship |
| **Cargo:** | Ballast |
| **Home Port:** | London |
| **Voyage:** | London to Cherbourg |
| **Date Built, Builder:** | c.1870 by Richardson Duck & Co. Ltd., Stockton-on-Tees |
| **Owner:** | H.E. Moss, London |
| **Ship's Master:** | G. Farmer |
| **Number of Crew:** | 9 |

---

At 10.45am on Saturday 30th September 1899 the *International* was being towed by the London tug *Gauntlett* in a very strong westerly wind and heavy seas in Seaford Bay, when disaster struck. The vessel had been sold by the Indiarubber and Gutta Percha and Telegraph Works Company of London and was being towed to Cherbourg for the new French owners.

During the previous night it had been discovered by the crew on board the *International* that it had sprung a leak and they had made distress signals to the tug *Gauntlett* but due to the terrible conditions and poor visibility these signals were not seen. However, when it became light and this leak had been communicated to those on the tug, it was decided to put in at Newhaven. Unfortunately, as the conditions deteriorated it became more and more difficult for the tug to control the large bulk of the *International.*

The vessels had got just to the west of Newhaven harbour when an enormous wave lifted the *International* right onto its crest but as the vessel descended down into the wave's trough, the strain on the towing hawser was so great that it snapped. The *International* was now adrift in mountainous seas but with quick thinking and expert seamanship, the tug *Gauntlett* managed to get another line on the drifting vessel again bringing it back under tow. However, this was not for long because the pitching and rolling of the *International* soon caused the towing hawser to snap for the second time. Once again the vessel was adrift and as it seemed unlikely that yet another line would be got on the *International,* the crew on board the drifting vessel displayed distress signals which were seen by Chief Officer Woolley of the Newhaven Coastguard Station.

Chief Officer Woolley, who had been watching the drama for some time, immediately notified the Newhaven Lifeboat Station. At 5pm the lifeboat *Michael Henry,* under the command of the coxswain Mr. C. Lower, set sail from the harbour towards Seaford Head where the drifting vessel had now reached. The Newhaven steam tug *Nelson* also left the harbour to give what assistance it could. Meanwhile the *International* continued to drift eastward until 6pm when the vessel struck the rocks at Birling Gap with terrific force.

While the lifeboat made for the scene, Chief Officer Woolley had notified the Birling Gap Coastguard Station of the situation. The coastguardsmen from Birling Gap soon made their way towards the *International,* together with their rocket life saving apparatus. Once the vessel ran aground on the rocks the coastguards managed, after one failed attempt, to get a line on the stranded vessel to enable the crew to get ashore. However, the crew decided that they would rather row their small boat out to the tug *Gauntlett* which was standing just off the *International.* The stranded crew then had second thoughts about this means of rescue as the waves were sweeping right over their vessel and in the darkness it was judged to be a perilous endeavour. The master of the tug *Gauntlett,* with incredible skill in these horrendous conditions, managed to get his tug alongside the *International* and get all the crew safely off.

The crew of the lifeboat *Michael Henry* had great difficulty in reaching the *International.* Having arrived at the casualty, the lifeboat dropped her anchor and drifted onto the vessel with the intention of taking off the crew. The tug *Gauntlett* then signalled the lifeboat to inform them that all the crew had been safely rescued. On answering, the lifeboat crew signalled a request that they be towed off the wreck as there was insufficient water for them now to manoeuvre as they were very close to the shore. Unfortunately, due to the terrible weather their signal was not seen on the tug, which meant that the lifeboat crew had to row for an hour to get out of their very perilous position before setting sail back to Newhaven. It was recognised as a particularly clever piece of seamanship by the coxswain and his boatman Mr. Richardson.

Over the following tides the vessel took a terrible pounding from the sea pushing it further up the beach with each tide, so that at low tide the vessel was high and dry. Several feet of water also got into the holds and it was clear that the vessel was not going to be floated again. It was subsequently sold by auction on Wednesday 11th October by Mr. J. Easter of Messrs. Easter & Wright of Eastbourne. The hull, masts, winches, windlass machinery, boilers, anchors, chains together *'with all other gear that may be on board'* were sold as one lot for £225 to Messrs. Blackmore & Co. of London. What property had been salvaged was sold in separate lots.

There was a particularly ironic twist to this incident because where the *International* ran aground, it cut through the very same telegraph cable it had laid some years earlier across the Channel to France from this very spot.

*Ref: SIBI; CNMM; SE 3.10.1899; HC 4.10.1899; HN 6.10.1899; EC 7.10.1899; EG 18.10.1899*

# TOPSY

| | |
|---|---|
| **Date:** | 27.12.1899 |
| **Wreck Location:** | 2½ miles/4km west of Newhaven |
| **Description of Vessel:** | |
| **Vessel Type -** | British fishing sailing smack |
| **Cargo:** | Ballast |
| **Home Port:** | Dover |
| **Voyage:** | Newhaven and return |
| **Date Built, Builder:** | c.1884 |
| **Owner:** | Alexander Instead, Walpole House, Folkestone |
| **Ship's Master:** | James Thomas Cloke |
| **Number of Crew:** | 3 |

During the afternoon of Wednesday 27th December 1899 the *Topsy* left Newhaven harbour for the local fishing grounds with a mate, cook, and James Hinchcliffe, an 18 year old seaman from Jersey. Although it was foggy that evening the vessel was displaying the proper lights.

At 11pm on Wednesday 27th December 1899 the cargo steamship *Dieppe,* under the command of the master Mr. Leber, left Newhaven harbour in calm but still very foggy conditions. It was because of these conditions that the steamer's look-outs were doubled before leaving the harbour. As the vessel cleared the harbour it set a course for Dieppe and steamed slowly out to sea with its fog siren constantly sounding.

The *Dieppe* was just 2½ miles/4km into the journey when out of the fog the fishing smack *Topsy* appeared right under the vessel's bows. The steamer's engines were immediately put into reverse but there was a smash and a shout heard from the fishing smack. The steamer immediately threw over the side ropes and lifebuoys. The boats were also lowered to rescue any survivors, because the impact of the collision had cut the *Topsy* in half. The rescue attempt found only one survivor, James Thomas Cloke the master, who was taken to Newhaven by the steamer.

The master of the *Topsy* was the first in the vessel to see the oncoming *Dieppe*, when it was about 100 yds/91m away. The *Topsy* already had a small boat out in case of emergency but when the emergency arrived, it arrived too quickly for the crew to get into the boat. As the *Dieppe* sliced right through the fishing smack from the starboard side, one of the crew, Hinchcliffe, just happened to be in the vessel's rigging at the time. He was quickly joined by the mate, and both men tried to climb on board the steamer but without success. As the *Topsy* sank the master went down with it, but managed to get to the surface to find a drifting oar which he held on to until he was able to get one of the ropes that had been thrown over the side of the *Dieppe*.

At 11am the following morning, Henry Scott, a local coastguardsman, saw a small boat drifting out at sea with something in it. At this stage he was unable to make out what was in the boat so he informed Chief Officer William Mellow of the Portobello Coastguard Station. Chief Officer Mellow gave instructions to follow the drifting boat which finally came ashore near Rottingdean. On checking the boat the body of James Hinchcliffe was found on board and taken to the White Horse Hotel by Police Constable Brown. The small boat itself had all the hallmarks of itself having been run down at some stage. On the stern of the small boat was the word '*Peter*' and on the starboard side was marked '*114 R.X.*'.

It was on New Years Day 1900, at the White Horse Hotel that the Inquest was held into the death of James Hinchcliffe by the Deputy Coroner Mr. Sprott. One of the witness at the Inquest was James Cloke, the master of the *Topsy*, who could give no account as to how Hinchcliffe came to be in the boat. He could only offer the possibility that Hinchcliffe had fallen out of the vessel's rigging into the small boat. He also told the Deputy Coroner that the *Dieppe* was travelling at about 7 miles an hour/11 kilometres per hour at the time of impact. The Inquest was adjourned until 17th January 1900 so as to enable witness from the *Dieppe* to give evidence.

*Ref: SIBI; HI 4.1.1900*

# Sources of Information

*Books*

Berry, Patricia, *Seaford Shipwrecks* (Seaford Museum)

Biggs, Howard, *Sound of Maroons* (T. Dalton)

Bouquet, Michael, *South Eastern Sail*

Duncan, A. *The Mariner's Chronicle – Vol. III*

Gosset, W.P., *Lost Ships of the Royal Navy 1793-1900* (Mansell Publishing Ltd)

Hutchinson, Geoff, *Martello Towers – A Brief History*

Larn, Richard and Bridget, *Shipwreck Index of the British Isles – Volume 2* (Lloyd's Register of Shipping)

Layson, J.F., *Memorable Shipwrecks & Seafaring Adventures* (Heyes, Lloyd Shuttleworth)

McDonald, Kendall, *Dive Sussex* (Underwater World Publications Ltd)

Morris, Jeff, *The Story of the Eastbourne Lifeboats* and *The Story of the Newhaven Lifeboats* (R.N.L.I.)

Philp, Roy, *The Coast Blockade – The Royal Navy's War on Smuggling in Kent & Sussex 1817-31* (Compton Press)

Surtees, John, *Beachy Head* (S.B. Publications)

Thornton, Nicholas, *Sussex Shipwrecks* (Countryside Books)

*Newspapers*

*Bexhill Chronicle*
*Bexhill Observer*
*Cinque Ports Chronicle*
*Eastbourne Chronicle*
*Eastbourne Gazette*
*Eastbourne Standard*
*Hastings & St. Leonards Chronicle*
*Hastings & St. Leonards Independent*
*Hastings & St. Leonards News*

*Hastings & St. Leonards Observer*
*Hastings & St. Leonards Times*
*London Jacket*
*South Eastern Advertiser*
*Sussex Agricultural Express*
*Sussex Express*
*Sussex Times*
*Sussex Advertiser*

*Other*

Brett Series of manuscripts held at Hastings Central Library, East
   Sussex
Lloyd's List
Newhaven Maritime Museum
Royal National Mission to Deep Sea Fishermen
Seaford Museum of Local History

# Acknowledgements

I wish to acknowledge the following for the assistance they have given me in the research and preparation of this book: the staff of the Reference Section, Hastings Central Library; the staff of the Reference Section of Eastbourne Library; Roy Philp author of *The Coast Blockade – The Royal Navy's War on Smuggling in Kent & Sussex 1817-31*; Jeff Morris of the R.N.L.I. Enthusiasts Society and author of *The Story of the Eastbourne Lifeboats* and *The Story of the Newhaven Lifeboats*; Richard and Bridget Larn for their co-operation in the use of information from their book *Shipwreck Index of the British Isles – Vol. 2*; members of the Newhaven Maritime Museum; Sue Sutton of the Seaford Museum & Heritage Society; Stephen Friend of York St. John College, University of Leeds; and my daughter Stephanie and Simon Mason whose invaluable assistance in the final preparation of this book, I could not have done without.

# Index

# Index

# Index

# Alphabetical Index to Shipwrecks

# Alphabetical Index to Shipwrecks

# Alphabetical Index to Shipwrecks

# Alphabetical Index to Shipwrecks